PRAISE FOR *SEVEN MORE MEN*

More deeply inspiring stories of extraordinary men who defied the odds and left an eternal impact on everyday life. Heroes anchored with purpose and resolve, worthy of our careful time and attention. A drink of cold water for the thirsty soul.

— Tim Clinton, president of the American Association of Christian Counselors, executive director of the James Dobson Family Institute

God often uses nobodies from nowhere with nothing to offer but hearts fully surrendered to him and uses them to change the world. Metaxas once again magically and masterfully illustrates God's guiding hand in the lives of seemingly ordinary men to produce great men who use their gifts and opportunities to bring glory to God and to serve others. This book will deeply inspire you to diligently serve God with all your heart, no matter your life's current circumstances, knowing that he knows the plans he has for you.

— Kirk Cameron, actor and producer

Eric Metaxas has done it again. In *Seven More Men* he has given us yet another masterpiece from a master biographer. You will laugh and you will cry as you read this amazing book. Above all, it is a page-turner. I was deeply impacted by Eric's first biographical book, *Amazing Grace*—so much so that I can verbatim retell the details of William Wilberforce's struggles to single-handedly abolish slavery. This book is a must-read for young and old alike; I am giving it to my grandchildren.

— Michael Youssef, pastor and televangelist heard 13,000 times a week in 196 countries

We need heroes more than ever. We all love superhero movies, but nothing is more inspiring than stories of real people who have stood courageously for nobility and virtue. Eric Metaxas's *Seven More Men* will inspire you to be the hero your world needs.

— Greg Laurie, author and pastor

In *Seven More Men* we are reminded of the courageous faith that has paved the way for this generation. With his newest list of seven heroes, Eric Metaxas engages the reader in a personal journey through our too often forgotten heritage! Another must-read for all who desire to engage our world for Christ.

— Allen Jackson, pastor of
World Outreach Church,
Murfreesboro, Tennessee

Another essential collection of people used by God to change the world whose stories we need to know. Eric's ability to uncover little-known details while also situating his subjects into the larger contexts where they belong is on full display here. I hope he keeps these "Seven" books coming!

— John Stonestreet, president
of the Colson Center for
Christian Worldview

MORE
MEN

MORE
MEN

AND THE SECRET OF
THEIR GREATNESS

ERIC METAXAS
with ANNE MORSE

ZONDERVAN
BOOKS

ZONDERVAN BOOKS

Seven More Men
Copyright © 2020 by Metaxas Media, LLC

Requests for information should be addressed to:
Zondervan, *3900 Sparks Dr. SE, Grand Rapids, Michigan 49546*

Zondervan titles may be purchased in bulk for educational, business, fundraising, or sales promotional use. For information, please email SpecialMarkets@Zondervan.com.

ISBN 978-0-310-35889-3 (hardcover)

ISBN 978-0-310-35891-6 (audio)

ISBN 978-0-310-35890-9 (ebook)

Cover/interior images: William Booth: Hulton Archive / Getty Images, George Whitefield: Hulton Archive / Getty Images, Alexander Solzhenitsyn: Auk Archive / Alamy Stock Photo, Alvin York: Stocktrek Images, Inc. / Alamy Stock Photo, George Washington Carver: World History Archive / Alamy Stock Photo, Billy Graham: Hulton Archive / Stringer / Getty Images, Martin Luther: Wikimedia / Public Domain

Printed in the United States of America

20 21 22 23 24 25 26 27 28 29 30 /LSC/ 15 14 13 12 11 10 9 8 7 6 5 4 3 2 1

Contents

Introduction

n the opening lines of Mark Twain's masterpiece *The Adventures of Huckleberry Finn*, the book's eponymous narrator and protagonist—meaning Huck himself, of course—tells the reader that if they know about him it's only because they have read Twain's earlier book, *The Adventures of Tom Sawyer*. Actually, Huck says it better than I can: "You don't know about me without you have read a book by the name of *The Adventures of Tom Sawyer*; but that ain't no matter. That book was made by Mr. Mark Twain, and he told the truth, mainly."

I think of those famous lines now because this book is a bit like that. Meaning, if you know what came before, you'll understand this one better. Of course, any book with the word *more* in the title presupposes a previous *something*. In the case of this book, that previous something is my book *Seven Men: And the Secret of Their Greatness*. This book is a continuation of that book. Or you could say this book is a sequel to that book. But unless you already knew that, you'd wonder why *more* is in the title; and I thought I'd just be clear about that right up front. But nothing I say here can properly underscore the importance of the lives in this book. These are absolutely extraordinary lives that in most cases are tragically little known, and I firmly believe that our cultural ignorance of these lives—and the lives in my other books—has contributed greatly to many of the problems facing us today. So merely getting to know them will dramatically help you to be a part of the solution.

I'm happy to say that the response to my first book along these lines—*Seven Men*—was so wonderful that I soon knew I had to write another similar book. And since the response to my book *Seven Women: And the Secret of Their Greatness* was equally happily wonderful, I knew I had to write yet another similar book.

And so this book, *Seven More Men*, and my next book, *Seven More Women*—coming out in 2021—are both meant to do more of what the first two books did: put on the written page the lives of people who have lived in a way that warrants our admiration and, to some extent, our emulation. These are people whose lives inspire us, and who doesn't need that?

So the principal reason for my telling these stories about the lives of amazing men is that any of us encountering these lives can't help but be inspired. If we are honest, we know we all need this sort of inspiration desperately. We need to know that those who have gone before us have struggled in ways that might help us in our own struggles and have succeeded in ways we too can succeed.

Of course, spending time with real flesh-and-blood heroes is better than reading about them. Many of us have had parents or grandparents—or aunts or uncles or family friends or pastors or coaches or teachers—who have been real heroes in our lives, who have helped us understand what's important in life and how to deal with adversity and how to be people of character and integrity. Nothing can ever beat that. But the next best thing is reading about the lives of people like that.

One of the reasons I wrote the first two books—and now write this one and the next one—is that we are living at a time in which the concepts of nobility and virtue and heroism are either ignored or maligned and mocked. This is part of why we are suffering many of the problems we face in our culture. And so this book is simply meant to be a small antidote to that problem. So please read about these men and be encouraged and inspired!

As with the previous book, I must up front and openly aver the naked subjectivity of these choices. There are so many wonderful figures whose stories I would have loved to tell and might have told, but when you can choose only seven, you are forced to make some choices, and so I have. I have little doubt you will be so impressed with their lives that you will at least temporarily forget about the ones I might have included but didn't!

I should also say that most of the men in this book have real flaws. Naturally, every man but Jesus is a sinner and therefore will have flaws, and the flaws in some of the figures herein are significant. For example, Martin Luther at the end of his life said a number of awful things about Jews that can't easily be waved away. George Whitefield approved of slavery. General William Booth had an authoritarian side to him that caused great trouble to himself and his family late in life. In our time of politically correct madness, understanding that to err is human is vital, and we must always put our mistakes and the mistakes of others in context. For example, to expect Luther or Whitefield or Booth to bend to the standards we all seem to think of as self-evident in our own time is naive.

I have tried not to shy away from mentioning these mistaken beliefs where they apply. But the *au courant* idea that a mistake or blunder somehow destroys the value of all the good that someone has done is a deeply wrong idea that we must stand against strongly and boldly at every opportunity. Of course, it is disturbing to think that men we might otherwise consider moral giants and heroes—like Washington and Whitefield—were somehow still able to countenance slavery. But unless we see the big picture, we will be throwing the proverbial baby out with the bathwater. In other words, lives are at stake in our failure to take a broad view.

It takes wisdom and discernment to know what is truly great, and I hope the stories of the great men in this book will impart some of that to you. In fact, I'm quite confident they can't fail to do so.

Eric Metaxas
New York City
September 2019

ONE

Martin Luther

1483–1546

Here I stand. I can do no other. God help me. Amen.
—MARTIN LUTHER

Martin Luther was born in Eisleben, Saxony, on November 10, 1483. Actually, he was possibly born in 1482 or 1484. Scholars can't say for sure which year, nor did Luther or his mother—both of whom history records as present—seem to know.

Birthdays were rarely remembered in those days, but name days were something else. For this reason, we know that on the very next day—November 11 of one of those years—the one-day-old Reformer-to-be was trundled across the street to the magnificent Saints Peter and Paul Church to be baptized. This was to ensure that if he died young, as so many did in those days, he would escape the eternal flames of hell.

Luther was born at a time when the Church seemed far less interested in the happy idea of entering God's presence in heaven than in avoiding eternal punishment outside his presence in hell. As most know, this was something of an obsession with the Church of the high medieval era, so much so that it would eventually lead to the incident that would make Luther world-famous. Because Luther was baptized on the feast day of Saint Martin of Tours, his parents named him Martin.

Soon after his birth, the family moved to Mansfeld, twelve miles north, where his father, Hans, would begin a thriving mining business. Hans borrowed a significant sum of money from his wife's family to purchase four refining operations, called "smelt works." Although Luther in later years often referred to himself as "the son of a poor miner," his father hardly labored with a pick or shovel. The Luthers worked hard and were not aristocrats, but we now know they were far from poor.

In fact, just twenty years ago, an archaeological dig discovered that the historic home in Mansfeld, to which visitors have been pointed for centuries, was only one-third of a much larger home in which Luther grew up. A second dig discovered the food, toys, and silverware from their time there, all of which indicated a family of considerable means. We also know the brilliant boy was sent to the very best schools of that time so he could learn Latin and prepare for university, for it was his father's ambition that he should one day study law and then come back to work in the family business.

While away at these boarding schools, young Martin encountered many people who were deeply serious about following God, and there can be no doubt that this affected him. Although his father's plan for him was clear, Luther sometimes wondered whether God might be leading him in another direction. After all, if the picture of hell that the Church so often and so vividly presented was real, what could be more important than doing everything to avoid that everlasting nightmare? It was generally thought at that time that the only certain way to be assured of salvation was by devoting one's whole life to God by becoming a priest or a monk or a nun. But because his father had other plans for him—and because the Bible commands us to honor our father and mother unconditionally—Martin knew he must continue toward studying the law.

He entered the University of Erfurt in 1501 and in 1505 earned his master's degree, at which point he finally entered his legal studies. Martin appreciated his father's "bitter sweat and toil"[1] in making his education possible and dutifully continued along the path set out for him until a particular hot afternoon in early July 1505.

We don't know precisely what frame of mind Martin was in that day, but we have some clues. Two young lawyers whom he knew well had died that year, and on their deathbeds both expressed grave doubts about their eternal destinies, even saying they wished they had become monks and not lawyers. Young Martin didn't have the courage to bring up the subject with his father, but he must have been tortured to think of continuing this path toward becoming a lawyer, because he knew if he did, his eternal destiny would remain a horrifying and all-too-real question in his mind.

So one day, while riding back to law school after a visit to his parents' home, everything changed. He was just six miles from the university—just outside the village of Stotternheim—when a lightning storm of monstrous proportions descended on him. He was in a flat open area where a thunderbolt might at any moment have snatched him from this life and into the next, where for all he knew he would immediately be torn apart by the talons of hideous demons. The fear that overtook him was so dramatic that when one bolt struck very near, Luther was undone. The terrified young man fell to the wet ground trembling and abjectly shouted a prayer to Saint Anne, the patron saint of miners. "Help! Saint Anna!" he shouted through the moaning wind and rain. "If you save me, I will become a monk!"[2]

As it happened, Luther survived this frightful episode and rode on to Erfurt. But a heavenward oath wasn't something he could take lightly. He knew he must keep his word and immediately told his friends at Erfurt that in two weeks he would join the local Augustinian monastery—and disappear from them forever. They tried to dissuade him, but in vain. And so—without breathing a word of this news to his father—Martin one day knocked on the doors of the Augustinian monastery, offering his life to God's service forever.

When word of this extraordinary deviation from his plans for his son reached Hans Luther, he was predictably furious. He couldn't fathom that his brilliant son would openly disobey his father by throwing away the promising career toward which both of them had already devoted so much. But that's precisely what Martin Luther had done.

However, the peace Luther expected to find in becoming a monk eluded him. His whole being was focused on prayer and worship every day, from the dark predawn hours until dusk. But the harder he worked to earn God's approval, the further from heaven he felt. No matter what he did, he felt condemned. For example, he might pray for many hours—but then have a flicker of pride that he had prayed for so many hours. He knew this pride was sinful, and he would have to confess it, else it might damn him to hell forever. But he never felt that his confessions were sufficient. There almost always lingered another thing he thought he should confess. He never seemed to get closer to his goal of peace with God, so he simply tried harder. Luther later wrote that if ever a monk could have gotten to heaven through "sheer monkery,"[3] Luther would have done it. He prayed and confessed—and fasted so much that he became skin and bones. But somehow he only felt more wretched. Eventually he became exasperated and resentful, convinced that it was "impossible to please God through monastic efforts."[4]

On April 4, 1507, Luther was ordained to the priesthood. By now his father's ire had cooled somewhat, and both of Luther's parents came to the service where Luther would celebrate his first Communion. But during the ceremony, Luther faltered noticeably. The idea of his unworthiness to handle the body and blood of Jesus himself was so terrifying that Luther froze. If the priest attending him at the time had not urged him on, he might still be standing there. His terror of a holy God who judged him made his existence nearly impossible.

Luther's superior at the monastery was Vicar General Johannes von Staupitz—to whom Luther would grow especially close. Staupitz saw that Luther was especially brilliant, and uniquely troubled, and tried to help. So he invited Luther to leave Erfurt to join him at the newer

University of Wittenberg. Staupitz had recently been named dean there, and recognizing Luther's great gifts, he wanted the twenty-five-year-old to join him and to go on to teach theology there. So Luther went, earning his bachelor's degree in biblical studies in 1508.

But he continued to be tortured by the question of his own salvation, still unable to feel God's love or approval. During his weekly confession with Staupitz, he would go over and over the tiniest details of the previous week, trying to be absolutely sure there wasn't anything he might have forgotten and left unconfessed. Staupitz himself almost lost hope that he could ever get Luther to see that God really loved him. To Staupitz, Luther behaved as though God hated him, and as though he secretly hated God. But who wouldn't hate a God who was a cruel judge and who put us through such endless misery?

In 1510 Staupitz needed someone to travel to Rome to settle a bitter dispute between two rival groups of Augustinian monks. Perhaps sending Luther would break the young man's cycle of obsessive spiritual navel-gazing. The trip had to be made on foot, and since it was eight hundred miles, it would take two months to get there and, of course, two months to walk back. Surely such a journey would provide Luther a different perspective on himself and on God. Yet, amazingly, it didn't. When Luther returned, he was quite the same as ever.

Nonetheless, what the young monk saw during his weeks in Rome was eye opening. Luther was horrified at "the chaos, the filth, and the practice of locals who urinated in public and openly patronized prostitutes."[5] This last activity even included members of the clergy. Luther also observed corrupt and incompetent priests racing carelessly through their Masses. Since Luther took his faith so seriously, this was all greatly depressing and dismaying. It is often said that Luther's time in Rome propelled him to think about reforming the Church, but this is simply not true. He was a deeply loyal son of the Church and had no idea in 1510 about the things he would say and do a decade in the future.

Staupitz felt that Luther's tremendous zeal to read the Bible would make him an ideal candidate to earn his doctorate and then teach the

Scriptures at the university. He knew how Luther hated teaching Aristotle and how he loved teaching the Scriptures. So one day, under a pear tree in the cloister, Staupitz broached the subject. Luther was unable to accept the idea that he could be worthy of such a great honor, but Staupitz was relentless. He knew Luther better than Luther knew himself. And soon afterward, Luther began his studies. In October 1512 he officially became a doctor of theology and days later joined the theological faculty. He began intensely reading and meditating on the biblical letters of Paul. It was in these epistles that he would eventually notice things he had never seen before and would at last find the God he had never believed existed, a God who was not only a Judge but also a loving Father and gracious Savior. It was as though Luther would one day see a thread and pull at it and pull at it until—to his own shock—he had unraveled the entire tapestry of medieval Christianity. The particular thread concerned the New Testament idea that we aren't saved by what we do but by believing in what Jesus did on the cross. When we cease trying to reach God by our own efforts and simply realize we can never reach him that way, we finally turn to him in earnest and are welcomed into his arms.

The famous verse in Paul's epistle to the Romans that became a key for Luther was Romans 1:17 (KJV), "For therein is the righteousness of God revealed from faith to faith: as it is written, The just shall live by faith." By faith! Not by our own efforts! And in Paul's letter to the Galatians, Luther read: "We also have believed in Christ Jesus, in order to be justified by faith in Christ and not by works of the law, because by works of the law no one will be justified" (2:16 ESV). When Luther finally saw what the Bible said—that it isn't what we do but our faith in what Christ did—everything changed. The scales fell from Luther's eyes, and at last he could see God as he really was. God is a God of infinite grace, who wants to reach every sinner, including the miserable monk named Martin Luther.

While this theological cataclysm was rumbling through Luther's soul and changing him from the inside out, something else was happening too, and this would affect Luther's thinking about grace in a more practical sense. It would also cause the historic controversy that catapulted him into the forefront of history. It had to do with the issue of so-called indulgences.

By way of background, the practice of indulgences began as a good idea. If one had sinned and wanted to repent—and do penance for one's sins—one had several options. One might pray certain prayers or make a pilgrimage or do a good work, such as donating a certain amount to the Church. Some of these donations took the form of "indulgences." But over time the use of indulgences grew twisted from its original intentions. Indulgences became such a significant source of income for the Church that it preached about indulgences more and more. After all, there were many important things that needed financing—such as the building of St. Peter's Basilica in Rome—and what better way to raise funds than to preach indulgences all across Europe? But finally the practice had gotten so far out of hand that to Luther and a few others, it was a theological and moral horror that must be stopped. But how?

Luther saw the trouble with indulgences not just on a theological level but on a practical one. After all, he was not just a theologian; he was also a priest. Sometimes when the faithful came to him to confess, they would pull out an indulgence certificate they had purchased, expecting it to get them out of doing any further penance for the sins they were now confessing to Luther. These people had been told that they could pay in advance for sins they hadn't yet committed. He knew such beliefs were corrupting the souls of the faithful.

Staupitz had seen these problems for some time and often taught that "true repentance must begin with the love for justice and for God."[6] So now Luther too spoke out against indulgences, but nothing was done. Eventually it occurred to him that the best way to draw attention to this problem might be via an academic debate. Wasn't this what theologians were supposed to do? The problems would be confronted in the proper academic environment, and the results would be sent to the archbishop, who would surely see the situation and do what was necessary to change it. So Luther took the initiative and wrote up ninety-five provocative debate theses—as was the custom—to advertise the upcoming debate.

Because these theses were in Latin, very few could read them, but, of course, they were intended to be read only by the theologians who might join the debate. The common people weren't supposed to know about the theological disagreements among their leaders. After all, that might well undermine the Church's authority, which is precisely what happened.

In the five centuries since these now-famous Ninety-Five Theses were written, there have been innumerable images showing Luther dramatically nailing the document to the door of the Castle Church in Wittenberg. It appears as though he intends this act to be loud and public and provocative, especially to the pope and anyone else supporting the practice of indulgences. By daring to post the inflammatory document right on the door of the most important church in Wittenberg, he was essentially poking his finger in the eye of the ecclesiastical authorities. But this is all far from the truth.

For one thing, the large wooden door of the Castle Church was simply the bulletin board for the town. Anyone posting anything would have posted it there, so this was hardly a provocation. As far as Luther was concerned, he was simply and politely posting a Latin document advertising an academic debate. Further undermining the ideas we have about this captivating image is the fact that Luther may not have used a hammer and nails but a jar of paste. And he may well not even have posted the document himself but may have simply given it to the church sexton to post. Finally, it is almost certain that the date on which Luther is always said to have done this—October 31, 1517—is not the date he did it, if he did it himself at all. But what Luther did do on that date—something far less memorable than noisily hammering something onto a door—is post a letter.

Luther felt it his sworn duty as a "doctor of the Church" to inform his archbishop—Archbishop Albrecht of Mainz and Magdeburg—of the theological debate about to occur, so he wrote him a humble letter on the subject of indulgences and with it enclosed a copy of the Ninety-Five Theses, mailing it on the date now reckoned as the beginning of the Reformation.

In the letter, after extremely humbly referring to himself as "the dregs of humanity,"[7] Luther graciously suggests that the archbishop might not realize that these corrupting indulgences were being circulated in his name. He expresses his concern over "the wholly false impressions which the people have conceived from [the indulgences]."[8] These "unhappy souls believe that if they have purchased letters of indulgence they are sure of their salvation; again, that so soon as they cast their contributions into the money-box, souls fly out of purgatory. . . . Thus souls committed to your care, good Father, are taught to their death."[9]

Luther was a deeply devoted monk, and whatever his thoughts toward those in power would become, he was at this time still humble and deferential. He wanted to give the archbishop the benefit of the doubt regarding what was happening in his name and tried to help him see the difficult situation. Luther thought it likely that the busy archbishop didn't realize the extent of the problem and simply felt it was his duty to speak up.

In his letter, Luther went on to clarify the problem these indulgences had created. He pointed to the New Testament verses that spelled out the deeply serious nature of one's salvation, including Peter's words that "the righteous scarcely [shall] be saved" (1 Peter 4:18 KJV). Therefore, treating salvation as lightly as the indulgence preachers were doing was scandalous. "Why, then, do these preachers of pardons," he asked, "by these false fables and promises, make the people careless and fearless? Whereas indulgences confer on us no good gift, either for salvation or for sanctity, but only take away the external penalty."[10]

Luther also said that to push the sale of indulgences, the Church ignored infinitely more important things, such as the preaching of the gospel itself. "How great then is the horror," he wrote, "how great the peril of a bishop, if he permits the Gospel to be kept quiet, and nothing but the noise of indulgences to be spread among his people!"[11] Finally, Luther asked the archbishop to look into the matter and take action.

But what Luther didn't know was that the man to whom he appealed for help was far from ignorant about what was happening, much less unbiased on this explosive issue. Indeed, Albrecht knew all about the indulgences being preached in his district and desperately needed every penny coming from them. And the corruption underlying the situation was even worse than that. Although almost no one knew, Albrecht had paid a vast sum of money to the pope so he would overlook a certain rule Albrecht had broken. To pay this money, Albrecht took out a gigantic loan—and to pay it back he got the pope to agree that he, Albrecht, could keep half the money from the indulgences sold in his district. The other half would, of course, go directly to the pope, who wanted to fund the building of the new St. Peter's.

So we can only imagine what Albrecht thought when he read Luther's letter. But whatever he thought, he surely thought even less of the enclosed Ninety-Five Theses because their tone was dramatically different from the humble tone of the letter. The theses were meant to provoke debate among Luther's fellow academics, and they hardly pulled punches on what their author really thought.

"Most people," the theses read, "are necessarily deceived by that indiscriminate and high-sounding promise of release from penalty. . . . They preach only human doctrines who say that as soon as the money clinks into the money chest, the soul flies out of purgatory. . . ."[12] This last sentence was a clear and pointed reference to Johannes Tetzel, who preached indulgences under Albrecht's authority. Luther continued, turning the now-infamous epigram on its head: "It is certain that when money clinks into the chest, greed and avarice can be increased. . . . Those who believe that they can be certain of their salvation because they have indulgence letters will be eternally damned, together with their teachers. . . . Any truly repentant Christian has a right to full remission of penalty and guilt, even without indulgence letters."

The phrase "together with their teachers" of course implied that Tetzel—and perhaps the archbishop too—would go to hell for what they were doing. Surely that caught the archbishop's attention. Even more shocking, Luther's criticism of the pope was explicit. "Why does not the pope empty purgatory for the sake of holy love," Luther wrote, instead of doing so only "for the sake of miserable money with which to build a church?" Luther then asked, "Why does not the pope, whose wealth is today greater than the wealth of the richest Croesus, build this one basilica of St. Peter with his own money rather than with the money of poor believers?"[13]

What was a deeply compromised archbishop to do? He did exactly what many do when handed a hot potato: pass the flustering tuber to someone else. And so Albrecht sent the whole kaboodle on to Rome, to the pope himself. If Albrecht was lucky, the pope might simply ignore it.

But something happened in Wittenberg that would ensure that this issue would be anything but ignored. Someone who understood Latin and had read the Ninety-Five Theses decided they were so juicy and interesting that they must be translated into German. Of course Luther had never dreamed this would happen, but they were indeed translated—and then printed and distributed! Thus, in violation of all Luther thought possible, this private notice of an academic debate, with all its provocative language about the Church and the pope, was suddenly being read and discussed by everyone across Germany! For Luther, it was a waking nightmare, the medieval equivalent of mistakenly hitting "Reply All" when sending a vicious email.

What really began the trouble was when the Ninety-Five Theses fell under the eyes of the man so obviously referred to in them, the burly indulgence preacher named Johannes Tetzel. Tetzel became so outraged that he loudly declared that this archheretic Luther would be burned at the stake in no time. In Tetzel's view, Luther was far from someone humbly wanting to right a theological error. He was a self-aggrandizing troublemaker who brazenly had disrespected the Holy

Church. And for good measure, Tetzel now wrote 106 provocative theses of his own, attacking Luther and all he had written.

To be clear, what made everything that followed possible—in the cacophonous back-and-forth between Luther and his innumerable critics—was the relatively recent invention of the printing press. The idea of printing was so new that there were no laws regarding copyrights, so any printer was free to print and sell anything they liked. And what could be better than anything written on this suddenly red-hot topic of the Church's selling of indulgences?

In the beginning, Luther did what he could to cool the situation. When he first realized his provocative theses were being read widely, he knew he should carefully and in a moderate tone clarify what he meant, hoping to nip the scandal in the bud. So Luther preached a theologically buttoned-up sermon on indulgences and quickly had it printed and distributed. But somehow this effort only opened other theological cans of worms and caused more trouble. Before Luther knew it, people in England were talking about the controversy—and about the intemperate Saxon monk who had started it all. Some thought he was a villain, plain and simple, but many others thought him a hero, thrilled that someone was finally speaking against the corruption they had seen for years.

As the controversy rattled all of Europe, the attacks from Rome grew increasingly vicious. They were so vicious and unreasonable that eventually Luther himself wondered whether a spirit of antichrist had indeed taken hold of his beloved Church. If so, then the end times were at hand, and he had better speak the truth at any cost. At this point, figuring things couldn't get worse, he threw caution to the wind and replaced his humble tone with a bellicose one that gave no quarter to his opponents. As the attacks on him increased, Luther became less and less diplomatic in what he said and wrote. It was at this point that Luther had to reckon what he feared more—God's judgment or humans'. In the end there was no contest. Better to die a horrible death by burning at the stake for speaking the truth than to go to hell forever for staying silent.

Eventually, Luther even dared to question the pope's authority and the primacy of the Roman Catholic Church. What historical evidence existed, he wished to know, to warrant putting Rome's authority above that of the Eastern churches? Or to give the pope nearly dictatorial powers?

Staupitz would help Luther in many ways in the years ahead. Staupitz enjoyed a close friendship with Frederick the Wise, the elector of Saxony, and this relationship would prove very important as Luther continued the dangerous habit of criticizing the pope and church doctrine. In fact, now there were threats to Luther's life. Staupitz feared for Luther as he made the trip to Heidelberg, so Staupitz persuaded Frederick to write a letter guaranteeing Luther's safe passage. Luther got to Heidelberg safely, and his talk there went very well, adding more converts to the cause.

When Pope Leo X initially heard about Luther's stand against indulgences, he dismissed him as a "drunken German monk." But in time, he realized Luther was bringing real trouble to him and to the Church. He eventually felt he must strangle this monster in the cradle before it was too late, so he put a Dominican friar named Sylvester Prierias on the job. It was Prierias's job to respond to Luther's attacks, and Prierias did, promptly labeling Luther a heretic and demanding that Luther carry his impertinent carcass to Rome to address the serious charges against him.

When Frederick learned of this, he was rightly concerned. A trip to Rome might well result in Luther's death. After all, heretics were frequently burned at the stake. A hundred years earlier that was precisely what happened to Jan Hus, who had said many of the things Luther was saying. So Frederick decided he would play a political card. He was one of the seven electors in the Holy Roman Empire, and his vote was extremely important in choosing the next emperor. Pope Leo had a certain candidate in mind for the job—and wanted Frederick's vote. So when Frederick asked the pope to consider moving the meeting with Luther to a location in Germany, the pope understood it was in his best interest to do so—and did.

If the meeting were in Germany, the odds of Luther's being killed were much less than they would be in Rome. But what would that German location be? It so happened that the next Imperial Diet, an annual gathering of all nobles and ecclesiastical dignitaries to discuss and vote on the issues of the empire, was to be held in Augsburg, Germany. So instead of requiring Luther to travel the eight hundred miles south to Rome, the pope would send his legate, Cardinal Cajetan, up to Augsburg.

Staupitz never spoke publicly against the Church, but he supported Luther nonetheless, and now, before this historic confrontation, he took the dramatic step of freeing Luther from his Augustinian vows. Thus, Luther was able to travel and speak out publicly against the authority of the bishops, which a monk still under discipline was forbidden to do.

Shortly after arriving in Augsburg, Urban de Serralonga, on behalf of the cardinals, paid Luther a visit. He had some instructions for this meddlesome monk: Luther was ordered to meekly recant all he had said.

But Luther quickly dismissed this advice. "If I am convinced out of the Sacred Scriptures that I have erred," he said, "I shall be but too glad to retract."[14]

Naturally, Urban was infuriated. "The Pope could, by a single nod, change or suppress articles of faith," he said.[15] So Luther would do well to accept this prudent advice if he wished to stay alive.

But Luther was unmoved by the threat. "I shall still have heaven," he answered.[16] His fear of God was real, more real than his fear of what any man might do to him, and this is clearly what kept Luther from yielding on any of the points that seemed so clear to him.

On October 11, 1518, Luther appeared before Cajetan. After acknowledging that he had written the Ninety-Five Theses, Luther said, "I am ready to listen most obediently to my accusation, and if I have erred, to submit to the instructions in the truth."[17]

"Observe," Cajetan growled, "in the seventh proposition you deny that the Sacrament can profit one unless he has faith."

Luther responded, "That the man who receives the holy Sacrament must have faith in the grace offered him is a truth I never can and never will revoke."

A furious Cajetan responded, "Whether you will or no, I must have your recantation this very day, or for this one error I shall condemn all your propositions."

"But I demand proof from the Scriptures that I am wrong," Luther said. "It is on Scripture that my views rest."

"Do you not know that the Pope has authority and power over these things?" interrupted another papal representative.

"Save Scripture," Luther replied.

"Scripture!" the cardinal sneered. "The Pope is above Scripture—and above Councils."

Here, of course, was the rub of rubs. Where did the final authority rest? Was it in the Scriptures more than in the decisions of the Church? Luther said it was in the Scriptures, but Cajetan was saying it was the pope himself who had the final say.

Of course it was true that the Church had overseen which books became part of the canon of Holy Scripture. Had not God deputized the Church to do that, and had he not spoken to its leaders via his Holy Spirit at the Council of Nicaea? So if the pope was the head of the Church, did he not have authority that trumped that of Scripture? On this very unforgiving point was the Church broken in two.

Eventually, Cajetan, after making more threats of punishment if Luther didn't recant, offered the monk safe conduct if he would travel to Rome for judgment. Luther, no fool, knew this "safe conduct" would likely deliver him directly to a dank Vatican dungeon. The offer was politely declined.

Cajetan had been ordered to arrest "this beast,"[18] as he called Luther, if he refused to recant, but he simply didn't act quickly enough, and Luther, sensing the noose tightening, secretly slipped out of Augsburg under cover of night.

Luther's next encounter with Rome was instigated by Duke George of Saxony, who organized another disputation with the monk in 1519 in a city he considered hostile to Luther: Leipzig. Here, Johannes Eck, a skilled debater with access to power, would debate Luther's ally Andreas Karlstadt. Luther himself would also be given an opportunity to speak.

As Luther prepared for the confrontation, he and his allies remained on the offensive, making increasingly bold charges against the pope. Luther's incendiary statements, with which more and more people were agreeing, threatened to destabilize not merely the church authorities but the civil authorities too. What he was unleashing could easily boil over, with harmful and unintended consequences far beyond his control.

The debate took place at Pleissenburg Castle. In a strong, clear voice, Luther began by quoting Matthew 16:18 to back up his assertion that popes didn't have the exclusive right to interpret Scripture and that, therefore, neither popes nor church councils were infallible. Eck countered by trying to link Luther to the heresies preached by Jan Hus a century before. If Eck's strategy succeeded, Luther likely would have followed in Hus's footsteps and been immolated at the stake. The debate ended with partisans on both sides claiming victory. But Eck wasn't through. Once he returned to Rome, he worked diligently to convince Church officials to aggressively pursue this man who had even dared to call the pope "antichrist."

By June 15, 1520, Pope Leo had had enough. He wrote a papal bull titled *Exsurge Domine*, in which he warned Luther that unless he promptly recanted forty-one sentences from his various writings—including the Ninety-Five Theses—he would be excommunicated, which to anyone who believed in the pope's authority meant an eternity in hell. But by this time, Luther was convinced that those attacking him were animated by the spirit of antichrist rather than by God, so he didn't take the threat of excommunication as the pope had hoped he would. Luther responded to this threat by publicly setting fire to the papal document at the Wittenberg city dump. For good measure, he also incinerated some books of canon law. "Since they have burned my books," Luther now declared, "I shall burn theirs!"[19] University students got into the act too, gleefully hurling writings attacking their favorite professor into the roaring bonfire.

Soon after this, Luther kicked out every theological trace by penning three works that would inflame his critics further still: *Address to the Christian Nobility of the German Nation*, *The Babylonian Captivity of the Church*, and *On the Freedom of a Christian*. In the first, he laid out the shocking idea of a "priesthood of all believers," declaring that the baptized were equally worthy to stand before God and that they could forgive others and pray for others themselves, not requiring any official priestly mediation.

Seeing that Luther had publicly mocked the pope's threat of excommunication, the pope made good on the threat and excommunicated him from the Roman Catholic Church. The papal bull that announced Luther's excommunication called on Emperor Charles V to carry out the excommunication. This meant Luther would be put on trial and perhaps executed. But when the bull arrived in Wittenberg, Luther read it and immediately wrote a peppery response, saying that the bull "condemns Christ himself."[20]

Once again, Frederick of Saxony was sympathetic to Luther, but papal nuncio Girolamo Aleandro insisted that secular authorities must keep their noses out of Church business. The Church had found Luther guilty of heresy; the state must now hand him over. Luther appealed to Emperor Charles V himself, whose first reaction was to tear up Luther's letter and stomp on the pieces. But later, in a more pensive mood, Charles considered how the German people might react if they learned that Luther had been condemned without a hearing. After all, most of them were now his enthusiastic supporters. So Charles—not merely ruler but politician too—invited Luther to travel to the city of Worms to "answer with regard to your books and your teaching."[21]

Luther's friends, fearful Luther would not survive the journey, beseeched him to stay put. But Luther had set his face toward Worms. This is not to say he wasn't frightened. History records that he traveled to Worms in a simple wagon, "physically fearful and trembling."[22] But along the journey, his spirits were lifted again and again: he was cheered in town after town by enthusiastic followers. Unbeknownst to him, his writings had circulated so thoroughly around Germany that he was greeted everywhere as a hero, a voice of the people, whose cause he had taken up.

The diet to which he was traveling convened in early 1521 at the Imperial Palace. The pope had directed his representatives in Worms to force "the wild boar" to play defense and under no circumstances to allow the shrewd monk to turn the somber occasion into a colorful debate. There were to be no tricks or shenanigans! Luther must either recant or not recant.

The scene greeting observers on the day Luther was brought to the palace is described (very probably by Luther himself) as follows:

> At four in the afternoon, the imperial chamberlain, and the herald who had accompanied him from Wittenberg, came to him at his inn, The Court of Germany, and conducted him to the town hall, along bye-ways, in order to avoid the crowds which had assembled in the leading streets. . . . Many persons had got upon the roofs of houses to see Dr. Martin. As he proceeded . . . several noblemen successively addressed to him words of encouragement. "Be bold," said they, "and fear not those who can kill the body, but are powerless against the soul."[23]

At last Luther, dressed in the habit of a humble monk, entered the candlelit room filled with scores of the most powerful men in Christendom wearing bejeweled robes and furs and ornate gold crosses. Above them, on a magnificently decorated dais, sat the emperor himself.

Luther stood before a table piled high with all his writings. Johannes von der Ecken—who was secretary to the archbishop of Trier and is not to be confused with Luther's earlier interlocutor, Johannes Eck—sprang immediately to the business at hand. "Are these books yours?" he asked.[24]

"Yes," Luther replied. "The books are mine."

Now Ecken would ask the question of questions. He wasn't interested in philosophical meanderings but demanded a simple yea or nay. "Do you wish to defend the books which are recognized as your work?" he asked. "Or to retract anything contained in them?"

Luther was flummoxed. The books contained many things that even leaders in the Church had commended. It would, he said, "be rash and dangerous to reply to such a question until I had meditated thereupon in silence and retreat, lest I incur the anger of our Lord." This reply was certainly unexpected. But it was clever too. The annoyed Ecken knew he had no choice and told Luther he could have precisely twenty-four hours; and so the assembled spectacle of people had to scatter until the next day.

When they gathered again, Ecken repeated his question and pushed harder. "Explain yourself now!" he said. "Will you defend all your writings, or disavow some of them?" This time, Luther was ready.

"Most Serene Lord Emperor, Most Illustrious Princes, Most Gracious Lords," Luther began, in that conciliatory and humble tone that must have rankled his foes as much as anything he would say. "To this day I have thought and written in simplicity of heart, solely with a view to the glory of God and the pure instruction of Christ's faithful people."

Then Luther asked his audience to observe that his books "are not all of the same kind." Some dealt with piety in faith and morals, "with such simplicity and so agreeably with the gospels that my adversaries themselves are compelled to admit them useful, harmless, and clearly worth reading by a Christian. . . . If I should begin to recant here, what, I beseech you, would I be doing but condemning . . . that truth which is admitted by friends and foes alike?"

Others of his books dealt with "writings leveled against the papacy and the doctrine of the papists," Luther explained, "as against those who by their wicked doctrines and precedents have laid waste Christendom by doing harm to the souls and the bodies of men . . . and are to this day being devoured without end in shameful fashion." Were he to recant the writing of these books, Luther observed, "the only effect will be to add strength to such tyranny, to open not the windows but the main doors to such blasphemy."

He wasn't through. A third category of books, he declared, were written against private individuals "who have exerted themselves in defense of the Roman tyranny and to the overthrow of that piety which I have taught. . . . But it is not in my power to recant them, because that recantation would give that tyranny and blasphemy an occasion to lord it over those whom I defend and to rage against God's people more violently than ever."

Luther concluded, "I shall be most ready . . . to recant any error, and I shall be the first in casting my writings into the fire" if—and of course this was the condition on which all hung—if he, Martin Luther, could be convinced of any scriptural errors.

This wasn't the answer for which Ecken was angling. He sternly demanded a plain reply to the following question: Was he, or was he not, prepared to recant? These were the sole options before him, and he must choose one without further delay.

Luther's response, offered up without notes, is recorded as follows: "Your Imperial Majesty and Your Lordships demand a simple answer. Here it is, plain and unvarnished. Unless I am convicted of error by the testimony of Scripture or (since I put no trust in the unsupported authority of Pope or councils, since it is plain that they have often erred and often contradicted themselves) by manifest reasoning, I stand convicted by the Scriptures to which I have appealed, and my conscience is taken captive by God's word, I cannot and will not recant anything, for to act against our conscience is neither safe for us, nor open to us." He concluded with the famous words for which he is most well-known. "Here I stand," he said. "I can do no other. God help me. Amen."[25]

After the people heard these words, the hall exploded in chaotic confusion. To Emperor Charles it was plainly hopeless to continue. The day's proceedings were at an end, and all now made their exits. Luther returned to his lodgings and gulped down an Einbecker beer brought to him by a thoughtful supporter.

Most accounts of Luther's life seem to imply that this is essentially where things ended, but that is far from the case. After Luther's historic stand, there was still much haggling to be done. In the days after his appearance before the diet, a committee met privately with Luther and tried to find a compromise. They acknowledged that Luther was correct on some counts and asked him to revoke some of his other points. But Luther had come too far and was unable to concede anything they asked.

Afterward Luther was allowed to make his way home from Worms, enjoying the same warm outpouring of support on the return journey as he had experienced in the other direction. Wherever he stopped, boisterous crowds assembled to hear the extraordinary preachings of this outlaw monk. Luther had been journeying for one week when he received a surprise. Actually, he had some idea it would happen, but he didn't know when it would happen, nor the details. Suddenly, two men on horseback, armed with deadly crossbows, appeared. They galloped up to Luther in his wagon, halting him and his companion dead in their tracks. They then blindfolded Luther, put him on the back of one of their horses, and galloped away into the woods.

Luther knew his own Duke Frederick had orchestrated this "kidnapping" for Luther's own safety and the preservation of Luther's cause. Frederick thought it best to pretend to kidnap Luther before anyone else could do so in earnest, and murder him—so he was now spirited to the eleventh-century Wartburg Castle, high on a crest in the endless woods of Thuringia, which bordered Luther's own province of Saxony. Here, in relative solitude and safety, Luther would wait until the trouble blew over, if it would blow over. He would grow out his tonsure and would grow a beard to be disguised as a knight so that even the others in the castle would not know who he was. The only one at the castle who knew his real identity was the castellan, Berlepsch, who was entrusted with feeding Luther and seeing that no one else knew anything about him. To any souls expressing curiosity about this mysterious castlemate, he was simply called "Junker [Knight] George."

While Luther was sequestered at the Wartburg, Emperor Charles V put forth the ominous Edict of Worms, which decreed, "We forbid anyone from this time forward to dare, either by words or by deeds, to receive, defend, sustain, or favor the said Martin Luther. On the contrary, we want him to be apprehended and punished as a notorious heretic, as he deserves. . . . Those who will help in his capture will be rewarded generously."[26] In other words, Charles had accepted the negative verdict at Worms against Luther, who was now officially not merely a heretic but a criminal too.

Of course, this was precisely why Frederick had "kidnapped" Luther in advance. His whereabouts were secret, except to a tiny group of friends in Wittenberg. In fact, many now believed him to be dead. But Luther, very much alive, put this time to what became historic use. He read and wrote voraciously. That spring—in the shockingly brief time of eleven weeks—Luther translated the entire New Testament into German. There had been other translations into German before, but never one that could be read by most Germans, and never one that was so well done. Five centuries later, it is still used.

While Luther labored at this monumental task, he also struggled with a host of maladies that would multiply and plague him for the rest of his life, including depression, constipation, and hemorrhoids. And during this time too, while Luther was in hiding, the revolution he had unleashed continued, albeit unfortunately without his wise oversight. For example, on one occasion, student demonstrators, under the "leadership" of Luther's overzealous colleague Andreas Karlstadt, hurled rocks through stained-glass windows of churches, smashed religious statuaries, broke pipe organs, and otherwise ran riot through Wittenberg. And they did it all in the name of their hero, Martin Luther. They wanted to eliminate every one of the church practices Luther had objected to, but when Luther himself learned of their violent activities, he was outraged. These intemperate radicals were threatening the success of everything Luther had worked for.

The news he kept hearing was so bad that less than a year after his involuntary confinement, he knew he must return home to "lead a more orderly process of change."[27] Returning was of course very dangerous. Still, despite even the stern disapproval of Frederick himself, who felt it reckless to leave the safety of the Wartburg, Luther made his way back to Wittenberg. It was one thing to have overseen a revolution, to have shown people what was wrong with what had become of the Roman Catholic Church; but it was another thing entirely to figure out how to govern a new church in an orderly and respectful way. In many ways, this would prove more difficult.

Immediately upon his return, Luther got to work, giving a series of sermons meant to offer the proper way forward—in the process rebuking some of those who had acted so rashly in his absence. He also published a book outlining how his followers, who despite Luther's protestations were now called "Lutherans," should best reform the church. Luther was quite clear that the vandalism and rioting didn't serve God's purposes. Instead, his followers must ever "act with fear and humiliation. . . . For here we battle not against pope or bishop, but against the devil. . . . And do you imagine he is asleep?"[28]

He continued, "Therefore all those have erred who have helped and consented to abolish the mass—not that it was not a good thing, but that it was not done in an orderly way. You say it was right according to the Scriptures. I agree, but what becomes of order? For it was done in wantonness, with no regard for proper order and with offense to your neighbor."[29]

It was now also necessary for Luther to define authority in the church, especially since he had repudiated the authority of the pope and other church officials. What was left, Luther wrote, was the Holy Scriptures themselves—the only inspired and authoritative Word of God. According to Luther, the Word of God was the single source of doctrine and the only infallible guide to salvation. The Latin term he used, *sola scriptura*, has served to express this theological position ever since.

———— ◆ ◆ ◆ ————

A nd so Luther lived in Wittenberg, unable to go beyond the borders of Saxony, wherein Frederick would protect him. In October 1524, Luther made a bold and highly symbolic change, giving up his monastic garb for ordinary clothing, signaling his refusal to make distinctions between pastors and parishioners. As he had said before, all baptized Christians were part of "the priesthood of believers."

As many have pointed out, Luther was a man with great virtues and great faults both, a man who made mistakes, some of which he acknowledged and others he didn't. Most biographers, in summing up his life, note that some of Luther's most dismaying actions had to do with what became known as the Peasants' War.

Luther famously cited Romans chapter 13, in which Saint Paul speaks of obeying the earthly authorities, urging all citizens to obey the government. But as a result of the social chaos that in part had grown out of Luther's own statements and actions, many peasants took matters into their own hands regarding the injustices they felt, both from the church and from the secular authorities.

Luther, the man who challenged church authorities and who proudly told everyone that his own ancestors were peasants, might well have been expected to be on the peasants' side in this grievance. He did speak out against the injustices of the ruling classes against the peasants, but when Luther saw how the peasants were behaving, often cruelly murdering everyone in their way, Luther took a harsh stand against them.

In a typically bluntly titled pamphlet, *Against the Robbing and Murdering Hordes of Peasants*, Luther charged that the peasants had murdered their enemies and had "committed their crimes under the cover of Christ's name, thereby shamefully blaspheming God."[30] He believed it was the role of the government to keep order and declared that like mad dogs, the peasants had to be put down. But these were words he would soon regret. When it was all over, a hundred thousand peasants had been massacred, and Luther was horrified. Now he thundered against the mercilessness of the ruling classes, but it was too little too late, and on this score, Luther's reputation would be permanently stained.

◆ ◆ ◆

Luther had often attacked the Roman teachings on priestly celibacy, which had been mandated only since 1123 and only in the Roman Catholic Church. The Eastern Orthodox churches never mandated it, except in the cases of those priests who wished eventually to become bishops. The Vatican had instituted the doctrine for three main reasons. First, Church authorities at that time held the view that all sexuality, including within marriage, was sinful; second, it was thought that an unmarried priest could better serve God; and third, married priests who became wealthy would want to pass their wealth on to their children instead of to the Church. By Luther's time, Church teaching on celibacy had become so entrenched "that to question it and then to promote clerical marriage struck very close to the social foundations of the church and government."[31] But Luther spoke out strongly in favor of both the good of human sexual expression within marriage as well as the benefits of matrimony itself for religious leaders.

Then in June 1525, at the age of forty-two, Luther decided to do more than speak and write on the subject. He married a runaway nun named Katherine von Bora, one of a dozen he helped rescue from their convent in Nimmschen. Luther had learned that as a result of his teachings, these nuns had tried to leave the convent but were prevented by force. Feeling responsible, he hatched a plan to free them. A man Luther knew named Leonhard Kopp would secretly carry the nuns away while they hid in his delivery wagon. Most accounts of this escape colorfully maintain that they hid in smelly herring barrels, but we now know this a fanciful and false addition.

Luther and his wife apparently had a genuinely happy marriage. "Katie," as her husband called her, bore him six children. "There is a lot to get used to in the first year of marriage," Luther wrote a friend. "One wakes up in the morning and finds a pair of pigtails on the pillow which were not there before."[32] But marriage and family life seem to have suited Luther extremely well. He seemed to love and respect and esteem his Katie tremendously. In his will, Luther broke with tradition once more when he left his whole estate to Katherine instead of to his children. He didn't want her to "have to look to the children for a handout, but rather the children should be obligated to her, honor her, and be subject to her as God has commanded."[33]

◆ ◆ ◆

By 1526, when Emperor Charles V was more able to focus on the troubles emanating from the monk in Wittenberg, it was essentially too late to do anything. Luther's ideas had spread so far and wide in the previous years, and had been embraced by so many leaders in so many areas of Europe, that rolling things back was no longer possible. And so, conceding defeat—at least in part—the imperial diet held at Speyer in 1526 only reaffirmed the Edict of Worms for Catholic territories. In other words, where Lutheranism couldn't be squashed, it would be officially tolerated. But the notion that another church besides the Roman Catholic Church could be legal in Europe was an epochal victory, and not just for Luther but for the future of religious liberty, which would spread slowly but surely until, after the United States' founding, it would be thought of as a right for all citizens.

Luther continued to think about church reforms and to write prodigiously. He developed a new definition of vocation—or of serving God. It was no longer merely about living in a monastery but could also be ordinary family life: feeding children, growing crops, and washing diapers. Everything could—and should—be done to the glory of God.

And just as everything should be done to the glory of God, so every man, woman, and child must take their own faith seriously—as seriously as any monk or nun or priest. So Luther used every means available to help the common people understand their faith and live it out. Music was one of the most effective. He declared that church music must no longer be considered the domain of chanting monks and nuns and taught his congregants to sing loudly and joyously. Luther knew that singing lyrics was one way to learn the basics of the faith, and he himself wrote many hymns, the most famous of which is "A Mighty Fortress Is Our God."

Luther was also a proponent of public education for children and of the idea of compelling parents to send their children to schools where they would learn about God and his gift of salvation, if their parents themselves didn't inform them. He wrote a small catechism, intended for teaching children, and a large catechism, meant for pastors and teachers.

While there is so much to admire about Luther—most notably his courage in the face of church authorities and his adherence to what he perceived as truth, whatever the cost—there is sadly enough to grieve us and infuriate us too. But how to explain this great contradiction? For one thing, it seems that the titanic force of will and passion Luther brought to everything also led him to think and say many greatly regrettable things, especially in his later years, as his health and circumstances changed. The very attributes in him that were good and helpful in battling his theological opponents were also sometimes very harmful.

Luther's attitude, for example, toward Jews, Muslims, and Anabaptists (who teach the so-called believer's baptism) is rightly shocking to modern Christians. As one biographer explains it, "In the case of volatile personalities, disappointment, frustration, and a sense of lost power can lead to rage, and Luther vented plenty of it in his senior years. His anger was never so evident as in his late attacks on three enemies beyond the protestant circle: the pope as Antichrist, the menacing Muslim or Turk, and the Jews, especially the rabbis."[34]

Toward the end of his life, Luther was convinced that everything happening in the world meant the second coming was imminent, which only exacerbated his already great impatience and cranky attitude toward everything and everyone. For example, in 1545, the year before his death, Luther grew irritated by the pope's attempt to scotch efforts by the emperor to create a church council. His response was to publish a rant titled *Against the Roman Papacy, an Institution of the Devil*, in which he labeled the pope the Antichrist. If his vicious words weren't enough, Luther's friend, the artist Lucas Cranach, was enlisted to illustrate the book with obscene drawings.

Luther also worried about the violent encroachments of Muslim armies into Christian Europe. Was the world about to end? The advancing Muslim armies strongly indicated this, as did his view that the pope and the Roman Catholic Church were apostate.

Luther's attitude toward Jews became grotesque, although it bears saying that not many years before, he sang a dramatically different tune toward them. In 1523 he authored a tract titled *That Jesus Christ Was Born a Jew*, which was very sympathetic. At that time he sincerely hoped that by reforming the church as he was doing, these brothers and sisters might be converted and drawn toward Jesus as their Messiah.

But in 1536 Luther allied himself with some provocative proponents of active anti-Semitism, including Elector John Frederick, who issued a decree banishing Jews from Saxony. Jews who had read Luther's earlier works naturally believed Luther would help them. Instead, in 1543 Luther wrote a screed titled *The Jews and Their Lies*. This book rehearsed monstrous calumnies about the Jews: that they ritually killed Christian children, poisoned wells, and profaned the Lord's Supper, all of which Luther sincerely believed. Most of all, Luther was angry that the rabbis had not accepted his earlier overtures to see the Old Testament as pointing toward Jesus. Their stubborn refusal to do so, in Luther's eyes, was the worst kind of blasphemy.

Luther attacked the Jews in still other tracts. Convinced that Christ would return soon, Luther called on civil rulers to chase the Jews out of Saxony to keep it "pure." So much for religious freedom, the very freedom Luther had in effect spent decades demanding from Rome.

What had happened, suggests biographer Martin Marty, was that Luther "had become so comfortable with his certitude that it took on the character of the very self-centered security, the intellectual and moral self-assurance, against which he had always warned. It served as his license to threaten others. The apostle of Christian freedom was not here free of his own theological prejudices," and his attitude toward the Jews, among others with whom he disagreed, "showed that he had not conquered his own worst self."[35]

Martin Luther died in 1546, at age sixty-two, in Eisleben, five hundred yards from the very place where he was born. His body was carried in a three-day funeral cortege back to Wittenberg, where he was buried in Castle Church, appropriately just beneath the pulpit where he had delivered himself of innumerable sermons through the decades, and where he lies to this day.

The year 2017 marked five hundred years since Luther wrote his Ninety-Five Theses, and 2021 marks five hundred years since his historic stand at Worms. There can be little question that we in the West live in the world to which Luther opened the door, although, of course, he would say it wasn't he but God who did the opening.

So what shall we make of his life, influence, and legacy? It's not too much to say that the life of this brash and fiery German monk served as the midwife not just to Protestantism but to the modern world itself. And just as his fiercest critics warned, by opening the door to a second church in the world, he opened a door to thousands, and to every kind of heresy Luther himself would have hated. But that was the inevitable price of freedom. And in the mostly free world we live in, one has the freedom to choose one's church—or to reject all churches—which is part and parcel of what it means to be free. So Luther's actions have had impossibly far-reaching consequences, both for good and for ill.

Luther is an example of extraordinary courage, of someone willing to die rather than sacrifice what he was sure God was saying in the Bible. In a nutshell, he looked to God for approval, and all else was immaterial.

Eight hundred million people today call themselves Protestants, most of whom trace their spiritual lineage to Martin Luther. But even those in the Roman Catholic Church today can trace some of their practices to Luther. Congregational singing has become a normal part of worship services, often with "Protestant" hymns. And the Church leadership has over the centuries and decades made a number of adjustments to their official teachings that can't fail to be traced back to the teachings of the intemperate maniac and "wild boar" who once raged against them.

◆ ◆ ◆

The story of Martin Luther is both breathtakingly inspiring and humbling. It can't help but remind us that even the most courageous soul, who nobly and bravely stands up for truth—and thereby looses incalculable good on the world—is also himself a sinner, capable of terrible thoughts and actions. Anyone familiar with basic Christian teaching will know this already, but to be reminded of it in the outsized life of this towering historical figure drives home the point all the more.

It was Luther himself who coined the Latin aphorism *simul justus et peccator*, which perfectly sums up this idea: those who trust in Jesus by faith are "just" (meaning "justified and righteous") and yet are "sinners" at the same time. We—all of us who believe—are both things simultaneously. All things considered, this concept is perhaps the most important thing anyone can ever remember—and it seems fitting that not just Luther's theology but his life too, should help us see that.

TWO

George Whitefield

1714–1770

If you are going to walk with Jesus Christ, you are
going to be opposed. . . . In our days, to be a true
Christian is really to become a scandal.

—GEORGE WHITEFIELD

Two and a half centuries ago—on the morning of September 30, 1770—a fifty-five-year-old man took his last breath in a home in Newburyport, Massachusetts. In no time, word of his passing went around the world, and encomiums were soon trumpeted from places as far away as Savannah, Georgia, where he had built an orphanage thirty years earlier, and London, where his old friend John Wesley preached a funeral sermon before a rapt "immense multitude." Living in London at that time was Ben Franklin, who wrote, "I knew him intimately upwards of 30 years: his integrity, disinterestedness, and indefatigable zeal in prosecuting every good work, I have never seen equaled, I shall never see exceeded." And in Boston, African American poet Phillis Wheatley, then a slave girl, published her first poem on the occasion of the man's death, praising his support for the American cause:

43

When his AMERICANS were burden'd sore,
When streets were crimson'd with their guiltless gore!
Unrival'd friendship in his breast now strove:
The fruit thereof was charity and love.[1]

To say the man who died was an evangelist is almost to do him an injustice. It would be like saying Homer or Dante was a "writer," or Washington or Lincoln a "politician." In this man's relatively brief life, he crossed the Atlantic thirteen times, preached eighteen thousand sermons, and gave twelve thousand other talks. The world he left in his wake, in which the American colonies were on the verge of declaring independence from Great Britain, was profoundly different from the one he entered back in 1714, when the idea of independence wasn't yet a gleam in any American's eyes. But owing to this man's preaching, this great sea change in history would occur. But before we go back to the beginning of his life, it's worth first entering a scene at the docks in Philadelphia when he came to the American colonies for the second time and began a preaching tour that launched what we now call "the First Great Awakening."

◆ ◆ ◆

I t was a day early in November 1739. A slight, cross-eyed twenty-four-year-old stepped off a ship in the bustling harbor of Philadelphia. His name was George Whitefield (pronounced WHIT-field), and nearly everyone in the city anticipated his arrival. Most had read of his exploits in England in the *Pennsylvania Gazette*, published by Benjamin Franklin, then a slim young man himself, and with a full head of hair. Few beyond Philadelphia had heard of Franklin, but the man coming down the gangplank was already an impossibly famous celebrity. Nearly four thousand souls stood jostling one another just to catch a glimpse of him as he stepped onto American soil. Not until the Beatles landed at New York's Idlewild Airport two centuries later would a British export create such widespread giddiness and portend a cultural revolution. But why all the excitement?

The boyish figure in question was a preacher, but he was a preacher unlike any the Philadelphia crowd had heard before. His voice was of such singular quality that across England, many who had heard it were quite undone, weeping and crying out to God in a way no one had ever seen. In England even such worldly sophisticates as philosopher David Hume had gone to hear Whitefield, who was reportedly drawing crowds of up to twenty and thirty thousand.

At the beginning of his ministry, Whitefield had been warmly welcomed into churches. But in time most respectable ministers found his message and methods shocking and objectionable, so they pointedly shut their doors to him. But their rebuff would backfire magnificently when Whitefield took to preaching out of doors. The effects of this were electric, and in no time numberless thousands were swarming to hear him. So the Church of England could do little besides sputter with indignant rage. How outrageous it was that its flocks should be siphoned away by this queer, otherworldly fellow! But now he had traveled to the colonies—and good riddance!

In fact, Whitefield had been to America a year earlier, at the invitation of his friends John and Charles Wesley, whom he had known at Oxford. He had preached extensively and tirelessly in the few months he was there, as he always did and would for the subsequent years of his life, but all of that was small beer compared with what lay ahead.

In the colonies, Whitefield first preached in churches, just as in England, and once the ministers decided they had had enough of him, he did in America what he had done in England, taking to open-air preaching. And now again in 1739, the numbers that came to hear him were historic. Ever the Yankee skeptic, Benjamin Franklin wondered how someone so physically insubstantial could be heard by twenty or thirty thousand. So one evening, soon after Whitefield's arrival, when he was preaching from the top of the downtown courthouse steps, the canny amateur scientist undertook one of his famous experiments and wrote of it in his *Autobiography*:

[Whitefield] had a loud and clear voice, and articulated his words in sentence so perfectly, that he might be heard and understood at a great distance, especially as his auditories, however numerous, observed the most exact silence. He preached one evening from the top of the Court-house steps, which are in the middle of Market Street, and on the west side of Second Street, which crosses it at right angles. Both streets were filled with his hearers to a considerable distance. Being among the hindmost in Market Street, I had the curiosity to learn how far he could be heard, by retiring backwards down the street towards the river; and I found his voice distinct till I came near Front Street, when some noise in that street obscured it. Imagining then a semicircle, of which my distance should be the radius, and that it were filled with auditors, to each of whom I allow two square feet, I computed that he might well be heard by more than thirty thousand. This reconciled me to the newspaper accounts of his having preached to twenty-five thousand people in the fields, and to the ancient histories of generals haranguing whole armies, of which I had sometimes doubted.[2]

When Franklin conducted this experiment in November 1739, Pennsylvania was one of thirteen colonies, none of which had any idea that three decades later they would be daring to think of independence from Britain. The American colonists were naturally deferential to authority but already markedly less so than their counterparts across the sea. The American character was emerging, and Franklin more than anyone embodied it. He was the proverbial self-made man who had left kith and kin in Boston to start life anew in Philadelphia at age seventeen and had by his own wits and ingenuity achieved tremendous things and would achieve dramatically more in the years ahead. But still, the idea of self-rule, of self-government—of throwing off the yoke of the British Empire and forging ahead alone—was at that time still quite far off, a cloud the size of a man's fist on the horizon. But it was the slight young man preaching who more than anyone would change that.

It took three decades of his tireless preaching, but by the time he died in 1770, he was the single figure everyone in the colonies knew and thought of as a celebrity. In fact, by the time he died, it is estimated that 80 percent of Americans had heard him preach at least once in person. As a result of his years among them, the colonies were united in a way that was unthinkable when he arrived, and their people so changed their attitudes toward authority and toward monarchy that they became a different kind of people than had ever before existed in the world. The small cloud on the horizon had become a torrential downpour.

———— ◆ ◆ ◆ ————

George Whitefield came into the world in December 1714, a few months into the reign of King George I. He was the youngest of seven, born in the small town of Gloucester, at the Bell Inn, which still stands today and which his parents owned and ran. Nine days after his birth, he was baptized a hundred yards away, in St. Mary de Crypt, the twelfth-century church that also still stands.

His father died young—George was just two—but six years later George's mother married again. George's stepfather wasn't much of an innkeeper and soon mismanaged the business into financial trouble, forcing George's elder brother Robert to take over.

At an early age, George was sent to the school connected with St. Mary de Crypt and was quickly seen to possess tremendous talent as an orator and actor. Everyone remarked on his voice, which was of such a quality that, in the decades to come, history itself would be shaped by it. In fact, once George was famous, no less a figure than actor David Garrick praised it, declaring, "I would give a hundred guineas if I could say 'O' like Mr. Whitefield."[3]

Because of his talent, George was often chosen to give special speeches at school. But it was drama that he loved best, acting in every play he could. George became so enamored of acting that he often skipped school to stay home and work on his lines.

George's love for acting was such that he wondered why he troubled himself with studying Latin and other subjects. So when he turned fifteen, he dropped out of school and began working at the inn full time, where he did whatever was needed, including cleaning rooms and washing mops.

Around this time, George was having a spiritual awakening too. His mother's strife with his stepfather had caused George to look to God for answers, so the bright young man read certain books, including the Bible. George also had problems getting along with his brother Robert's wife, who ran the inn with her husband. At one point things were so unpleasant that George decided to leave and visited his other brother Andrew in Bristol, thirty-five miles away.

While there, George attended St. John's church and one day during a service had a spiritual experience he would never forget. In writing about it he described "unspeakable raptures" in which he was somehow "carried out" beyond himself. What was God trying to tell him? During this time he also spent much time reading Thomas à Kempis's *The Imitation of Christ*, among the most popular devotional books of that time.

George's devotion to God became such that he even wondered whether he should abandon his dreams of acting and enter the ministry. But he knew entering the ministry required a college education, and under the circumstances there was simply no money to pay for one. As he was considering this, however, a visitor to the inn, who became acquainted with young George and his ambitions, said there might be a way for George to attend university after all. He asked whether George would be willing to be a "servitor" at Oxford University. This was what they called the young men who served the wealthier students, performing such tasks as polishing shoes and generally being butler and maid. Of course this role was looked down on by Oxford's elites, but George Whitefield was a humble young man and was certainly used to menial work. So he accepted the opportunity with relish, immediately resuming his schooling at St. Mary's to prepare for what lay ahead.

Meanwhile, he continued reading and thinking about God. So when George finally began his studies at Oxford's Pembroke College, he was of a noticeably pious bent, especially when compared with the other students, most of whom appeared to be in a perpetual contest to best one another in roguish behavior. When one day some of his chamber mates tried to pull him into their bad habits, George made it clear he wasn't interested. He would rather have no friends than do things he knew were wrong. But in time he would have friends, and they would share his views on God and other things.

At it happened there were two brothers at Oxford at this time—in Lincoln College, where their rooms are preserved to this day—named Charles and John Wesley. They were also of a religious bent, so much so that they had formed a group called the Holy Club, gathering to study the Bible and pray regularly. In the wild university atmosphere, they were often mocked, but whenever George heard someone saying something against them, he bravely leaped to their defense. He had heard about them and had come to admire them tremendously and wished to join their club himself. But the rules of that time didn't allow someone working as a servitor to speak directly with the other students.

The Wesleys eventually noticed George anyway, and one day Charles approached him and invited him into their society. What happened next is one of those things we may properly think of as a hinge in t'ıe history of the world.

There were then about fifteen members in the Holy Club. They prayed together several times per week and fasted Wednesdays and Fridays and took Communion weekly at St. Mary's church. They also studied the Scriptures and—as the Scriptures commanded—visited prisoners and did other good works, such as teaching orphans to read. They were so "methodical" in all they did for God that their fellow students sneeringly dubbed them "methodists," a term they would eventually adopt as a badge of honor—and that would eventually become the name of one of the most powerful movements in history.

George happily joined the Holy Club and outdid everyone in his zeal to pray and fast and do good works. But one day while he read Henry Scougal's *The Life of God in the Soul of Man*, a book already considered a classic at that time, a certain passage leaped out.

> Some place [the Christian faith] in . . . orthodox notions and opinions. Others place it in the outward man, in a constant course of external duties and a model of performances; if they live peaceably with their neighbours, keep a temperate diet, observe the returns of worship, frequenting the church or their closet, and sometimes extend their hands to the relief of the poor, they think they have sufficiently acquitted [themselves].[4]

But Scougal said there was much more to being a Christian. "True Religion," the passage continued, "is [a] Union of the Soul with God." It was the believer's privilege, he said, to be allowed "a real participation of the divine nature, the very image of God drawn upon the Soul, or in the Apostle's phrase, it is Christ formed within us." George wondered whether he had been missing the whole point of God's will for his life. So rather ironically—and almost comically, except that it nearly killed him—he decided that the solution to his dilemma was to do even more of what he was doing and to launch into a draconian program of "self-denial."

For example, he thenceforward staunchly refused to eat anything appealing, beginning with fruit. He also refrained from powdering his hair, then the custom, because taking pains over one's appearance struck him as vanity. And when his college gown was ripped, he decided it must not be repaired, nor must his muddy shoes be cleaned. It seemed that George Whitefield was determined to draw closer to God by allowing himself to become an unkempt, otherworldly vagabond, which naturally caused him to lose much of his work as a "servitor," since looking dirty and slovenly wasn't much of a recommendation for the work he was supposed to be doing.

In the midst of this seizure of religious madness, George was even determined to fast from laughing, believing the only joy worthy of a true Christian must be expressed in prayer and worship. And when he recalled that Jesus had spent all night praying on a mountainside alone, he felt this too must be heaped upon his groaning table of self-righteous acts. So one evening he left his room to kneel outside on the cold, damp turf of Christ Church Walk. After thirty minutes of kneeling, he went further, lying flat on the ground, after which the heavens rewarded his efforts by unleashing a cold rain. In the end, soaking wet and cold, he returned to his room, determined to do this again when the opportunity presented itself.

In the meantime, his active mind searched for what else he might do to deny himself. He settled on the capital notion of isolating himself from the joy of being with his friends. He wouldn't even let himself pray with them, because that might be pleasurable. So he now prayed alone in his room. But the Wesley brothers grew concerned for their friend, who seemed determined to enter God's presence by slowly killing himself. They visited George and tried to convince him that praying with them wasn't something God frowned upon. After all, didn't the Scriptures often talk of the importance of being with others to pray and worship? George finally agreed, but his austere dietary regimen would continue. At this point, he ate nothing but coarse bread and drank tea—without sugar.

Then one day something happened that at last got George thinking along different lines. He was near Magdalen Bridge in Oxford when he saw a bedraggled woman walking alone. He eventually recognized her as the wife of one of the prisoners he had been visiting. But the woman looked half dead and was soaked to the skin. What had happened to her? As he learned, she had just moments earlier tried to drown herself right there in the Cherwell. Because her husband was in prison, she had nothing with which to feed her children and decided she couldn't go on. But while she was trying to take her life, a gentleman had seen and had prevented it, after which she realized that what she was doing was no answer to her problems; rather, it was a horrible sin. She knew she must repent quickly, and she was at that very moment looking for Mr. Whitefield so that he could pray with her along these lines. She knew he could show her the way toward true salvation—and now here he was! But George wasn't quite ready to pray with her that minute, so he gave her some money and made an appointment to meet her and her husband at the jail later that day.

At the jail, George decided to read to the couple from the third chapter of the gospel of John. When he read John 3:16 (NKJV)—"For God so loved the world that He gave His only begotten Son, that whoever believes in Him should not perish but have everlasting life"—the woman suddenly declared, "I believe!" over and over. "I am born again!" she shouted. "I am saved!" Soon her husband joined her in these happy proclamations. The message was simple and clear. All they must do is believe! But George himself wasn't so sure what to make of it. Could it be that simple? Perhaps. But he wasn't entirely convinced, and although he was now thinking about this, he nonetheless continued his strange self-denying behavior.

Six months later, not surprisingly, he became quite sick. Day after day he lay in bed, praying and barely eating. During this time he picked up another old book, titled *Contemplations on the New Testament*. He read in it about the thief on the cross next to Jesus, and at last as he read, everything changed. He saw that the thief didn't do anything dramatic to draw toward God. All he did was hang there dying and believe in Jesus and say so. And this dying man's simple statement prompted Jesus to declare, "Today you will be with me in paradise" (Luke 23:43). Suddenly, George saw what he had never seen before: that it was only by putting his faith in Jesus that he could accomplish anything. That was all God required, and God would do the rest. The thief hadn't performed any good works. He had only believed in the One who had done—and was then doing—everything that was necessary for our salvation.

What followed from this piercing epiphany in a bed in Oxford's Pembroke College can hardly be calculated. It was as though the slightest finger of a divine breeze had blown that day. Over the course of the next months and years it grew and grew until eventually it became a sanctified tornado that would reconfigure the landscape in England. It would then leap across the Atlantic to light down in the New World where it would do the same, changing the history of the world forever.

Immediately after this moment in bed, George knew he must correct his course. First, he decided to leave Oxford, returning home to the Bell Inn, where—even as he recuperated—he told everyone he met of his new discovery. And he continued to minister to everyone and anyone who needed help too. Somehow, the bishop of Gloucester came to observe this curious twenty-one-year-old and was duly impressed. Although the age for ordination was twenty-three, the bishop happily made an exception, and George Whitefield soon became the Reverend George Whitefield.

His first official sermon was at St. Mary de Crypt, where he had been baptized and at whose school he had first learned the power of oration. Word got out about this precocious young fellow, so the crowd that assembled that day was considerable, but because of his shocking youth—for he looked even younger than he was—some heckled him when he began speaking. But soon enough his outsized talent and remarkable message gained the upper hand. The crowd had never heard anything to equal what they heard that day. Many were so affected that afterward someone complained to the bishop, saying fifteen of those in attendance had gone quite mad. And thus commenced a preaching career unequaled in the annals of Christendom.

This sparkling debut soon led to invitations to preach in London, and his reputation grew by leaps and bounds. Within mere months he wasn't less than a national celebrity, although it's not too much to say he was a phenomenon who had caught the attention of the nation, and someone famously remarked that George Whitefield's voice had "startled England like a trumpet blast." At the same time, however, some ministers grew peeved and began to find fault with this new golden boy.

By this time, John and Charles Wesley had crossed the ocean to minister to the Native Americans in the American colony of Georgia, but on hearing all this good news of their old friend, thought they should invite him to visit. George accepted their invitation and made plans for the journey. But when word got out that he was leaving England, the crowds who came to hear him only increased further. After all, what would they do when he was gone? There was no one in England like him!

It might be said that George Whitefield wasn't someone who preached only on Sundays. On the contrary, he preached every day and often many times per day. He even preached in prisons—something unheard of at the time, if not shocking. And although it is difficult for us to fathom, George's maniacal schedule didn't change for the rest of his life. As we have already noted, by the time of his death, he had preached eighteen thousand sermons, plus twelve thousand "talks and exhortations." No one in history had ever done anything like it, before or since, causing certain wags to declare that "compared to Mr. Whitefield, St. Paul and Billy Graham almost come across as lazy agnostics!"

One almost wonders whether Whitefield knew how to refrain from preaching. He even preached each day aboard the ship to America. And the moment the ship docked in Georgia, he simply continued, preaching twice daily and four times on the Sabbath.

After a few months he traveled to South Carolina, where the preaching continued until at last, on September 6, 1738, he boarded a ship in Charleston and began the journey home, preaching daily on the eastward crossing too. But now, when he arrived in England, he saw for the first time bitter opposition to him and his message. It didn't come from atheists or secularists, who hardly existed at that time, but from ministers and bishops in the Church of England, who finally saw him not as an ally but as a threat to their power and to the establishment in general, of which they were a vital part.

One of the reasons Whitefield's method of preaching was so unpopular with ministers at that time was that it was shockingly egalitarian, and therefore didn't uphold the status quo. In simply preaching the good news of Jesus, who said all must be "born again," Whitefield was inadvertently saying things that foreshadowed the United States Declaration of Independence, "that all men are created equal," and there was much about this radical idea that didn't sit well with everyone.

It was in the New Testament that Whitefield found such ideas. For example, the Scriptures say that "God is no respecter of persons" (Acts 10:34 KJV), that he regards the peasant and the criminal just as he regards the magistrate and the king. All are under his authority and are equal in his sight. All are his beloved children, for whom he sent his own beloved Son to die, that they might all be redeemed and reconciled to him forever. For those in the lower classes who never seemed to hear this, it was extraordinarily good news. Could it be true that God loved them as he loved the king? Whitefield said it was, and he used the Bible to back it up. But to those already in power, it was bad news, and the man who preached it must not be suffered to continue.

But it wasn't just what Whitefield said that was unorthodox. It was how he said it. This young man was nothing like the forbidding divines who glowered weekly from their stone pulpits. His message was beautiful and appealing and moving, and many who heard him went half mad with enthusiasm, crying out to God and generally carrying on in a way that embarrassed the upper classes. But there was no stopping what was happening. Whitefield's preaching signaled the first rays of a new order dawning in the world. But would that new order be something good or bad? Those in power believed the latter and did all they could to work against it.

Many ministers at this time imperiously leveled the accusation of "enthusiasm" at Whitefield. This was a derisive term for any expressions of faith that departed from the starched, constricting order of their traditional Anglican services, and anyone who took God too seriously was called "an enthusiast." Of course, for someone who had been dully laboring in a pulpit for decades to see this overly emotional stripling become the talk of English society must have been downright nettling. In any event, many of the churches that had initially invited him to speak now ceased to do so, fearing they had given oxygen to a fire that might never go out.

But even though the invitations were drying up, Whitefield hardly felt the need to confine his preaching to the dank interiors of medieval churches. Jesus himself had preached in the highways and byways and to all manner of people, to the lame and the halt and the deaf and the blind. He had preached on mountaintops and in the marketplaces and had even once preached to a crowd from a boat. Actually, the notion of taking his preaching outside church buildings first struck Whitefield while he was preaching inside one. He was in the pulpit of the Bermondsey Church in South London and—as was increasingly the case—so many had turned out that once the church was filled to capacity, people gathered outside in the churchyard, hoping to catch the sound of Whitefield's extraordinary voice through the church's open windows. That day there were over a thousand outside the church, trying to listen to him. It struck Whitefield that perhaps he might go out to them and stand on top of one of the larger tombstones. And why not? He didn't do it that day, but he mentioned the idea to some friends afterward. Was God perhaps calling him to do such a thing?

Two weeks later he traveled to an area near Bristol that was inhabited primarily by uneducated and unchurched people, many of whom labored in the coal mines there. George realized his time to preach outside had come. "I thought," he said, "it might be doing the service of my Creator, who had a mountain for his pulpit, and the heavens for a sounding board."[5] So one afternoon he climbed to the top of a mound in a place called Rose Green in Kingston and began to preach. He had done nothing to advertise his presence, but about two hundred walking home from the mines gathered around to see and hear him. Most of them had never been to a church in their lives. What was this odd young man saying?

Whatever he said must have appealed to them, because the next day he returned, and several thousand showed up. On the third day nearly twenty thousand were there. It was the beginning of something unknown since Jesus himself had preached seventeen centuries earlier.

As his listeners stood there, Whitefield saw that many of their faces were still blackened by the coal dust from the mines they had just left. No respectable minister in the Church of England would travel to such a godforsaken precinct, much less preach to these befouled savages. But Whitefield was doing precisely what he knew Jesus himself had done. He was taking medicine to those who knew they were sick and offering freedom to those who knew they were captives. His heart went out to them, and with everything he had in him, he preached to these men and women under the evening sky. He later wrote that the "first discovery of their being affected was to see the white gutters made by their tears, which plentifully fell down their black cheeks, as they came out of their coal pits."[6] Many thousands of these men and women received his message of salvation and freedom that day with great emotion.

To many churchgoers, the idea of preaching out of doors was a bold affront to decency, like attending a funeral without a shirt. But to those who never went to church, and hardly felt they would be welcome if they did, it was a tremendous opportunity, and one they didn't take for granted. For many of them it seemed like a dream, like eating strawberries and cream from a silver spoon. That the poor and uneducated have value is something we today take for granted, but it came into history only because of what began here, when this young man announced to the unwashed rabble that there was Someone who cared about them, who loved them, and who sought their company. To a man or woman born into that brutal world, where the poor were treated as deserving of their poverty, it must have been as though heaven itself had opened and they could hear their own names pronounced by the tongues of angels.

Many Church of England pulpits at that time preached a withering, pinched sort of castor-oil moralism that made hearers feel bad about themselves without offering much of a solution. Others preached a soapy lukewarm Deism, which was essentially nothing more than French Enlightenment rationalism, and said nothing much at all. Whitefield knew these counterfeit messages had left many longing for the truth of the gospel, and he would let nothing stop him from reaching these hungry souls, wherever they might be found.

Much of what made him so compelling was that his audiences could see that he himself was affected by the power of that about which he spoke. The God of whom he spoke and the love of God were so real to Whitefield that others were drawn into the powerful current of his own emotions. Cornelius Winter, Whitefield's assistant in later years, said, "I hardly ever knew him to go through a sermon without weeping. . . . Sometimes he exceedingly wept, stamped loudly and passionately, and was frequently so overcome, that, for a few seconds, you would suspect he never could recover."[7]

Of course with popularity came all manner of derision too, and at the height of his fame, Whitefield was attacked from all quarters. It wasn't just the ministers who were bothered by his popularity. Many others took to throwing stones too, some literally and others literarily. In a popular play of the time by Samuel Foote, titled *The Minor*, the principal character, "Dr. Squintum," was a barely disguised carica-ture of Whitefield. The unflattering moniker was meant to refer to Whitefield's noticeably crossed eyes. Others criticized him in verse for preaching that faith alone was necessary for salvation. One verse in an entire burlesque ballad, titled "Friendly Advice for Dr. Squintum," read:

> "Do nothing and be saved," he cries,
> His stupid audience close their eyes,
> And groan in concert to the lies
> Of canting Dr. Squintum.[8]

For those who didn't criticize his theology but only made fun of his crossed eyes, Whitefield's admirers had a positive answer, declaring that "even his eyes make the sign of the cross upon which Jesus died!"

Touché. But Whitefield wasn't one to let his detractors bother him or slow him down. In the course of his life, he endured every kind of attack imaginable. On more than one occasion, stones were thrown at him, and during one sermon someone hurled a dead cat at him. During another, "pieces" of a dead cat were reportedly thrown, along with an entire dog. On another occasion, one man was so fixed on putting an end to the preaching that he took the great trouble of clambering onto the upper limbs of a nearby tree, from which altitude he urinated at his target, apparently aiming to quench Whitefield's fire. He failed.

But it was mostly from the clergy and those in power that Whitefield was attacked. His preaching seemed the height of recklessness and folly. To them, the social order was ordained by God, and any threat to that order was a threat to everything. The Church of England at that time was in many respects an extension of the Crown, having a vested interest in the status quo. So to those with ecclesiastical power, Whitefield's egalitarian and emotional messages must have seemed as though Dionysus himself had arrived and was cavorting with his maenads through their congregations. It was all a great scandal.

But it was precisely this contrast that shows us Whitefield's subsequent appeal to the American colonists in the years and decades ahead. Just as jazz in the twenties and rock and roll in the sixties represented a threat to the social order, they also represented the very life and joy and freedom and wildness inherent in the promise of America. It was ever a two-edged sword and could always go too far. In France, for example, similar things would lead to the chaos and bloodbath of the French Revolution, and in the United States, the sexual revolution of the sixties would lead not only to greater personal freedom but also to the social chaos brought on by the breakdown of the family. The threat of these things wasn't merely imaginary.

Whitefield's principal message in his preaching concerned what he called the "new birth." After his own experience in Oxford, he knew the Christian faith wasn't about how one behaved but about what one believed, and if one truly believed one could do nothing to achieve salvation but believe in Jesus, one's behavior would follow. So everywhere he went, he preached what was for that time a revolutionary message.

But Whitefield understood what he was up against. Many, if not most, of the ministers in the Church of England were themselves merely going through their religious motions in jobs that were little more than sinecures. Many of them were complete strangers to this startling message of God's grace and redemption. But when they became openly hostile to Whitefield and his message, he pointed out their spiritual shortcomings in his writings, infuriating them the more. When the bishop of London wrote a letter criticizing Whitefield, Whitefield shot back that most Anglican clergy were "lazy, non-spiritual, and pleasure seeking."[9] And later on he specifically said that this bishop knew no more about Christianity "than Mahomet, or an Infidel."[10]

However much he battled, over the course of the next decades, his influence on Great Britain would be dramatic. His outdoor preaching and other efforts opened the door for the work of the Wesleys and the Methodist movement in general, which led to many social reforms, including the eventual abolition of the slave trade. His preaching also helped lead the people of Great Britain along the path toward greater democratization. But all this can't be compared to the influence he had on the thirteen colonies across the Atlantic.

During his lifetime Whitefield's many visits to the colonies would forever alter the landscape of the New World. His preaching began the process of uniting the thirteen colonies into something greater than the sum of their disparate parts, preparing them to become the United States of America.

As we have said, it all began during his second trip to America, in 1739. That first day in Philadelphia, he preached to six thousand in the morning and that afternoon to eight thousand. That Sunday fifteen thousand came to hear him. Benjamin Franklin was immediately impressed. "Every accent," Franklin said, "every emphasis, every modulation of voice, was so perfectly turned, and well-placed, that without being interested in the subject, one could not help being pleased with the discourse." He said it was much like listening to "an excellent piece of music."[11]

Whitefield was perpetually raising funds for an orphanage the Wesleys wished to build in Georgia. The legendarily thrifty Franklin counseled Whitefield that it would be far more prudent to save the money required for transporting the building materials to Georgia by building his orphanage right there in Philadelphia. Why not bring the Georgian orphans to Philadelphia? But Whitefield rejected this idea, and though he wished his friend well, Franklin vowed never to give money to the endeavor, however noble it might be. But Whitefield's abilities to persuade were very considerable, as Franklin tells us:

I happened soon after to attend one of his sermons, in the course of which I perceived he intended to finish with a collection, and I silently resolved he should get nothing from me. I had in my pocket a handful of copper money, three or four silver dollars, and five pistoles in gold. As he proceeded I began to soften, and concluded to give the coppers. Another stroke of his oratory made me ashamed of that, and determined me to give the silver; and he finished so admirably, that I emptied my pocket wholly into the collector's dish, gold and all. At this sermon there was also one of our club, who, being of my sentiments respecting the building and Georgia, and suspecting a collection might be intended, had, by precaution, emptied his pockets before he came from home. Towards the conclusion of the discourses, however, he felt a strong desire to give, and applied to a neighbor, who stood near him, to borrow some money for the purpose. The application was unfortunately [made] to perhaps the only man in the company who had the firmness not to be affected by the preacher. His answer was, "At any other time, Friend Hopkinson, I would lend to thee freely; but not now, for thee seems to be out of thy right sense."[12]

Although Franklin never quite accepted the whole of Whitefield's theology, the effect of Whitefield's preaching met with his approval. From his earliest years he had been a believer in virtuous behavior, and he saw that the hundreds who were being converted by Whitefield's preaching became model citizens, so he did all he could to promote Whitefield, publishing his entire sermons on the front page of the *Pennsylvania Gazette* and eventually becoming Whitefield's American publisher and friend. In preaching about the "new birth," Whitefield broke down denominational barriers. This egalitarian "born again" faith fit well with the American character because it supported the idea that denominations could coexist and respect one another, that their similarities were more important than their differences.

The historic eighteen-month-long tour Whitefield undertook during this time involved traveling two thousand miles on horseback. Indeed, his initial ride from New York to Charleston was at that time the longest such ever undertaken in North America by a white man. Whitefield was an adept rider and far preferred riding his own horse to being drawn in a carriage or coach, whose bumpiness he found disagreeable. In addition, Whitefield also traveled three thousand miles by boat during his American visit. He would officially preach 350 times and gave many smaller exhortations and talks to other smaller groups. Before he left America in January 1741, he had visited over seventy-five cities and towns, and everywhere he went, the message was the same— that people must choose to be "born again" and must accept their new identity in Christ.

Because Presbyterians and Congregationalists and Quakers and Baptists and others all heard the same message and were free to respond similarly, Americans became inadvertently united by his preaching. People were being offered a new identity that fit well with the American way of thinking. Some were German by background, and some were French, and some were English, but none of it mattered: they were all equal under God, they were all believers in Jesus, and they were all born again. This was something new, an identity that was separate from one's ethnicity or one's denomination. To be part of the thirteen colonies now meant to buy into a new set of ideas about one's equal status in God's eyes—and by dint of this to be accepted into a new community, to be something new in history: in short, to be an American.

In the 1730s, just before Whitefield's arrival in America, there had been a great revival in the area of Northampton, Massachusetts, fueled by the preaching of Jonathan Edwards. But by 1740 this religious ardor had cooled somewhat. But when Whitefield visited, the banked fires flared to live once more. Edwards's wife, Sarah, wrote:

> He is a born orator. You have already heard of his deep-toned, yet clear and melodious voice. O it is perfect music to listen to that alone! ... You remember that David Hume thought it worth going 20 miles to hear him speak; and Garrick said, 'He could move men to tears ... in pronouncing the word Mesopotamia.' ... It is truly wonderful to see what a spell this preacher often casts over an audience by proclaiming the simplest truths of the Bible.
>
> ... A prejudiced person, I know, might say that this is all theatrical artifice and display; but not so will anyone think who has seen and known him. He is a very devout and godly man, and his only aim seems to be to reach and influence men the best way. He speaks from the heart all aglow with love, and pours out a torrent of eloquence which is almost irresistible.[13]

From Northampton, Whitefield traveled south along the Connecticut River valley toward Hartford. The almost inconceivable effects of his progress through the colonies during this time may be glimpsed in an extraordinary firsthand account left to us by Nathan Cole, a farmer and carpenter in Middletown, Connecticut:[14]

> Now it pleased God to send Mr. Whitefield into this land; and my hearing of his preaching at Philadelphia, like one of the Old

apostles, and many thousands flocking to hear him preach the Gospel, and great numbers were converted to Christ; I felt the Spirit of God drawing me by conviction, longed to see and hear him, and wished he would come this way. And I soon heard he was come to New York and the Jerseys and great multitudes flocking after him under great concern for their Souls and many converted which brought on my concern more and more hoping soon to see him but next I heard he was at Long Island, then at Boston, and next at Northampton.

Then one morning all on a sudden, about 8 or 9 o'clock there came a messenger and said Mr. Whitefield preached at Hartford and Weathersfield yesterday and is to preach at Middletown this morning [October 23, 1740] at ten of the Clock. I was in my field at Work. I dropt my tool that I had in my hand and ran home and run through my house and bade my wife get ready quick to go and hear Mr. Whitefield preach at Middletown, and run to my pasture for my horse with all my might fearing that I should be too late to hear him. I brought my horse home and soon mounted and took my wife up and went forward as fast as I thought the horse could bear, and when my horse began to be out of breath, I would get down and put my wife on the Saddle and bid her ride as fast as she could and not stop or slack for me except I bade her, and so I would run until I was much out of breath, and then mount my horse again, and so I did several times to favour my horse, we improved every moment to get along as if we were fleeing for our lives, all the while fearing we should be too late to hear the Sermon, for we had twelve miles to ride double in little more than an hour. . . .

And when we came within about half a mile of the road that comes down from Hartford Weathersfield and Stepney to Middletown; on high land I saw before me a Cloud or fog rising. I first thought it came from the great river [Connecticut River], but as I came nearer the Road, I heard a noise something like a low rumbling thunder and presently found it was the noise of horses feet coming down the road and this Cloud was a Cloud of dust made by the Horses feet. It arose some Rods into the air over the tops of the hills and trees and when I came within about 20 rods of the Road, I could see men and horses slipping along in the Cloud like shadows, and as I drew nearer it seemed like a steady stream of horses and their riders, scarcely a horse more than his length behind another, all of a lather and foam with sweat, their breath rolling out of their nostrils in the cloud of dust every jump; every horse seemed to go with all his might to carry his rider to hear news from heaven for the saving of Souls. It made me tremble to see the sight, how the world was in a struggle, I found a vacancy between two horses to slip in my horse; and my wife said law our clothes will be all spoiled see how they look, for they were so covered with dust, that they looked almost all of a colour coats, hats, and shirts and horses.

We went down in the stream; I heard no man speak a word all the way three miles but every one pressing forward in great haste and when we got to the old meeting house there was a great multitude; it was said to be 3 or 4000 of people assembled together, we got off from our horses and shook off the dust, and the ministers were then coming to the meeting house. I turned and looked towards the great river and saw the ferry boats running swift forward and forward bringing over loads of people; the oars rowed nimble and quick, every thing men horses and boats seemed to be struggling for life; the land and banks over the river looked black with people and horses all along the 12 miles. I saw no man at work in his field, but all seemed to be gone.

When I saw Mr. Whitefield come upon the scaffold he looked almost angelical, a young, slim slender youth before some thousands of people with a bold undaunted countenance, and my hearing how God was with him every where as he came along it solemnized my mind, and put me into a trembling fear before he began to preach; for he looked as if he was clothed with authority from the Great God, and a sweet solemn solemnity sat upon his brow. And my hearing him preach gave me a heart wound; by God's blessing my old foundation was broken up, and I saw that my righteousness would not save me.[15]

What Whitefield set in motion came to be known as the Great Awakening. Wherever he went—and he went everywhere—he preached, and wherever he preached, hundreds and thousands like Nathan Cole came straggling to hear him and were changed by what he said. But it wasn't a mere mental assent to some theological doctrine. Many, like Benjamin Franklin, observed that after Whitefield's preaching in an area, people's behavior changed. Church rolls swelled—and those who had already been attending church suddenly understood why they were there. The gospel came alive to them and they to it; and their common faith in God became the central animating force of these colonies that in a few decades would become a new country. So it was no surprise that William Cooper, a prominent Boston minister, memorably hailed Whitefield as "the Wonder of the Age."

For reasons we have touched on, Whitefield's tireless preaching to multiplied millions set the stage for a historic eruption. Even before Whitefield arrived, the American people were generally more deeply devoted to the Christian faith than their European counterparts. Many had come across the ocean precisely for religious freedom. And because of their distance from Mother Britannia, the Americans had to some degree been governing themselves already. Nonetheless, it was the Great Awakening that would strengthen these inclinations significantly and would put forward additional ideas not previously considered.

For one thing, the ideas that everyone could have a direct relationship with God and that all were equal before God led to the idea that earthly authorities could be judged and should be judged. If God was the ultimate Judge—above all other judges—then surely each person could consider whether those in authority over them were exercising their authority in accordance with God's principles. And if they were not, their rule could be thought of as tyrannous. This was an unprecedented development.

Although his focus was overwhelmingly evangelistic, Whitefield was never shy in making the correlation between Christian faith and political freedom. He denounced the "popish tyranny" of the French and Spanish, who fought England in the Seven Years' War; and when in 1765 the Stamp Act drew the ire of the Americans, he showed his solidarity with them against the British.

So Whitefield's preaching—by causing people to look directly upward to God—greatly tempered their fear of worldly authority and went a long way toward solidifying what we today see as the American character.

But it wasn't merely that the American colonists became more religious and therefore more capable of—and inclined toward—self-government. The very message of Whitefield's preaching was itself inclined toward the ideas of liberty and self-government. Because his preaching led each person to see that God wished to have a direct relationship with every one of his children, no matter their social standing, the church authorities were effectively cut out of the equation. There was something empowering about knowing one might go directly to God. This message introduced what we may think of as a free market of ideas into the situation too, because each person could choose for themselves what church they thought best and what preachers or teachers they thought most closely adhered to the theology in the New Testament, as set forth by Whitefield. And there were many options to choose from, chiefly because Whitefield's success as he traveled throughout the colonies had spawned a host of imitators who themselves set out to preach in the vacuum created by his wake.

Wherever one hailed from, whatever church one belonged to, whatever birth one might claim, or social rank, all were equal in God's sight. Furthermore, someone who might be outwardly common could know that all God's children were the children of the sovereign of the universe, so they too were members of the only royal family that mattered. The Scriptures themselves said they were members of a "royal priesthood."

The most august dukes and earls were sinners who could be saved only by grace, the same grace that saved the commonest commoner. The gospel of Christ was the most powerful sociological leveler in history, and although the message had existed for seventeen centuries, it would burst into full bloom only now—at this crucial point in history—under the watering can of Whitefield's preaching. And over the decades this sociological leveling changed the colonies and created an American people.

The egalitarian strains of the gospel were even more shocking when they extended to women and blacks too. The Great Awakening spawned many female preachers and also many black preachers. Unlike most mainline ministers of his day, Whitefield often spoke to "Negroes" and once remarked that he was especially touched when one of them came to faith. One of them even asked Whitefield, "Have I a soul?" That Whitefield believed he did meant he was in this most important respect perfectly equal to whites, an idea staggering and incendiary to most at that time. Whitefield, like so many in his day, did not see that slavery was necessarily an evil institution but seems naively to have hoped that as slave-owners and slaves were both converted, the slave-owners would treat their slaves differently.

Whitefield's preaching was a great social leveler throughout the colonies. But it was a great uniter too. By the time Whitefield died in 1770, an inconceivable 80 percent of the population of the American colonies had heard him preach at least once. By traveling as he did, he accomplished what no one else had ever done. He became known to all in the colonies equally. He was the first American celebrity, but he was much more than a mere celebrity.

Harry S. Stout reminds us that before "Whitefield there was no unifying inter-colonial person or event," and "before Whitefield, it is doubtful any name other than royalty was known equally from Boston to Charleston." So his impact on the culture and thinking of early and mid-eighteenth-century America can hardly be overstated. Stout says that "by 1750 virtually every American loved and admired Whitefield and saw him as their champion."[16]

For example, while not brazenly antiestablishment, Whitefield often and openly criticized ministers and pastors whom he thought were merely going through the motions and not living out the kind of real and vibrant faith he preached about. They were not only not "saved" but also guilty of preventing their parishioners from finding God—in Jesus's words, they were the blind leading the blind (Matthew 15:14). Such sentiments did not sit well with the authorities, but Whitefield wasn't cowed by their threats and even dared to publicly cross swords with bishops in the Church of England, which must have made many cheer. So to the common person who saw the Church as a mere extension of the oppressive power of the state, Whitefield was a hero.

We can see that Whitefield's preaching was a dramatic element in the uniting of the colonies and the articulation of what they came to believe. Everyone who accepted these views about liberty and independence—with all their ramifications and corollaries—became a part of something larger, of an "American" way of seeing things. Thus, all who believed these things began to think of themselves as Americans as much as—or more than—they thought of themselves as citizens of any one of the thirteen colonies. And so the various members of those colonies slowly became a people who would eventually seek political independence and become a nation.

George Whitefield has been called the spiritual founding father of the United States, but his travel and the effects of his preaching went far beyond the American shores. Fifteen times he traveled to preach in Scotland and twice to Ireland. He also preached in the Netherlands, Gibraltar, and Bermuda; and shortly after his death, Augustus Montague Toplady, author of the famous hymn "Rock of Ages," deemed him "the apostle of the English empire." Still, nothing can compare to the effect of his preaching in the American colonies. After Lexington and Concord, he was almost regarded as a patron saint, the Protestant American saint of liberty.

One example of the high regard in which he was held by those on the side of American independence concerns Benedict Arnold. Before the action that made his name become synonymous with being a traitor, Arnold was a hero of the Revolution, and on his way to begin the campaign in Quebec, he made a pilgrimage to the grave of Whitefield in Newburyport, Massachusetts. This was in September 1775. Arnold wasn't content simply to visit the grave, but along with his officers opened the tomb to gaze upon the mortal remains of the great man. Most of Whitefield was gone, but his moldering clerical clothing remained, so Arnold and his officers cut what they found into small pieces and distributed it among themselves as good luck relics for what lay ahead. That this was a decidedly "Catholic" action of which Whitefield would not have approved—and that this action might have uncomfortably echoed that of the soldier's who at Christ's death greedily divided his clothing—was obviously lost on Arnold. But the military campaign that followed did not go well, and of course we know what befell Arnold himself.

◆ ◆ ◆

Over the decades, the boyish slip Whitefield had been was transformed into a somewhat heavy man. "I dread a corpulent body," he wrote to a friend, "but it breaks in upon me like an armed man."[17] Even at forty he was growing tired—of the endless activity and traveling and of the battles with theological opponents, including his old friend John Wesley, who had taken up homiletic arms against him over the issue of predestination and election. Eventually, their squabbling died down and they were reconciled, but wherever he went, Whitefield had detractors, many of them publicly vicious. "God knows how long I am to drag this crazy load along. . . . I am sick of myself, sick of the word, sick of the Church and am panting daily after the full enjoyment of my God."[18]

But his influence not just over history but over innumerable individual men and women too cannot be overstated. During his 1764 tour of New England, a Native American of the Mohegan tribe named Samson Occom came to faith under Whitefield's preaching and entered the ministry to reach his own people. The following year Occom sailed to London where he stayed in Whitefield's home and preached before such dignitaries as King George III himself, and then returned to America to continue his ministry.

In 1765 an African slave named Olaudah Equiano was visiting Savannah on a trip for his master, who had encouraged him to buy his own freedom, which he would do the following year. When Equiano passed a certain church, he saw that the churchyard was overflowing with people, some of whom had climbed ladders to look in the windows. When he found out the cause of this spectacle, he fought his way inside and heard Whitefield preach, being much taken by what he saw and heard. Soon thereafter Equiano bought his own freedom and two decades after that emerged as one of the most powerful allies of William Wilberforce in working against the British slave trade.

That same year, Whitefield was passing through Virginia when the twenty-nine-year-old Patrick Henry spoke out against the draconian Stamp Act, which seemed to be the last straw for many American colonists already incensed at King George's harsh policies. That next February, Benjamin Franklin sailed to London to tell Parliament what he thought about the Stamp Act, and as he did so, his old friend Whitefield showed up to lend moral support. Whitefield wasn't directly involved in the political situation that arose from England's crushing tax policies, but there was no question that the high passions against tyranny in any form had over the decades been coaxed into existence via Whitefield's preaching in the colonies.

Whitefield's final trip to America was in 1769, and his final sermon before he boarded the ship included the themes people had come to expect in his preaching: "Christ does not say, are you an Independent, or Baptist, or Presbyterian? or are you a Church of England-man?

nor did he ask, are you a Methodist? All these things are of our own silly invention."[19]

It seems fitting to close with that quote from his final sermon in England because it encapsulates one of the principal things Whitefield's nonstop preaching over the decades achieved: the idea that one's simple faith in Jesus outweighs any denominational affiliations. Of course sectarianism did not vanish, for it is yet with us, but Whitefield struck a blow against it that still reverberates. By focusing on the message of the "new birth" in Jesus and the idea of having a personal relationship with God, Whitefield created the concept of the born-again—or "evangelical" as we now often refer to them—Christian, meaning someone whose zeal for God in Christ is central and who is less interested in denominational affiliation.

As we have seen, this also helped created the concept of the "American," whose fealty was to something beyond their own colony or state—to an idea called "liberty." There is little question that Whitefield's time in the colonies prepared the way for the next act in the story of the American people. When he arrived among them in 1738, they were already suspicious of authority and were used to a measure of freedom in governing their own affairs, but by the time of Whitefield's death in 1770, they were ideologically more prepared to defy the aggressions of the mother country, even if that meant taking up arms against her. Because of Whitefield, the colonies had become united as never before; and their citizens had a far greater sense of how their Christian faith could—and should—lead to a form of government that was "of the people, by the people, and for the people" and that guaranteed liberty and justice for all.

THREE
George Washington Carver

ca. 1864–1943

Nature in its varied forms are the little windows through which God permits me to commune with him, and to see much of his glory, by simply lifting the curtain, and looking in. I love to think of nature as wireless telegraph stations through which God speaks to us every day, every hour, and every moment of our lives.

—GEORGE W. CARVER

George Washington Carver was born during the Civil War and died during the Second World War. He was born as the son of slaves and died one the most famous men in the world, a self-taught scientist so brilliant and creative that even Thomas Edison tried—and failed—to hire him. During his lifetime he met with three presidents, and in 1941 *Time* magazine heralded him as a "black Leonardo [da Vinci]."[1] Five years after his death, his face appeared on a US postage stamp. But humbler beginnings for such a widely celebrated figure can hardly be imagined.

His extraordinary story begins with a white man, Moses Carver, who was a hardworking farmer and horse breeder who did every job on his Ozark farm himself, for he didn't believe in slavery. In fact, in his youth he lived in Springfield, Illinois, and knew the young Abraham Lincoln. Nonetheless, when Moses's wife, Susan, complained of aching loneliness on their remote farm and then begged her husband to solve the problem by buying a young slave girl to help with the chores and keep her company, Moses reluctantly agreed. He bought a thirteen-year-old named Mary from a neighbor for $700. But because Susan and Moses had no children of their own, they treated Mary with great affection. Still, the honorable Moses knew this couldn't make up for the fact that he had trafficked in human flesh, and it continued to trouble him.

In a few years young Mary fell in love with a slave named Giles, who lived on a neighboring plantation. She bore several children with him, and although two died in infancy, two other children survived: a boy named Jim[2] and a girl named Melissa. Then Mary bore one more baby who struggled for breath and constantly coughed and wasn't expected to survive. This tiny sickly child, whom Mary named George, was just weeks old when tragedy struck. His father, Giles, was killed in a farming accident. And soon afterward there was more trouble: a gang of vicious bushwhackers came to the Carver farm. Bushwhackers were roaming criminals who took advantage of the chaos of war, and the stealing and reselling of slaves could be particularly lucrative. Mary fled with her children and hid in a nearby cave. But the bushwhackers figured Moses must know their whereabouts, so they tortured him, hoping to get the information. They hung him from his thumbs, whipped him, and even burned the soles of his feet with hot coals. But Moses heroically endured the pain and said nothing. Thinking they heard an approaching posse, the bandits set fire to the Carver barn and galloped away.

But Moses knew they would return, and there was little he could do on their lonely outpost but wait. He and his wife felt toward Mary and her children as they might feel toward their own children, and the idea of losing them to bandits was a painful thought. But on a cold December night, the nightmare happened. The bushwhackers returned and snatched Mary and her two youngest children. Only little Jim was saved.

Moses knew he must rescue Mary quickly, before she could be resold far away. So he immediately went to nearby Diamond Grove and approached a former bushwhacker named John Bentley. If Bentley could help recover Mary and her children, Moses promised him forty acres of timberland. Bentley agreed. Moses also gave him a valuable horse with which to ransom Mary and her two babies.

The Carvers waited impatiently for six days, but when news came, it was bad. Bentley returned and told Moses and Susan he had been unable to catch up to the bandits who had stolen Mary. But then, pulling open his coat, he handed Susan something wrapped in damp rags.

"It's all I got," Bentley said. "I don't know whether it's alive or dead."[3]

It was tiny George, hardly breathing. Susan stripped off the wet rags and lifted his little naked body before the fire. When she tried to get him to take some warm milk, it simply ran down his chin. Then, suddenly, the child "choked, cried feebly, and sucked for more."[4] As Susan continued to feed George, drop by drop, between the spasms of his coughing, Bentley explained that, after losing the trail of the marauders, he had given up and turned back. Mary and little Melissa were lost forever, and Moses's and Sarah's hearts were broken. But they took some small consolation in still having the two little boys.

And where, Moses asked, had Bentley found George?

"They just give him to some womenfolks down by Conway," he replied. "He ain't worth nothing."[5]

But he was worth a great deal to Susan and Moses, who were grieving the loss of the baby's mother, their beloved Mary. And so, just as they had done with Mary, they treated George as their own child. But the first years of his life were a constant struggle for survival. He continued to cough horribly, which damaged his vocal cords and would give him, to the end of his days, a pronouncedly high, feminine-sounding voice. But Susan nursed him through his endless illnesses. George also suffered from a stutter and was slow to develop physically.

When the Civil War ended, Moses told George and his brother Jim that they were now free and could leave the farm if they wished. But they hoped the boys would stay with them. Although the boys were too young to fully understand what freedom meant, they agreed to stay on with the Carvers.

George continued to be weak and sickly and was never strong enough to join his brother working outdoors alongside Moses, shearing sheep and milking the cows. So "Aunt Susan," as George called his foster mother, taught the frail, skinny child how to do other things that would end up helping him in the years ahead. He learned how to do a vast array of things, including tanning hides, curing bacon, dipping candles, washing clothes, and even crocheting and knitting. Susan also taught him how to plant and raise vegetables, and when they were ripe, how to can them. When little George observed Susan digging up and grinding roots, which she brewed into medicines, the future scientist got his first lessons in botany.

George seemed to enjoy learning. He had an extraordinary mind—in time it would become clear that he wasn't less than a genius, capable of inventing innumerable things. But his first invention was a humble one. He made a special pair of shoes for Uncle Moses. Moses had always cobbled his own shoes but could never seem to fashion a pair that gave him relief from the endless blisters that resulted from hard farm labor. So one day, without being asked, George took the shoes apart, redesigned them, and put them back together. They were a huge improvement over the old ones, and Moses was amazed and grateful. But with every day that passed, he and Aunt Susan saw that the child in their midst was far above the ordinary. For one thing, George constantly asked questions about the world around him, questions that eluded easy answers. Why were some roses yellow and others red? Where did the sun go at night, and what caused the rain to come down?

As he grew older, George spent more and more time wandering in the woods, studying everything he saw—not only the wildflowers but also the birds and the beasts, unusual stones, and insects. His active mind continued to overflow with questions nobody seemed able to answer.

One day George simply sat and observed a fern, amazed at how it rose out of the ground and through the accretion of dead leaves. More and more he lost himself in the natural world around him, although in retrospect it seems that in losing himself this way, he would find himself, and his future.

George began caring for Aunt Susan's plants, deadheading her geraniums and pruning her roses. When Mrs. Fred Baynham, a friend of Susan's, came to visit, she noticed that her friend's roses were impressive. Susan quickly gave the credit to George and said she would one day send him over so that he could show Mrs. Baynham what he was doing.

When he went over, George immediately knew why Mrs. Baynham's roses weren't thriving as they should be. So he dug them up and replanted them where they would get the needed sunlight. When he went inside to tell Mrs. Baynham, he was stunned by the rooms in her house, which were filled with beautiful furnishings and paintings. George had never seen a painting in his life, and he stared at them in amazement until Mrs. Baynham interrupted to thank him for his work in her garden.

Immediately after this visit, George decided he would like to create some paintings himself. Lacking paint, he now did what he would do the rest of his life: he creatively improvised, using pokeberry juice to paint on stones. Little could he imagine that one day he would become quite famous for his paintings of flowers.

Other neighbors asked George to help with their gardens too, soon earning George the title "the plant doctor." Even now, while still a child, George began the observations and experiments that would one day make him the most famous black man in the world. As one biographer put it, "He learned that petunias planted in pure loam paled, and some died. When he mixed in sand they recovered, and he decided that some plants couldn't digest so rich a diet, just as he couldn't eat too many of Aunt Susan's corn biscuits without getting a stomachache. . . . He tracked down grubs and worms that fed on roots, and got rid of them. That summer Uncle Moses fretted because his best apple tree was withering, and George crawled among the limbs until he found the one where a colony of [codling] moths had made a home."[6] George told Uncle Moses that if he just sawed that branch off, the tree would improve, so Uncle Moses sawed it off and it did.

His foster parents continued to be amazed at the depth of the child's knowledge and his rather uncanny ability to observe plants and teach himself about them. It seemed to be a divine gift and they marveled at it.

It was around this time, however, that the brilliant little boy had an experience that would inform everything he did afterward. He was just ten years old when it happened, but it wasn't until he was an old man that he wrote about it.

He wrote to a friend in 1931:

God just came into my heart. . . . [It was] one afternoon while I was alone in the "loft" of our big barn while I was shelling corn to carry to the mill to be ground into meal.

A dear little white boy, one of our neighbors, about my age came by one Saturday morning, and in talking and playing he told me he was going to Sunday school [the next day]. I was eager to know what a Sunday school was. He said they sang hymns and prayed. I asked him what prayer was and what they said. I do not remember what he said; only remember that as soon as he left I climbed up into the "loft," knelt down by the barrel of corn and prayed as best I could. I do not remember what I said. I only recall that I felt so good that I prayed several times before I quit.

My brother and myself were the only colored children in that neighborhood and of course, we could not go to church or Sunday school, or school of any kind.[7]

It wasn't just church and Sunday school that George couldn't attend because of his skin color. Not far from the Carver farm was a cabin that served as both a church and a school. George would now and then sit on the cabin's steps and listen, entranced, to the teacher leading the children through their ABCs and arithmetic. Running home one day, George asked Moses if he was old enough to attend. Looking at the boy sorrowfully, Moses told him he couldn't. It was a school that was only for white children.

On hearing this, George broke down in tears. He so longed to learn. Why should they keep him out just because of his skin color? But George didn't dwell on this long. He was determined to get an education somehow, and by God's grace, he would. In the meantime, Susan and Moses did their best, teaching him how to read and write and do simple sums. But this was far from enough.

A few years later, George walked eight miles to a town called Neosho and was amazed to discover a small school for black children. He could hardly believe it, and in great excitement, he ran home and told Moses and Susan that he wanted to attend. But how could he walk sixteen miles round trip each day? George thought he could just move there. Moses worried how George would support himself so far from home, but George was determined. He figured he could perform chores for local families to support himself.

So the Carvers watched George walk away from their humble farm and into his future.

George arrived in town on a Friday afternoon, and school was closed. He spent the night in a barn and the next morning met the extraordinary woman who owned it. Mariah Watkins was a black woman of tremendous dignity who earned her living washing clothes and delivering babies. She and her husband, Andrew, had no children of their own, and she was taken with this bright, skinny boy who was all alone in the world.

Learning that George wanted to attend school, she fed him a huge breakfast and, after discussing the matter with her husband, told George he could live with them. Of course, he must work to earn his keep. George got teary-eyed with gratitude and began to thank her, but she wouldn't have it. "God brought you to my yard," she said. "He has work for you. And He wants Andrew and me to lend a hand."[8]

Andrew was glad to have the boy live with them. "You call me Uncle Andy, hear?" he said. "And her Aunt Mariah. We're mighty happy to have you, son."[9]

The schoolhouse was right next door to the Watkinses' home, and George attended on weekdays. On Saturdays he helped Mariah with housework, bringing in firewood and learning to wash and iron clothes for her customers. On Sundays the couple took George to church, a new experience for the boy. At first George was nervous, but when the voices of the congregation rose to sing the beautiful hymns of the faith, George's heart was filled with joy. He listened eagerly as the preacher spoke and for the first time began to understand who God was and how he loved his children.

At school George became one of seventy-five children of all ages, all hoping for an education. George loved learning and was seldom found without his reader, eagerly studying it even as he did his chores.

That Christmas, Aunt Mariah gave George a gift he would cherish for the rest of his life—a leather-bound Bible. George read it every day, even memorizing long passages. Aunt Mariah seemed to know that God had special plans for George and said so. "You must learn all you can," she said, "and then go back out in the world and give your learning back to our people."[10]

After two years in this wonderful environment, George had learned about as much as his teacher at the school could teach him. He wondered whether there was another school where he might get answers to his thousand questions about the plant world and so many other things.

As it happened, his neighbors, the Smiths, were planning a trip to Fort Scott, Kansas. George knew this was his chance and asked whether he could go with them. So in January 1877 he climbed aboard their wagon with his few possessions and waved goodbye to Uncle Andy and Aunt Mariah.

Just as with Moses and Susan Carver, Andrew and Mariah Watkins hated to see George go. But they knew it was right he do so. They knew he would go far and felt privileged to have been part of his journey along the way.

Four days later George arrived in Fort Scott and was staggered by the crowds and noise. On his own, he immediately looked for work, knocking on doors and asking whether the owners needed help with chores. After many rejections, he knocked on the door of a Mrs. Payne, telling her that he could sweep and wash dishes.

"Can you cook?" she asked.[11]

George really didn't have any experience cooking, but he was so desperate for work that he told a fib. "Oh, yes, ma'am," he said.[12]

Mrs. Payne invited him into the kitchen, where the hungry, tired boy nearly fainted at the aroma of beef roasting in the oven. And then, suddenly, Mrs. Payne was telling him to make bread pudding, biscuits, apple pie, and coffee. Thinking quickly, George told Mrs. Payne he wanted everything to be exactly right, so would she show him how she liked these dishes prepared? She would, and George watched carefully as she demonstrated how to make one thing after the other. George's brilliant mind remembered everything, and it wasn't long before he was going beyond what he had learned and was experimenting, just as he had in his garden back home, adding herbs to flavor the meats and making other improvements to the meals.

A few months later, George had saved enough money to begin attending school again. During his free time, he went into the woods to sketch pictures of plants and animals, gather rocks, press wildflowers, and search for other subjects to paint.

Whenever his money ran out, George went to work again, this time at a hotel doing laundry, earning enough to go back to the classroom that September. He continued this pattern, going to school until his money ran out and then going back to work. His perseverance and his drive for self-improvement and education were simply extraordinary.

But then something happened that traumatized George so badly that he would never fully recover, a turning point in his life. He witnessed a crowd of white men attempting to break into the local jail. At last the jailer gave in to their brutal demands and threw the black prisoner out to them. The men then kicked and beat him. As the man screamed for mercy, the crowd poured oil over him and threw him into a fire. George had never seen such evil and it scarred him. How could such injustice be allowed to exist?[13]

Shocked and terrified, George collected his possessions and escaped Fort Scott in the night.

For the next several years, George Carver wandered throughout the country, thinking bitter thoughts about what it meant to be a black man in a white country. But his overwhelming desire for education was unabated, and he continued attending schools in one town after another, all the while taking on odd jobs to support himself, just as he had done in Fort Scott. In time George grew tall—six feet—but was always rail thin. In time, he even lost his stutter.

Wherever George went he kept up his habit of observing unusual plants and of sketching them. Occasionally, he was himself mistreated by whites. George couldn't swim, and a gang of boys once threw him into a pond and laughed as he struggled to keep from drowning.

When he arrived in Olathe, Kansas, George moved in with an older black couple named Christopher and Lucy Seymour, where things improved. He attended school, helped Lucy with her housework, and went to church with the couple. When the Seymours moved to Minneapolis, Kansas, George went with them. In this town, although older than most of the other students, George was able to attend high school, generously helping other students with their schoolwork and even joining the dramatic society. And to support himself, he opened his own, very successful, laundry business.

George's education had hardly been typical. In 1885, as he was finally about to finish high school, he was already in his twenties. George decided it was time to apply to college, so he applied to Highland College in Highland, Kansas. George waited anxiously to find out if his education—gathered through countless schools across the country—would be good enough to allow him to take this next step. One joyful day in June, George opened a letter from Highland College. They were inviting him to enroll in September.

George bid adieu to the Seymours that summer and headed for Kansas City, where he immediately took typing and shorthand classes to prepare for college that fall. He also took a job at the union depot, typing messages, and then, just prior to traveling on to Highland, he returned to Neosho to visit the Watkinses and then to Diamond Grove to visit the now elderly Carvers, who were deeply proud of the fine young man their George had become.

At last George said goodbye and boarded the train to Highland, and college. On arrival, he immediately made his way to the office of the principal, Rev. Duncan Brown, and introduced himself. But on seeing George, the principal's face fell.

"There has been a mistake," he said.

Years later George recalled Brown "groping for words and finding only lame half-sentences."

George helpfully produced the letter inviting him to enroll.

Brown was embarrassed. "You didn't tell me you were Negro," he said. "Highland College does not take Negroes."[14]

George walked out, staggered. He sat miserably on a bench for hours, devastated and confused. He wanted to leave Highland immediately, but he couldn't even afford train fare to do so. So he simply walked until he found a barn to sleep in.

The next day, George went to work for a family of fruit growers, the Beelers, and attended church with them. His life took a new turn: George became a farmer, homesteading 160 acres of land by himself. He built a sod house with some help from Frank Beeler and spent two prairie winters in it, enduring the blizzards, and two summers sweltering under the blazing sun as he planted rice, corn, and fruit trees. During this time, George's spirit began to heal from the years of wandering and rejection. He began to dream again. Perhaps—if he couldn't attend college—he might start a greenhouse business and surround himself with his beloved flowers.

Eventually George mortgaged his homestead and hiked northeast. As ever, he picked up odd jobs along the way until he reached an Iowa village called Winterset, where he took work as a hotel cook. One evening, he decided to attend a white Baptist church, and here God intervened once more, bringing the right people into George's life at exactly the right time—just as he had done first with the Carvers and then with the Watkinses.

Among the church members were Dr. and Mrs. John Milholland, a white couple who were impressed with George's beautiful singing voice. They invited him to their home where George immediately spotted a piano. Mrs. Milholland played and sang for George, and as he listened, old memories rose up in his mind. George had to struggle not to cry.

George was in for a second surprise when they moved to the study, where he immediately noticed an easel, on which sat a painting of a flower: violet jimsonweed.

"You paint!" George exclaimed.

"I try," Mrs. Milholland replied, noting that her paintings were not as good as she would like.[15]

From years of experience, George knew a lot about painting and offered suggestions on how she could improve her technique, deftly grabbing a brush and demonstrating. Mrs. Milholland asked George if he would give her painting lessons in exchange for singing lessons. George happily struck a deal and from then on became a regular visitor to the Milholland home, teaching painting, practicing his singing, playing the piano, devouring books from the family's library, and playing with the Milholland children. And, of course, he was unable to keep himself from working in the family's garden.

One evening, George felt close enough to the family to tell the Milhollands about the shattering episode of being accepted at Highland College but then being rejected because of his color.

The couple sympathized and encouraged George to try again at Simpson College in nearby Indianola.

"They will take you there, George," Dr. Milholland said. "This next semester—if you have the heart to try it."[16]

But George wasn't sure what to do. For one thing, he loved these friends, who were like family, and he would hate to leave them. And his experience at Highland had so stung him that he wasn't sure if he still wanted a college education.

One day, however, while working in his laundry, George made his decision. He would apply to Simpson College after all, and God willing, he would be accepted. So that September 1890, George walked about thirty miles to Indianola.

When he arrived, George rather nervously presented his records to the school's president, the Rev. Edmund Holmes. Of course Holmes was white, and if George was accepted, he would be the only black student of the three hundred enrolled. The Rev. Holmes examined George's records for a while and then looked up at him. His demeanor was dramatically different from the Rev. Duncan Brown's back at Highland. "Welcome to Simpson," Holmes said brightly and extended his hand.[17] It was a life-changing moment, and deeply gratifying when George considered all he had been through up to that point.

George explained to Rev. Holmes that he would need a place to stay and said that to support himself he would launder clothes, as he had done in the past. It so happened that Rev. Holmes knew of a cottage— really more like a shack—not far away. It could serve as both George's home and his laundry, if he liked. Holmes even promised to let George's fellow students know where to take their clothing to be washed and ironed. The Rev. Holmes seemed to forget this promise, though, so when George opened for business, the customers were slow to come. As his food supplies ran low, George panicked.

"For quite some time," George wrote humorously to the Milholland family when this crisis had passed, "I lived on prayer, beef suet, and corn meal, being, at the last without the suet and meal."[18]

As for his classes, George had signed up for mathematics, etymology, grammar, and composition. He also hoped to study art but was told by the art instructor, Miss Etta Budd, that she first needed to see samples of his work.

Life as the only black student at Simpson was hardly easy. The other students mostly ignored him, adding to his sense of isolation. And if he didn't earn money soon, George would be unable to continue with his studies. The only good news at this time was that Miss Budd told him she thought his sketches were excellent and that he was welcome to attend her art class. But when she learned of his dire financial situation, she immediately came to his rescue, becoming another in the long line of kind mentors to this gifted young man.

Miss Budd did what Holmes had forgotten to do and told almost everyone on campus about George's laundry service. And she raved to her friends in town about George, asking them to offer him odd jobs—and any winter clothing and furniture they didn't need. One day, while George was away, Miss Budd's friend Mrs. Arthur Lister, organized efforts to find furniture and clothing for George and furnished Carver's humble cottage with chairs, a bed, a table, dishes, warm clothing, and even some meat and a fresh loaf of bread. Walking into his cabin and discovering these gifts, George was overwhelmed. While he was still adjusting to the generosity of his new friends, his first laundry customer showed up.

George believed in paying his debts to his friends (whether they wanted to be paid back or didn't). He paid back Miss Budd by cutting her firewood each week. He also thanked Mrs. Liston by working his magic in her flower beds and then presenting the delighted woman with a painting of her garden.

George's laundry service, now patronized by a number of his fellow students, slowly led to friendships with them. George began to believe his future would be in his art. He loved painting and was good at it. But Miss Budd gently explained how difficult it was for *any* artist to make a living, never mind a black one, given the attitudes of the times. She suggested he consider an alternative.

"George," she said, "I showed your picture to my father. He's a professor of horticulture at the Iowa Agricultural College at Ames. I told him about your skill with plants. He believes you could have a useful, rewarding career in agriculture. He thinks you should be at Ames."[19]

Once again, George had an important decision to make. He loved painting, but what was God's will for him? Suddenly, something Mariah Watkins had told him came into his mind: "Go out in the world, and give your learning back to our people. They're starving for a little learning."

George made up his mind. Believing it was God's will for him to help his people—something he thought he could best begin to do at Ames—he packed his bags once more.

It was a time of great change in agriculture, and the work being done by Ames scientists was at the forefront of finding new and more efficient ways of farming. Among them was James G. Wilson, Dean of Agriculture and one of America's most respected botanists. He also directed the experimental station, and one day would become Secretary of Agriculture for presidents William McKinley, Theodore Roosevelt, and William Taft.

George arrived in May and was given a room but discovered he wasn't allowed into the campus dining hall with the white students. He was told to eat in the basement alongside the black men and women who labored in the kitchen and in the fields. While George was hurt by this decision, he went along with it.

But when Mrs. Arthur Liston, one of the women who had gathered furniture and clothing for George, heard of his situation, she was outraged. She promptly traveled to Ames and asked George to give her a tour of the school. When it came time for dinner, Mrs. Liston made it clear to the dining hall director that she intended to eat in the basement with George.

"But—but madame," he pleaded, "What will the dean say? And Professor Wilson . . ."

"You ought to have considered that when you arranged Mr. Carver's dining facilities," she said. "And please bear in mind that I expect to be visiting here again."[20]

The next day, George was invited to dine in the dining hall, where he immediately became popular with fellow students, who enjoyed his conversation. They soon invited him to join a literary society and to sing in a college quartet. George also became the official trainer for Ames's athletic teams, learning to massage the aches and pains from their bodies.

In the classroom, George was carrying a heavy load, including zoology, botany, chemistry, bacteriology, and entomology, the study of insects. At last he was finding answers to his childhood questions about plants and their environment.

As with all male students at Ames, George was required to join the National Guard Student Battalion. George knew perfectly well that, as a black man, he would never be allowed to become an officer. Nevertheless, he trained hard, earning the top student rating and deeply impressing his commander.

George also continued to impress Miss Budd, his art teacher back at Simpson. During his first winter break at Ames, he returned to Simpson to take another of her classes. But Miss Budd knew George's ability had already outstripped her power to teach him anything, and she looked on proudly as George painted one masterpiece after another.

Miss Budd's father, professor of horticulture at the Iowa Agricultural College at Ames, suggested he exhibit his paintings at the all-Iowa art exhibition of the Iowa State Teachers Association, which would take place in Cedar Rapids. George confessed he couldn't afford the trip, and in any case, he didn't have the proper clothes to wear to such an event. But the day before the exhibit began, his fellow students at Ames "kidnapped" George, took him into town, and bought him a new suit, shirt, tie, hat, gloves, socks, and shoes.

Next they took him to Professor Wilson's home, where George was presented with a train ticket to Cedar Rapids. Miss Budd had also secretly taken four of George's finest paintings and wrapped them up.

When George wondered out loud how he would even begin to repay the money being spent on him, Professor Wilson stopped him.

"You have already repaid it," Wilson announced. "The small sum each of your classmates and teachers contributed is little enough for the honor of your friendship. We believe in you."[21]

As he always did when deeply moved, George cried.

At the exhibition, each one of George's four paintings won a prize, and George's painting *Yucca Gloriosa* was later exhibited at the Chicago World's Fair, where it won an honorable mention award—a staggering achievement considering that his competitors were all professional painters.

In 1894, when he was approximately thirty years old, Carver proudly received his bachelor of science degree. His thesis was titled "Plants as Modified by Man." According to the dean of agriculture, Dr. Louis Pammel, George was "among the most brilliant students he had ever taught."[22] This explains why he promptly hired Carver as assistant botanist at the Ames experiment station, where he suggested Carver take over the greenhouse, which he did.

The humble young botanist sometimes found it hard to believe he wasn't in the greenhouse merely to sweep the floor. He taught biology to freshmen and, always one to make good use of his time, also began working on a master of science degree, with a focus on mycology (the study of fungi), which he finished in 1896.

Carver found the academic atmosphere extremely stimulating. Biographer Lawrence Elliot noted, "Around Professor Wallace [assistant to the dean of agriculture] there clustered a band of young intellectuals whose energies were channeled into the search for a strain of corn that would withstand assaults of disease and drought. Pammell's [*sic*] published studies on plant pathology—on two of which his new assistant collaborated—were to become landmarks in their field." And Carver's "skill at hybridizing rendered whole families of fruits and plants resistant to fungus attack."[23]

In what spare time he had, George traveled around the state to teach farmers how to better care for their crops.

George enjoyed spending time with Professor Wallace's small son, Henry, teaching him how to cross plants—grafting, for instance, a red rose onto a yellow rosebush. But why would anyone want to do such a thing? Henry asked. To speed up growing time, George replied, or to help a more delicate plant survive, by grafting its root onto a hardier plant. (Little did either of them know at the time that little Henry would grow up to become vice president of the United States under Franklin Delano Roosevelt.)

At Ames, George was happier than he had ever been. The work was extremely gratifying, and his colleagues valued him tremendously. But George continued to wonder: Was this truly where God wanted him? He still believed God wanted him to use his agricultural knowledge to help poor black farmers.

As he was finishing his master's degree, George had no way of knowing God was preparing him for new and important work—the most important of his life. In faraway Alabama, an ambitious black educator named Booker T. Washington, a former slave who had organized and was the principal of the Tuskegee Normal and Industrial Institute, dreamed of helping not just the handful of students who could attend his school but the millions of impoverished black farmers all over the South.

"These people do not know how to plow or plant or harvest," Washington noted in one of his books. "I am not skilled at such things. I teach them how to read, to write, to make good shoes, good bricks, and how to build a wall. I cannot give them food and so they starve."[24] But Washington had heard of someone—a black agriculturist—who could teach them to plow and plant and harvest. He wanted this man at Tuskegee but doubted he could convince him to leave his plum position at Ames.

He would try nonetheless, and on April 1, 1896, he wrote to Carver, asking him to consider coming to Tuskegee to head up the new agriculture department. He offered Carver an annual salary of $1,500. But Washington didn't minimize the difficulties of such a move, nor did he suggest the new position was anything but a step down from Ames.

"I cannot offer you money, position, or fame," Washington wrote.

"The first two you have. The last, from the place you now occupy, you will no doubt achieve. These things I now ask you to give up. I offer you in their place work—hard, hard work—the task of bringing a people from degradation, poverty, and waste to full manhood."[25]

When Carver read Washington's letter a few days later, Carver's heart soared. He simply had no doubt that this was God's plan for him. "To this end," he wrote back to Washington, "I have been preparing myself for these many years; feeling as I do that this line of education is the key to unlock the golden door of freedom to our people. . . . I pray my work at Tuskegee become my reason for living."[26]

Of course Carver's friends at Ames tried to talk him out of leaving, but they soon saw that he couldn't be dissuaded and gave him a microscope as a parting gift.

On his train ride south, Carver saw with sorrowing eyes the huge swaths of land planted with nothing but cotton—and the equally huge number of poor blacks bent over as they picked it in the sweltering sun. This one-crop system "had ruled the South for 100 years, and year by year it had drained the good from the soil, producing an ever-smaller yield from the same enfeebled piece of ground, so that more fields had to be planted, and great forests felled to make room for still more fields."[27] The loss of the trees resulted in the precious topsoil being washed or blown away.

Carver knew the work at Tuskegee would be demanding and that the school was quite new. Nevertheless, he was taken aback when his buggy pulled up in front of a single frame building. Surely this couldn't be his destination. But it was. Wandering down the dusty road, stopping occasionally to examine unfamiliar plants, Carver encountered a few shacks and a small handful of other buildings, including a four-story brick building called Alabama Hall, built by the students. Dr. Booker T. Washington, whose simple office was housed in the first building Carver had seen, welcomed him and asked him what he thought of the school.

"There seems much to be done," he answered graciously.

"Yes, of course," Washington replied, "but we can now believe it *will* be done."[28]

Carver, accustomed to the modern laboratories and equipment at Ames, now discovered that Tuskegee's agricultural building existed only on paper, although there was a little land for farming—what Carver would later call the worst twenty acres in Alabama. The "dairy" actually consisted of but a single churn, and the "equipment" amounted to a broken-down nag and a pitiable handful of tools.

Nor was Carver pleased to learn that he would have to live in the same room he did his work in. But he reminded himself God wanted him here and that this place represented hope for his people, most of whom existed in poverty on hardscrabble farms, with no idea how to improve their yields. Remembering this changed everything.

Shortly after his arrival, Carver told his students—there were thirteen of them—that they were going to have to create supplies for their laboratory since no money was available to purchase what they needed. He led them to the school dump and instructed them to pick up bottles, pots and pans, the lids of jars, boxes and wire, and other odds and ends. Under his direction, they gathered more junk from the nearby town and carried their plunder back to the school.

As his students marveled, Carver applied his genius and decades of experience in making do—to work what looked like magic. Taking an ink bottle, he pushed a piece of string through the cork. This would serve as a wick, and suddenly the bottle became a Bunsen burner. An old teacup was repurposed as a mortar. Punching holes into pieces of tin, Carver showed his class how they could strain soil samples. Suddenly, Carver and his students had all the laboratory equipment they would need.

Among the first lessons he taught his students—beyond the general lesson of creative improvising—was that they should measure their success not by how much money they ultimately made but by how much service they could offer to those less fortunate than themselves.

Carver hounded the Tuskegee administration until they relented and purchased a two-horse plow, and he showed his students how to use it, constantly urging them to "plow deep!"[29]

Carver taught them how to identify plants and about soil and fertilizer. "The ground can give back only as much nourishment as there is in it," he explained.[30] His students also learned that there were many ways to fertilize crops beyond the animal manure everyone knew about. He then turned his attention to the twenty acres of farmland Tuskegee owned. To improve it, Carver asked Dr. Washington to contact a fertilizer company in Atlanta to see whether it would be willing to donate a few hundred pounds of phosphates for "a three-year agricultural experiment."[31] The company agreed to do so once it discovered that Carver, whose work at Ames they were familiar and impressed with, would be conducting the experiments.

Carver taught his students about the need for balanced nutrients for the soil and—since fertilizer companies were unlikely to hand out phosphates to every farmer in Alabama—told them their goal should be to identify fertilizing materials available to the poor.

First he showed them that leaf mold and muck could be used in the creation of a compost heap. He then added sandy soil to it, then organic waste—such as vegetable peels and kitchen grease—and once the mixture had rotted, the students spread it over the twenty-acre farmland. They were stunned when Carver announced they would not be planting cotton on it, which would bring in good money, but would be planting cowpeas instead. As far as they knew, cowpeas—also known as black-eyed peas—were only good for feeding hogs.

Carver explained that while most crops—especially cotton— "Drained life-giving nitrogen from the earth," cowpeas possessed "the unique ability to absorb nitrogen from the very air and feed it back to the soil."[32] That wasn't all. When the crop was harvested, Carver cooked his students a delicious meal of pancakes, potatoes, and meat loaf—all made from mashed cowpeas.

By year's end, the farm showed a profit of four dollars an acre and supplied Tuskegee's dining room through late fall. The following spring

Carver gave his students more lessons in crop rotation—planting sweet potatoes, soy beans, and something that very few people at that time consumed: peanuts.

When the sweet potatoes were harvested, the yield was a whopping 265 bushels an acre. But what happened the following spring grabbed the attention of local farmers. Carver had finally allowed his students to plant cotton, but as a result of how he had rejuvenated the soil, the cotton was far beyond what anyone had ever seen. Many local "farmers, black and white, came to the experiment station and stared at the perfect stalks and plump bushes, some of which bore as many as 275 great white bolls. The yield was an incredible 500-pound bale per acre—so rich a crop had never been grown in that part of the land."[33]

When the farmers asked how Carver had achieved this, he told them the same thing he'd been telling his students: "A plant needs certain things, and the soil has certain things to give, and it is the farmer's job to make the right adjustment between them."[34]

A year after Carver was hired, the number of students grew from thirteen to seventy-six. Carver found himself being asked to take on many other responsibilities at Tuskegee, such as testing well water, helping with the design of the soon-to-be-built agriculture building, doing landscaping work, measuring rainfall, and even serving as a veterinarian.

But despite his hard work and impressive success, not everyone at Tuskegee liked George Carver. Although they had hired him for his expertise, some constantly told him what to do, what to plant, and where to focus his energies. And despite much proof to the contrary, many simply thought his farming ideas outlandish.

In frustration, Carver wrote directly to Washington, with whom he also clashed frequently: "As to your office people, I do not mind them scoffing at my experiments, but you can see that I cannot have them deciding what is to be done and you will oblige me by telling them so."[35] Carver also asked Washington for more space for his books and other possessions—a request Washington granted, assigning Carver a room to serve as his laboratory. He also managed to stop others from meddling in Carver's work.

Carver also found ways to save the college money. When he learned how much money was being spent on a formula used to exterminate bedbugs, Carver concocted his own formula for about a third of the cost.

When he wasn't teaching students, he was in his laboratory, testing and experimenting with molds and soils. He also developed a way of extracting paint pigment from clay. His curiosity and creativity with plants and chemicals seemed boundless.

Whenever the stresses and challenges of work took their toll, Carver headed for Alabama Hall, where he played the piano and remembered each of the dear individuals, black and white, who had helped him through the years. Eventually students gathered in the evenings to hear their professor perform. His repertoire was impressively eclectic, ranging from Handel to such gospel hymns as "Swing Low, Sweet Chariot."

Carver's heavenly playing sparked an idea in the mind of Warren Logan, the school treasurer. Would Carver consent to helping the school raise money with a concert tour? Thinking of all the things the agriculture department desperately needed—and couldn't afford—he agreed. The tour took him to towns and cities all across the Deep South, where he performed in all kinds of venues, including in some beautiful homes and sometimes in barns too. In just over a month, Carver was thrilled to find that he had earned $350 for the college.

But the professor was also saddened as he traveled. Everywhere he went, he saw the emaciated faces and forms of fellow blacks who lived in miserable shanties and who labored long hours in the fields, neither expecting nor receiving anything better. Carver knew this was wrong, and he determined to help in whatever way he could.

He published popular agricultural bulletins based on his research findings, giving farmers practical advice—and farmers all over the world wrote to Carver, asking for it. He started the Farmer's Institute, in which local farmers could come to Tuskegee once a month to learn how planting only cotton, year after year, exhausted the land. It could be restored by treating it with materials that were available to all, he explained, things such as leaf mold, cornstalks, and potato peelings.

He also suggested that each subsistence farmer plant a kitchen garden so that their families would have a good supply of healthy vegetables to supplement their diets of meat, molasses, and meal.

He also explained that tomatoes, which were widely believed to be poisonous, were not only not poisonous but actually nutritious and would help protect them against scurvy. Carver enjoyed using humor to make his points and often shocked his audiences by sinking his teeth into a chunk of tomato, which he then chewed and swallowed. After a perfectly timed pause, he would then announce: "You will please notice that I have not died."[36]

But the most impressive thing for most of the farmers who visited him was what he called his "experiment station." All who saw it gasped at the impossibly enormous cabbages, onions, cantaloupes, watermelons, and potatoes. Carver expanded farmers' ideas about what was possible by showing them what he had already achieved. He wasn't just proposing theories. He had already tested his theories and had proved their worth—and here were the results for all to see.

The profit per acre was four dollars the first year, but in a few years, it had soared to an impossible seventy-five dollars per acre. Carver explained how planting cowpeas had enriched the soil, and he passed out recipes for cooking them too.

When farmers noticed that the crops of neighbors who had learned from Carver were of much higher quality than their own, word quickly got out about his new and manifestly successful ideas. But Carver wanted to reach even more small farmers, especially the thousands who lived far out in the swamps and couldn't attend the Farmer's Institute meetings. He determined that if they couldn't attend meetings at the school, he would haul the school out to them.

Carver designed a wagon for the job, and his student carpenters and wheelwrights built it. He stocked it with charts on soil improvement and stock raising, farm equipment, seed packets, and boxes of plants. This humble self-taught genius then hitched a mule to it and one evening rode off into the swamps and thickets.

He already knew trying to get these folks to give up planting cotton was essentially a lost cause. So when he located these isolated farmers, Carver reminded them how much fuller the cotton bushes had been just decades before. The land was tired and needed a rest, he said. The farmers understood that, but how could they let the land rest when they had hungry children to feed? What choice did they have but to plant more cotton and hope for the best?

When they said something along these lines, Carver would produce a sweet potato and hold it up to them. "Put ten acres in yams," he said, "and you'll have nourishing food for your table the year round, and the vines and culls and peelings will feed your hogs."[37] If they were willing to do this, within three years they could plant cotton again and would get a far greater harvest than they were getting now.

And since sweet potatoes were perishable, Carver taught these farmers how to preserve them.

The mobile farm idea caught on, not just in the South but all over the world, and Carver considered it the most important work he'd ever done, because it helped so many people, which was—as he had continued to teach his students—the true measure of success.

It took some farmers a long time to believe Carver knew what he was talking about. But some of them listened carefully, their eyes widening in wonder as Carver showed off the huge vegetables his students had grown at the experiment station. He even went into their homes and taught farmers' wives ways to prepare the cowpeas, bringing bags of vegetables as his contribution to the meals he shared with them.

Carver also urged farmers to try to save five cents every working day so that at the end of a year, they would have saved $15.65—enough to purchase three more acres of land. There was, he told them, "no other way to break the grip of the landlord or the plantation commissary."[38]

When it came to sharecroppers and tenant farmers, Carver's

ultimate goal was to help them improve their crops yields enough so that "they could afford their own farms, decent homes for their families, and modern equipment to make their lives less wearisome while improving production even more."[39]

At Tuskegee, Carver was irritated when equipment promised many months before never arrived, and while his overloaded schedule led him to sometimes complain that he shouldn't have to teach students along with everything else, Carver was a brilliant teacher who believed that the best way for students to learn was to get their hands dirty. As he said in his 1902 booklet, "Every teacher should realize that a very large proportion of every student's work must lie outside the class room. . . . The study of nature is both entertaining and instructive, and it is the only true method that leads up to a clear understanding of the great natural principles which surround every branch of business in which we may engage. Aside from this, it encourages investigation and stimulates originality."[40]

Carver so inspired his students that many would say his classes had changed their lives. They had other reasons to be grateful to him. Living in such close quarters with their professor, they quickly came to realize what a kind man he was, one who was willing to offer encouragement and to advise them when they needed advice—such as the need to put off marriage until they could support a family. Work hard, Carver advised his students, and follow your dreams. He urged graduates to stay in touch to let him know how they were doing.

Carver would frequently lend desperately poor students money, or would simply give it to them as a gift. His own expenses were low, and he could be the proverbial absentminded professor, forgetting sometimes even to cash his own paychecks.

Knowing his students would one day return to the outside world of prejudice and discrimination, Carver tried to help them develop the right attitude—trusting God and doing the right thing. "When our thoughts—which bring actions—are filled with hate against anyone, Negro or white, we are in a living hell. That is as real as hell will ever be. While hate for our fellow man puts us in a living hell, holding good thoughts for them brings us an opposite state of living, one of happiness, success, peace. We are then in heaven."[41]

Carver never wavered in his faith in God and always credited him with creating the world and everything in it and then giving humans the ability to understand it. While other scientists believed in evolution, Carver, because of his profound knowledge of the details of so much of creation, believed something else. The more "he learned about the beauty, complexity, and interconnectedness of the world, the more convinced he was that it would only have been formed supernaturally, by the hand of God."[42]

Carver brought these beliefs into the classroom and in 1907 was asked to begin teaching a Sunday evening Bible study class. Fifty students attended the first meeting. Instead of going into theology and opening a Bible, Carver brought along his plants and drawings and talked about "nature in its varied forms," which "are the little windows through which God permits me to commune with him, and to see much of his glory, by simply lifting the curtain, and looking in. I love to think of nature as wireless telegraph stations through which God speaks to us every day, every hour, and every moment of our lives."[43] Another time he said that the out of doors was to him "more and more a great cathedral in which God could be continuously spoken to and heard from."[44] Within a few months, some three hundred students were weekly attending Carver's Sunday school class.

Carver also kept up a regular correspondence with graduates, who continued to share their joys and sorrows with their old mentor. Replying to one who was evidently going through a rough time, he wrote, "You are now in the midst of a great struggle. You are fighting for freedom, you will win, God is on your side. . . . There are times when I am surely tried and am compelled to hide away with Jesus for strength to overcome. God alone knows what I have suffered, in trying to do as best I could the job he has given me in trust to do. . . . Many are the strange paths God led me into. He is and will lead you likewise."[45]

Over the years, Carver and Washington clashed regularly, and more than once, Carver tendered his resignation. Despite their skirmishes, however, the two men deeply respected each other. Washington understood that Carver needed regular doses of attention, respect, and praise, and Carver understood the endless strain Washington was under. When a troubled Washington, unable to sleep, occasionally knocked on Carver's door late at night, Carver would willingly get up, dress, and accompany Washington on long walks across campus.

And every morning, before the sun came up, Carver took a walk by himself, talking to God and ever on the lookout for interesting plant specimens to take back to his laboratory.

In 1917, despite his staggering gifts as a teacher, Carver—now in his mid-fifties—gave up teaching to devote himself entirely to doing research and carrying out experiments in his beloved laboratory. The list of his inventions—all created out of natural ingredients—is almost unfathomably long.

Among them were whitewash and paint, which were used on Tuskegee's own building to save money. A wood stain Carver developed was 90 percent cheaper than a commercially manufactured stain. He made dyes from radishes, tomatoes, and maple bark and announced that no fewer than fifty-three products could be made from chicken feathers, which were routinely thrown away. He even developed a new and improved strain of cotton that was resistant to disease.

A former student named Alvin Smith wrote that Carver's faith was "the key to all that he had been able to do. . . . Knowing the background from which students of the rural South, Africa, and other lands came [many of them nonbelievers], he was anxious that they have this key, without which they could not unlock the kingdom of good things they desired, or that they deserved."[46]

Talk of spiritual things led to questions such as, "If God is a Spirit, did this mean they would never be able to see him?"[47]

In response, Carver pointed to the flower he always wore in his lapel.

"When you look at this flower," he said, "you see thy Creator. Students at Tuskegee who are studying to be electricians are not able to see electricity, but when they make the proper contact . . . you can make a bulb light up, can't you, because the electricity is always there."[48]

As interested in developing his students' character as he was their brains, Carver developed what he called "eight cardinal virtues," which he urged his students to uphold:

1. Be clean both inside and outside.
2. Who neither looks up to the rich or down on the poor.
3. Who loses, if need be, without squealing.
4. Who wins without bragging.
5. Who is always considerate of women, children, and old people.
6. Who is too brave to lie.
7. Who is too generous to cheat.
8. Who takes his share of the world and lets other people have theirs.[49]

His mind never far from the poor—and often hungry—farm families, Carver continued research on peanuts and black-eyed peas, both of which contained many nutrients and were easy to grow in the South. He enjoyed creating new recipes from these items, and getting the school to prepare them, as a means of showing what they really tasted like. He invented "peanut pie" and even "peanut milk," which was of great use to families too poor to own a cow.

Carver once gave Washington a taste of meat that he had dried himself. Washington admitted that it tasted infinitely better than the canned meats Tuskegee was purchasing and determined to use Carver's method from then on.

As more and more farmers grew peanuts, Carver found himself developing even more uses for them, lest the farmers he had persuaded to grow them end up with more than they could sell.

Sadly, none of Carver's inventions were marketed commercially, because while the professor was a genius at developing new products from natural materials, he had little idea how to market them. Promotion and marketing were simply not among his gifts, nor did such activities interest him. Nor was anyone available to help him promote his inventions, and so—in what became a pattern—Carver would simply shrug his shoulders, abandon the project, and move on to the next one.

On November 14, 1915, Booker T. Washington died, an event that so upset Carver that he was unable to teach for a time. He donated a year's salary to a memorial fund for his old friend and paid his friend the ultimate honor by taking Booker T.'s surname as his own middle name. It wasn't until then—when he was in his fifties—that he became George Washington Carver, which is how he's been known ever since.

At the time of Washington's death, the eyes of Americans were increasingly focused on Europe, where the First World War was raging. When the United States entered the war in April 1917, there were shortages of products that the US had been importing from Germany. Carver immediately plunged into experiments to replace these products. In the process he created five hundred substitute dyes—made from roots and stems—to make up for the loss of aniline dyes from Germany. He even attempted to create rope from peanut hulls and rubber from sweet potatoes.

In the years after the war, Carver went from being a rumpled, absentminded professor known principally only to Tuskegee students and other scientists to a world-famous botanist. But this fame arose primarily from what was meant to be a ten-minute presentation in January 1921.

It came about when the United Peanut Growers organization asked Carver to speak to the Ways and Means Committee of the US House of Representatives. This was part of an effort to convince Congress to place a tariff on the import of cheap peanuts. When it was time for him to speak, Carver carried two heavy boxes into the House of Representatives office building. The committee chairman, taken aback by what he saw, politely reiterated that Carver had just ten minutes for the presentation.

Most members of Congress had no idea of the genius who stood before them, and after two days of sometimes agonizingly boring testimony, they were looking forward to wrapping things up as quickly as possible.

But as they soon understood, this was hardly to be. Dr. Carver first unpacked his boxes, placing innumerable exotic objects onto the table before him. Then he began. He held up a block of "crushed cake"—crushed peanut meat—which, Carver announced, made a delicious cereal, among many other things. He picked up ground peanut hulls: good for burnishing tin, he declared. Carver plucked a chunk of chocolate-covered peanuts off the table and showed it to his audience. "You don't know how delicious this is, so I will taste it for you," Carver said, putting the candy into his mouth.[50]

The congressmen—now wide awake—laughed.

"What is that other stuff?" the committee chairman asked curiously.

"Here is ice cream powder made from the peanut," Carver responded. "Simply mixed with water, it produces an unusually rich and delicious ice cream. . . . In these bottles are dyes extracted from the skin of peanuts. . . . They have been tested in the laboratory and found to hold their colors and to be harmless to the skin."[51]

Carver snatched up a bottle. "Here is a substitute for quinine," he said, adding, "We can hardly overestimate the medicinal properties of the peanut. . . . These are various kinds of food for livestock. You will find that cattle thrive on them and the increase in milk is pronounced."

By now Carver's ten minutes were up, but the committee couldn't pretend to be bored and asked him please to continue. And he did, such that most in the room eventually could hardly believe what they were hearing.

"Here is milk from peanuts," he said. "And here is instant coffee which already has in it cream and sugar." He then indicated other things that he claimed were "buttermilk, Worcestershire sauce," and "pickles—all made from the peanut."[52]

Carver, appreciating the warm reception, suddenly sang paeans of praise to the lowly sweet potato, from which he had made 107 products, including, he said, "ink, relishes, pomade," and "mucilage."[53]

Then returning to the subject for which he would soon be world-famous, he told his audience about the many recipes he had created from peanuts, even mock oysters and mock meat dishes.

Where, one congressman asked, did Carver learn all this?

From a book, Carver promptly answered.

But what book? the congressman wanted to know.

"The Bible," Carver responded. "It says that God has given us everything for our use. He has revealed to me some of the wonders of this fruit of His earth. In the first chapter of Genesis we are told, 'Behold, I have given you every herb that bears seed upon the face of the earth, and every tree bearing seed. To you it shall be meat.' . . . There is everything there to strengthen, nourish, and keep the body alive and healthy."[54]

In the end, Carver had spoken to his mesmerized audience for an hour and forty minutes, eventually showing them his peanut vanishing cream, rubbing oils, stains, fruit punch, and milk flakes and telling jokes and stories as he did so. When Carver indicated he was through and began to pack up his boxes, the committee gave him a standing ovation and invited him to come back another time. Congress soon thereafter placed a stiff tariff on imported peanuts.

Even despite his obvious brilliance and his academic credentials, Carver encountered the same ugly bigotry in the nation's hallowed capital as he had encountered years earlier in rural Alabama. Just before his talk, he had heard someone in the room laugh scornfully and say, "I reckon if he gets enough peanuts to go with his watermelon he's a right happy coon."[55]

But this truly great man—who had long before decided to cast out any bitterness in his heart, lest it cause damage to his own character—ignored the vile comment. And it is well that he did, because his subsequent inimitable performance before this previously fatigued and irritable all-white committee showed that, contrary to the ugly beliefs of some, blacks were capable of doing magnificently and almost impossibly creative and valuable things—and at the very least, of doing infinitely more than cleaning house and picking crops.

As his fame grew after this spectacular exhibition, Carver was invited to speak all over the country, and visitors would stop at Tuskegee to meet the "wizard chemist." Because he wore rumpled, mismatched clothing and dye-splashed cornstalk ties as he wandered about outside examining plants, he was sometimes mistaken for a gardener, which bothered him not at all. His love for humble people, and his own inveterate humility, caused him to rise above these things that might have irritated or offended so many others.

But his humility was always on display, no matter the audience. "I didn't make these discoveries," he told anyone who would listen. "God has only worked through me to reveal to his children some of his wonderful providence."[56]

Strangely, to the end of his days, Carver—who had frequently gone hungry as a youth—didn't care about saving money. He repeatedly refused to allow Tuskegee to raise his salary, and rather than selling his discoveries, he gave them away for free to companies that had been willing to pay large sums for them.

He continued to act as a father figure to students, and long after they had graduated from Tuskegee, his students remembered the lessons Professor Carver had taught them. As one graduate, who had evidently experienced bigotry, wrote him: "I never retaliated one bit; I used righteousness, patience, and self-control, and won out. . . . Now, this is not my victory; it is yours; because, had you not impressed my whole life, I am sure I would have retaliated."[57]

In the 1920s awards and honors began pouring in. Great Britain elected Carver to a fellowship in the Royal Society of Arts, honoring him for his discoveries. The NAACP gave Carver the Spingarn Medal, given each year for "the highest achievement in any field of human endeavor." And Simpson College, where Carver had been a student before leaving for Ames, awarded him an honorary doctorate.

Over the forty-seven years he spent at Tuskegee, Carver had several opportunities to leave the school. For instance, Thomas Edison himself offered Carver a job that would have paid literally ten times what his salary was at Tuskegee. But Carver declined.

For many years, Carver consulted with Tom Huston, who was the founder of Tom's Peanuts, and he discovered why Virginia peanuts didn't thrive in the Deep South. Carver determined that a combination of funguses was damaging them. As a result, Huston was able to make some adjustments, and his crop yield improved dramatically. Like Edison, Huston wanted to reward Carver with a lucrative job. But again, Carver declined.

Toward the end of Carver's life, Thomas Edison, Henry Ford, John D. Rockefeller, and Franklin Roosevelt all considered George Washington Carver a friend. Theodore Roosevelt publicly praised his accomplishments. Followers of Mahatma Gandhi came to Tuskegee to visit with Carver and asked him to recommend a vegetarian diet for Gandhi, whose hunger strikes weakened him. Even the Crown Prince of Sweden came to Tuskegee, just to study with Carver.

Now in his sixties, Carver continued to travel the country, talking to government leaders, farmers, students, and teachers. And yet, despite the many honors given to Carver, he, like every other black American, still had to endure being seated in segregated train cars, as well as the infinity of other indignities of life in the Jim Crow South. But he never demanded anything, knowing there were many who suffered far more. For example, black soldiers who had served honorably—and who had even risked their lives for their country—during the First World War were often treated as second-class citizens upon their return home.

Carter generally remained quiet on such issues, but what he did each day in his laboratory spoke more powerfully than any words he might have said and demonstrated the patent absurdity of the idea that blacks were anything but the equals of whites, and they would one day be rightly legally recognized as such.

By 1930 Carver's perseverance and quiet genius had turned him into the most famous black man on the planet. Many jockeyed for an opportunity to meet him in his laboratory and shake his hand. But Carver continued doing what he had always done, teaching Tuskegee students the Bible every week and living in the same two rooms he had lived in for decades. One was a bedroom, and the other was a study for his books, art, rock samples, and various other collections. His beloved flowers blossomed in every window.

Each morning, the old man still rose before dawn to walk in the woods, searching for and gathering new specimens, after which he ate breakfast and then spent time in prayer, asking God to open his eyes as he worked. Then he would head for his laboratory. Later Carver might meet with students or visitors or respond to the many letters he received. Most evenings were spent alone, reading and sketching.

In the last years of his life, Carver traveled less, choosing instead to speak on coast-to-coast radio broadcasts, where he could reach far more people. He suffered from pernicious anemia, and other illnesses forced him to spend much of his time in the hospital. Tuskegee built a museum to honor their most famous professor, one that would hold his plants, paintings, and equipment. On July 25, 1939, some two thousand guests attended its dedication.

And yet, just six weeks later, when Carver traveled to New York to be a guest on a radio program, he was told there was no vacancy at the New Yorker hotel, even though his traveling companion, Austin Curtis, had already made reservations. Curtis refused to take "There's been a mistake" for an answer, as Carver might have done. While an exhausted Carver waited in a chair near the men's restroom, Curtis called someone at the publishing company of Doubleday, Doran and Company, which was working with a writer on a biography of the great man. When the Doubleday employee arrived at the hotel and asked for a room, he was immediately offered one, but when he turned around and offered it to Carver and Curtis, the manager once again told them there was "a mistake": there were, he claimed, no rooms available.

For six hours Carver sat in a chair in the washroom hallway until

—after a threat to sue the hotel by a senior executive at Doubleday—this living legend and friend of President Roosevelt was shown to his room.[58]

That very year, the Theodore Roosevelt Association honored Carver with a Distinguished Service Medal, given for his contributions to southern agriculture; and he was awarded honorary memberships from the American Inventors Society, the Mark Twain Society, and the National Technical Society. And to add to his old friend's comfort and convenience, Henry Ford financed an elevator in the building in which Carver lived.

As he considered the legacy he would leave, Carver in 1940 created the George Washington Carver Foundation, which he intended for the continuation of his work. He endowed it with a founding gift of $32,374.19, half his savings at that time. (At his death, Carver left the remainder of his savings—another $32,000—to the foundation. The two donations are the equivalent in today's money of more than $1 million.)

In December 1942, Carver took a final trip to visit his friend Henry Ford in Dearborn, Michigan, and then came home to Tuskegee. But just a few days later, he slipped on a patch of ice and was put on bed rest to recover. But his pain from the fall continued, and his appetite and health waned. Tuskegee's home economics teacher, Juanita Jones, brought over a number of Carver's favorite foods, hoping to get him to eat something, but even those attempts didn't succeed.

In what would be his final hours, Carver reached for the old Bible that Mariah Watkins had given him a long lifetime ago. He read from its pages for the last time, and on January 5, 1943, the man who had been born into slavery during the Civil War died in his sleep.

Condolences from fans of the "plant doctor" poured in from around the world, and many were read at his funeral, held in the campus chapel. There, long lines of grieving people came to bid farewell to the gentle scientist, artist, musician, humanitarian, and Christian pilgrim they had long admired and loved. He was buried near his old friend Booker T. Washington.

Following his death, many stories came in of things Carver had helped accomplish that he himself hadn't even known about. For example, he had saved the lives of hundreds of Africans in the Belgian Congo, simply by responding to a letter he received from a missionary there. The missionary said it was impossible to keep farm animals in central Africa because of attacks from tsetse flies and tigers, and without farm animals, there was no milk. So when new mothers were unable to nurse, their babies died. The missionary said Carver had written "with detailed information on the procedure for deriving milk from the nuts. Hundreds of infants were so saved from death, and for this we can never properly express our thanks."[59]

Today Carver's 265 uses for the humble peanut seem like little more than a novelty, but at the time this was an incalculably important gift to the poorest farmers, whose openness to Carver's ideas about crop rotation would lift innumerable thousands of them out of poverty. By giving farmers so many commercial uses for their new crops, Carver almost single-handedly broke the back of "King Cotton" once and for all.

Carver encouraged and guided generations of students, teaching them that God, their heavenly Father, created the tremendously varied plant life. He loved his neighbor, turned the other cheek, forgave those who persecuted him, prayed without ceasing, and gave God the glory in all things. He understood that "Whoever is generous to the poor lends to the LORD" (Proverbs 19:17 ESV).

This man who was born into slavery humbly lived out the words that are often attributed to Saint Francis of Assisi: "Preach the gospel at all times; if necessary, use words." When we look at the scope of Carver's life, and especially at his profound dedication to helping the poor—through his own scientific genius and through his humble efforts in visiting them personally—it is hard not to come to the conclusion that George Washington Carver was a modern-day saint, a man who put God and others first in all he said and did and who then trusted his Creator with the ultimate results.

FOUR
General William Booth

1829–1912

You cannot warm the hearts of people with God's love if they have an empty stomach and cold feet.

—WILLIAM BOOTH

I t was one of the most catastrophic storms ever to hit the United States. It was a Category 5 hurricane named Katrina that made landfall in Louisiana at the end of August 2005, causing such flooding that nearly two thousand people were killed. Hundreds of thousands were left homeless, without access to food or shelter, and the city's communication and transportation networks were rendered useless.

While politicians were busily pointing fingers at one another, thousands of volunteers quietly arrived in white trucks each bearing a red shield. The Salvation Army was about to embark on its biggest disaster response effort in its long, extraordinary history.

Men and women wearing red caps and aprons served 5.7 million hot meals at 178 canteen feeding stations and 11 field kitchens across the Gulf Coast. Other volunteers helped locate more than 25,000 survivors using a network of amateur ham-radio operators. And pastoral care counselors were on hand to meet the emotional and spiritual needs of 277,000 people.

A year later, the camera crews were gone, but the Salvation Army was still there because—they said—there was still much work to be done.

The organization had started in London 154 years earlier by a man who was recently named one of the one hundred greatest Britons of all time. His name was William Booth.

◆◆◆

William Booth was born on April 10, 1829, to Mary and Samuel Booth in Nottingham, England. Samuel was a well-to-do house builder, which meant they could afford to send their son to school, and when the time came, he went to Biddulph's School for Young Gentlemen. While in school he also helped his father in his house-building business; and every Sunday, William's mother took him and his three sisters to St. Stephen's Anglican Church.

But one day William's headmaster invited his students to attend Broad Street Chapel, a Methodist church. William was astonished at the difference between the two churches. Instead of droning on in difficult religious-sounding sentences—as his own pastor did at St. Stephen's—the Methodist minister spoke quite simply, explaining his points. And the congregation seemed engaged, chiming in with shouts of "Hallelujah!" and "Praise the Lord!" And instead of murmuring the prayers in their prayer books, this congregation prayed loudly and extemporaneously. Nor were the hymns funereal; they were lively and joyful. Could this really be church? Whatever it was, William couldn't wait to come back—and so he returned, attending Broad Street Chapel for many years.

But in the summer of 1842, William's father lost most of his money in a business deal, and to help with the family's finances, the thirteen-year-old was suddenly obliged to abandon his schooling and find work. He was soon apprenticed to a pawnbroker in the Goosegate area of the city, where he worked for the next five years, living above the shop.

The job was the boy's first experience in dealing with poor people, and it would have a tremendous impact on him and his future. Every day customers brought in items to sell—or "pawn." If they didn't come back within two weeks to pay for the item and reclaim it, it became the pawnbroker's property. And so he sold it at a substantial profit. To William, however, the business seemed built on the idea of taking advantage of others in their suffering.

William noticed that at first, people brought in the sorts of possessions they didn't need very much, such as umbrellas or certain pieces of furniture. But as these people's situations worsened, they would return with things more difficult to part with, such as dishes. Finally, in their direst straits, often unable to buy food for their families, they returned again, only to pawn the very tools of their trade, such as "the carpenter's level and saw, a bricklayer's trowel, or a butcher's knives."[1]

As he swept the floors and folded clothing, William felt pity for these people.

That fall his own family's fortunes took another brutal blow when William's father died. His mother, Mary, had little time to grieve before she was obliged to open a small shop where she and her three daughters sold small household goods, such as sewing needles, hatpins, and handkerchiefs. Meanwhile, William continued at the pawnshop.

He also continued worshiping at Broad Street Chapel and attended a Bible study class. During this time, a number of famous preachers visited the church. One was the Reverend James Caughey, an American. Another was Isaac Marsden from Yorkshire. William was inspired by their preaching and after listening would go off by himself and privately attempt his own sermons. But in his estimation, his attempts somehow fizzled. He knew there was one major difference between him and those he heard from the church pulpit. They all seemed to believe what they were saying, while he wasn't quite sure what he believed.

Then one evening, when he was fifteen, William walked into his church's Bible class just in time to hear his teacher, Henry Carey, say, "A soul dies every minute."[2] These words electrified William. Suddenly, he came face-to-face with the biggest question imaginable. If he died that day, would his soul enter heaven? And the question forced a second question: Was he going to fully commit himself to the God he had so often heard about—or keep on with his halfhearted worship?

The answer seemed to explode into his mind. From all he knew, there could be only one answer, and he wrote it in his diary soon thereafter: "God shall have all there is of William Booth."[3]

And in the classroom that day, he would take his first step. His teacher invited anyone who wanted to come forward and ask God to forgive their sins and surrender to his love. William stood and did just that. As he prayed, something deeply shameful came into his mind, something he had done a few years earlier, when he was still attending school.

A classmate and friend of his, Robert Powell, had lost a pouch containing the money his father had given him to pay for the next term. It was a devastating loss. When William happened to find the pouch, he didn't tell his friend. For some reason, he instead announced that out of his friendship with Robert he would give him the money out of his own pocket. Robert was so grateful for this extraordinary generosity—not knowing he was only getting his own money—that he gave William his cherished silver pencil case. So now, as William knelt in prayer, he promised God that he would make the situation right immediately and come clean with his old friend. And soon thereafter, he did.

As soon as he had committed his life to God, William felt his spirits lift. At the pawnshop, he frequently quoted Scripture verses to customers as a way of comforting them. And he would invite them to church with him too. Most of them declined his invitation, and he wondered: How could he possibly reach these people for God if they refused to set foot in church? There must be some way, but what?

Two years later William was trying to figure out exactly how he was meant to serve God. He didn't expect to spend his lifetime working in the pawnshop. Perhaps the Lord wanted him to become a pastor. But his impoverished mother and sisters needed his income, so he could hardly quit his job and go back to school, which would be necessary if he were to pursue a pastorate. He also knew he wasn't especially disposed to the intense study required of those working toward the degree to become a minister. So what did God want from him?

The answer would come to him one day when he was sick in bed. His friend Bill Sansom came to visit and told William that when he recovered he must join Bill and other young men from their Bible class who were going into poor neighborhoods to preach. The idea appealed to William, and two weeks later he joined them in their venture, which they called "the Mission." At first, few people were interested in their message, but they kept at it, going into the slums regularly to preach.

They eventually decided to hold actual services—"Meetings," as they called them. Being unable to find anything like a church, they held them in a widow's cottage, where they would preach and pray for people. When it was William's turn to speak, he was nervous, but finally, he "took a deep breath, picked up his Bible, and launched into the first sermon he had ever preached to an audience."[4]

William urged his audience not to become discouraged if they fell back into sinful behavior, but simply to keep trying to do what was right in God's eyes. So it wasn't a condemning message but an encouraging one, and his listeners, many of them recent converts, seemed to enjoy it considerably.

Not long after this, William's friend Bill died of consumption. It was a blow to all of them, but the other boys now turned to William to become their new leader. As the weeks passed, he grew in confidence, preaching more and more. It was during this period that he realized he had found what God wanted him to do with his life. He was to preach to the poor, not from a church pulpit but rather wherever they lived and worked. He was to take God's message to them. Among his first converts was a well-known, ill-tempered alcoholic and broom-seller who went by the name "Besom Jack." (*Besom* was the word for a broom.) Jack spent whatever he made from his trade on drink. When he was intoxicated, he often beat his wife and children.

But one day Jack heard William preach, and suddenly he saw himself through God's eyes. He dropped to his knees and shouted, "God, forgive me, for I am a terrible sinner!"[5] William went to his knees too and prayed beside Jack. The man's conversion was obviously sincere, and his neighbors were astonished to see the dramatic change in his life. In time many of them too came to hear William's preaching and knelt on the cobblestones, asking God to forgive their sins.

It wasn't long before William saw why so many of these poor souls had declined his invitations to church. They didn't have the "proper" clothing to wear to church, and because they had no regular source of water in which to bathe, they smelled. They knew they would not be welcome in the churches to which William had been inviting them. But William persisted. He knew these converts needed to be discipled, and one Sunday he finally got some of them to join him at the Methodist church.

But it was the first and last time they would do so. As these poor souls rightly suspected, the "nice" churchgoers didn't welcome these wretches who carried the stench of the docks and the slaughterhouses into church with them. William knew Jesus would have welcomed these people, but apparently these Jesus-loving Methodists didn't. How could that be? But the pastor and deacons—wanting to make sure there was no misunderstanding on this matter—immediately after the service sternly told William not to bring these "riffraff" back.

William left quite discouraged and walked the streets trying to figure out a solution. But before he did, he got news that temporarily took his mind off the poor. He learned that he had been relieved of his position at the pawnshop. His apprenticeship there was over, and his boss knew it would be far cheaper simply to hire a new apprentice rather than pay the now-experienced William a higher wage.

So William was forced to return to his mother's house and immediately looked for work. He continued to preach Sunday evenings, either at the cottage meeting or on street corners, but he knew he couldn't make his living doing this since his "congregation" consisted of the city's poorest residents. In financial desperation, William eventually moved to London and found another job with a pawnbroker. Though he disliked the job, it paid his bills, and whenever he was free, he went into the London slums to preach.

Eventually, William came to the attention of London's Methodist Church leaders, who invited him to become one of their lay preachers. Though the job paid nothing, he took it, and a year later applied to become a full-time minister. But when the church leaders realized Booth lacked interest in the usual training for preaching—learning Latin and Greek, for example—they turned him down flat.

Booth was frustrated and wrote to an old friend. "How can anybody with spiritual eyesight talk of having no call," he asked, "when there are still multitudes around them who have never heard a word about God, and never intend to, who can never hear without the sort of preacher who can force himself upon him?"[6]

In 1852, just before his twenty-third birthday, Booth preached at another Methodist church, the Walworth Road Chapel. He had no idea at the time, but preaching there would change his life because afterward a well-to-do man named Edward Rabbits, obviously taken with what he had heard, offered to support William for at least three months. That way he could leave his job and preach full time. The young man leaped at the chance and quit his position in the pawnshop.

Soon thereafter, Rabbits would change William's life equally dramatically once more. One day Rabbits bumped into William on the street and invited him to tea that very afternoon. William went and there met a number of figures who would become important to him, but none nearly so much as a certain dark-haired beauty named Catherine Mumford. At the tea, William conversed with her for a considerable time, and when it was over he escorted her back to her home.

It didn't take any time for him to think about marrying this woman. She was not only attractive; she was bright, lively, and opinionated too. In fact, she surprised her new acquaintance by voicing the radical idea— which she seemed to take from the Bible—that men and women were equal. Her father was a prosperous coach builder, and Booth—a gangly six-footer with wild black hair—couldn't help but wonder whether he would be able to convince her that he was worthy of her.

But somehow he did, and quickly too. They were engaged a mere month after first meeting. Still, they couldn't marry until Booth's prospects improved. But his prospects would improve, because already that year, the Reformed Methodists invited Booth to pastor what was called "the Spalding circuit," a collection of small Lincolnshire churches some one hundred miles north of the city. William was hardly eager to be taken so far from Catherine, but he was suddenly obliged to take the offer. This was because he had discovered a difference of theological opinion with his friend Rabbits, causing Rabbits to withdraw his support. And so William went to Lincolnshire.

But the new pastorate seemed to be God's plan because William's preaching met with immediate success. People flocked to his churches, with many being converted each week. When he spoke at "cottage" meetings, attendance often overflowed so that William was forced to take his preaching outside—always a welcome turn of events for him, as he considered the streets to be his natural preaching habitat. He and Catherine wrote each other frequently during this time, a habit they continued whenever separated throughout their lives.

It was a year and a half from arriving in Lincolnshire that William met a guest evangelist named Richard Poole, whom he invited to join him in his circuit preaching. Booth was impressed with Poole's theological learning and now determined to study theology himself. He would do so at a college associated with the New Connexion. Even with Catherine's considerable help, he found the study difficult, but persisted.

The college's principal, Dr. William Cooke, became impressed with the young man's preaching—and with the numbers of people coming to faith upon hearing it. So Cooke invited Booth to "become the superintendent of the New Connexion's London circuit."[7] Booth felt unqualified for such a position and humbly suggested becoming deputy superintendent instead. Cooke agreed.

This new position allowed Booth and Catherine, who had been engaged for three years, to marry immediately. They did so June 16, 1855, honeymooning on the Isle of Wight and afterward taking part in "a series of preaching services on the nearby island of Guernsey."[8] Soon thereafter they found out they were expecting a child. Unfortunately, Catherine's morning sickness was such that they thought it best for her to go to her parents' home, where she could stay while Booth continued his superintending duties and took part in revival meetings all over England.

During this time Booth considered a serious problem he had noticed: new converts lacking any real support after their important decision. Many subsequently fell away from their faith. At last he hit on a solution. It would work so well that—a century later—the evangelist Billy Graham would employ it, with similar success. Booth's idea was that when someone expressed interest in learning more about following Christ, he would invite them to come down to the communion rail. There deacons met them and led them to another room, where they gave their names and addresses and "paired up with someone in the congregation who promised to make sure the new convert got a Bible and came to church regularly."[9]

The following March, Catherine gave birth to their first child—of an eventual eight. They named him William Bramwell and called him Bramwell. Their second child, Ballington, was born just over a year later.

Once William had finished his two-year preaching tour, he and his family moved into their first home. Soon thereafter their first daughter—whom they named Catherine and called Kate—was born.

Booth was next assigned to minister at a church in Yorkshire and then in Gateshead (near Newcastle), where another daughter, Emma, was born in January 1860.

While Booth enjoyed his church work, his mind frequently wandered back to all the people who never set foot in churches, and he continued to wonder: How could the saving gospel message be taken to those who needed it most?

God seemed to answer this question in an unexpected way. At the end of a Sunday morning service in 1860, Catherine Booth suddenly stood up and approached the altar. "I want to say a word," she told a surprised William. But he trusted his wife's judgment in all things and happily stood aside for her. She spoke directly to the congregation: "I dare say many of you have been looking at me as a very devoted woman, but I have disobeyed God. I have made a promise to God that I will obey Him from now on, and it was His Holy Spirit who urged me to stand up and speak to you all. I, like my husband, have been called to preach the gospel from the pulpit, and I am ready to do that, even if it means that I look like a fool—at least I shall be a fool for Christ."[10]

Many were shocked at the idea of a woman preaching, not only because it wasn't done but because many believed the Bible forbade the practice. But William didn't interpret the Scripture that way, so when his wife said this, he didn't doubt what she said. He promptly announced to the astonished congregation that she would be speaking at that evening's service. Many thought this was a mistake—and told Booth so. But William disagreed. He believed that anyone who could bring the good news to listeners—even if they were listening only because a woman was doing the preaching—should do so.

Not long after this William fell ill, but Catherine felt quite capable of stepping into the pulpit to do whatever preaching was needed until he recovered. She even visited congregants during the week. And even once he recovered, they would now work as a team. But because the idea of a woman preaching was so controversial, it wasn't long before the leaders at New Connexion decided it was time to part ways with Booth, and he was dismissed from his duties.

Booth was disappointed but remained convinced he was following God's will, and so he was confident that in prayer God would show him the way forward. In the meantime, he and Catherine and the children returned to London to live with Catherine's parents. During this time William again looked for nonpastoral work to support his family, and for a time they struggled. Then one day an old friend, John Stone, asked William if he was interested in preaching regularly at his chapel in Hayle, Cornwall, warning that the pay would be little and the congregation quite elderly. Nonetheless, William accepted the position, traveling with Catherine to Cornwall and leaving the four children for long stretches with Catherine's parents.

The couple remained in Cornwall for the next eighteen months and felt God was with them in this new venture. William now proposed the idea that anyone who wished to repent of their sins—and give themselves to God—should come to the front of the sanctuary and stand at what was called the penitent rail. There they would identify themselves as sinners needing a Savior. The New Connexion leaders had disapproved of this practice, feeling it "made too much of a show over sin,"[11] but Stone was in favor of it, and the idea was adopted.

Somehow word of what was happening in that humble Cornwall chapel got out: "Each day the number of people attending the special services grew, until fishermen were rowing ten miles across rough seas to reach the chapel, while others . . . hiked over the coastal trails to get there. At every meeting a mixture of people from burly miners to little old ladies to young people stood together at the front of the chapel, weeping and asking God to forgive them for their sins."[12]

As word of their preaching spread, the Booths were asked to speak in other local churches. In one town, as a result of their preaching, over a thousand people became members of local churches; and the *Wesleyan Times* soon reported that throughout the whole of Cornwall, "7,000 souls have been awakened and saved."[13]

Despite the great success of these revival meetings, however, the Methodist leaders disapproved of their usually emotional tone, thinking it "undignified." So they ordered Methodist pastors to refuse the Booths access to their pulpits. Disappointed in this development but nonetheless more determined than ever to find a way to continue the work to which they were convinced God had called them, the Booths returned to London, where they now welcomed their fifth child, Herbert.

In January 1863, the couple traveled to Wales to preach. When they found the doors of the churches closed to them there, they decided on a way around their impasse. They rented a circus tent and advertised their meetings. At last William would get his wish of taking the good news to those who refused to go to a church. Vast numbers of just these kinds of people were quite happy to show up at the tent. Among those now attending were "drunks, pickpockets, and bookies."[14] And many of these same souls responded to the Booths' preaching.

William made another discovery now, by doing something never done before. He dared to invite former drunks—along with former poachers and former wifebeaters—to tell their stories of sin, conversion, and subsequent victory. The audiences paid especially close attention to these speakers, never having dreamed that others like them might have found a way out of their difficulties, and their responses to these speakers were beyond the ordinary.

The Booths spent the next two years preaching all over England and Wales, being helped financially by the wealthy coal merchant brothers John and Richard Cory. Still, they struggled, which meant that at times William had to go off alone to conduct revival meetings while Catherine stayed home with the children. Their sixth—named Marian—was born in 1864.

At home, Catherine was a typical Victorian mother. "Her primary goal was to bend the will of the child to the will of the parents" for the ultimate goal of preparing "the children to bend their will to the will of God when they reached an age of religious accountability."[15] But after Marian's birth—while William conducted revival meetings elsewhere— Catherine for the first time conducted revival meetings by herself, once again breaking a barrier into a realm previously closed to women.

In 1865 the family moved back to London, partly so they could be near Catherine's parents and partly because Catherine was tired of living as "God's gypsy," as she put it.[16] Catherine was also excited about having been invited—by the Southwark Circuit Free Church Methodists—to conduct an evangelistic campaign in the Rotherhithe neighborhood.

The London move was significant, leading as it did to the next stage of the Booths' ministry. During this time Booth took an eight-mile walk through London's East End. He was horrified to see that the city had deteriorated tremendously since he had last been there. It was a blighted and poverty-stricken area, quite unrelieved by any government safety net. As one biographer put it: "The row houses were dirty and dilapidated. Often as many as forty or fifty people were living in one house. They had little or no running water and used the gutter as a bathroom. And every fifth store in the area was a gin shop."[17]

A historian described the East End of that time:

> Famine stalked back streets. . . . The unemployed lived in East End warehouses. In 1867, as shipyards closed, unemployment in Poplar and Bromley was up nine thousand over the previous year. . . . As many as one hundred thousand unemployed, uneducated children became petty thieves. Girls and some boys became prostitutes. Lack of sanitation bred cholera; London's sewerage emptied into the Thames, from which inhabitants drew drinking water. In the summer epidemic of 1866, eight thousand died. . . . Smallpox was common.[18]

Perhaps most shocking of these grim sights was that of small children buying glasses of gin, drinking them, and then passing out on the street. These children became alcoholics quickly because "their tiny livers were much more affected by alcohol than those of the adults who callously introduced it to them."[19]

Because of the influence of William Wilberforce some decades earlier, there were now many charitable groups ministering in the East End. What they could do, however, was a proverbial drop in the bucket. But the members of these groups—knowing they needed help—had been praying for a powerful and effective leader. Years earlier many of these people had been impressed with Booth's open-air preaching in front of the Blind Beggar pub, as well as at the Garrick Theatre, both in Whitechapel. So the East End Revival Society now approached Booth and asked him if he would be willing to hold tent meetings in Whitechapel.

Booth knew he would speak after an assortment of other preachers who had apparently not made much of an impression on the million or so residents of the area. But he was undeterred. Rather, as he prepared for the first sermon, he grew excited at what lay before him.

His first sermon under the big tent was on Sunday, July 2, 1865. "Imagine a man going down a river in a boat," he said to the crowd, still trickling in. "He is headed for the Niagara Falls, but he does not know what is ahead of him, nor does he care. The weather is nice, the sun is shining, and he's not worried about a thing. He paddles out into the stream, and suddenly he feels the current tugging him. He is going, going . . ."

Booth leaned over, as though he were peering over the falls. "My God!" he shouted. "The boater has gone over—and he never pulled at an oar! That is the way people are damned: They go on, they have no time, they don't think—they neglect salvation—and they are lost!"[20]

Booth had the crowd's attention and told them that if they were willing to confess their sins, Jesus would save them, giving them eternal life. Listeners lined up at the penitent rail, where Booth prayed with them and explained how they should go about living their new lives for God.

At home that first evening, Booth excitedly told Catherine that he had at last discovered how God intended him to use his gifts. He was to preach not in elegant churches, where preachers often only struggled to keep the already-converted awake on Sunday mornings, but rather to the least, the last, and the lost of East London. He named his new ministry the East London Christian Mission, although they typically just called it "the Mission"—and in time it would take the name most of us know today, the Salvation Army.

Under this Whitechapel tent, William preached night after night, converting many of his neighbors even as urchins threw rocks and firecrackers into the crowd, once even setting a woman's dress on fire. But Booth didn't only preach. He also did dramatically unconventional and creative things that no other minister of the gospel had ever thought of.

For instance, he sometimes led his new converts to stand outside a nearby pub, where they would sing hymns loudly. When men emerged from the pub to see what the fuss was, they were invited to come hear William preach. This tactic proved so successful that furious pub owners paid boys to pelt Booth with rotten fruit and even to try to knock him down. But Booth wasn't about to let this stop him. Even when knocked down—and he was—he would simply get up again and resume preaching. In time, it became almost impossible "to enter a pub without first being offered a pamphlet by a worker or to leave one without an invitation to a soup kitchen or Christian tea room."[21]

The Mission also now did something never done before—something we have associated with William Booth ever since. They formed brass bands to march down the streets. When they had the attention of passersby, they announced upcoming preaching campaigns. Members also recycled popular songs with biblical lyrics, singing them at their meetings and in public, and wore sandwich boards with slightly nutty invitations on them, such as "Come Drunk or Sober." Even nuttier were some of the stunts Mission members pulled. The Booths' eldest son, Bramwell, for instance, sometimes allowed himself to be carried solemnly in a casket to St. Paul's Cathedral, where he "popped out of the coffin and preached on the text, 'O death, where is thy sting?'"[22]

When such tactics were criticized as unbecoming to the gospel, Booth retorted, "If I thought I could win one more soul to the Lord by walking on my head and playing the tambourine with my toes, I'd—I'd learn how!"[23]

Newspapers wrote about Booth's meetings, expressing admiration for his ingenuity and for what he was achieving among the desperate and destitute.

When a storm blew the Whitechapel tent down, William moved

elsewhere, preaching anywhere he could. He would preach in every place from a dance academy to a carpenter's shop, to a wool warehouse, to a stable, to a pigeon shop, and even in a skittle alley. In a place called Poplar, he even preached in a farm shed near a foul-smelling pig-sty.

By 1867 Booth found a more permanent place for his Sunday meetings—the Effingham Theatre on Whitechapel Road. "East Enders felt comfortable here because they were used to visiting it during the week for other than religious purposes."[24] And Booth soon after acquired a place of his own in which to preach and serve soup to the poor: a former tavern called the Eastern Star."[25]

William always encouraged new converts to attend local churches, but their reaction was often the same as it had been years before. They said they weren't wanted at the fine churches because they didn't have anything "proper" to wear. So they continued to attend William's meetings instead.

Eventually, Booth's work was making a tremendous impact: the Mission boasted thirteen "preaching stations" by the end of 1868, and Mission preachers were speaking to more than fourteen thousand people each week. But the work came at a cost. As the Mission was saving souls by the barrowful, the attacks eventually became more vicious, with thugs throwing not merely clods of dirt and rotten eggs but also bricks, rocks, and dead rats. As Catherine wrote of this time, William would "stumble home night after night haggard with fatigue, often his clothes were torn and bloody bandages swathed his head where a stone had struck."[26] But William wasn't deterred. After one especially nasty attack, Booth's first words to his audience expressed forgiveness for his attackers.

Among the gangs that organized violence against Salvationists were the Skeleton Army and the Unconverted Salvation Army. Some were simply hooligans; others took their orders from the brewers and pub owners whose products the Salvationists were trying to get Londoners to give up. Still others feared that the Booths were teaching the poor to rise up against the upper classes who were, apparently, content for the poor to remain hungry, ragged, and homeless. And some simply disliked the Mission workers because they were different—possibly crazy—with their brass bands and their singing and marching down the streets.

The worst assaults occurred in 1882. An explosion of mob violence resulted in the beating of 669 Salvation Army officers,[27] and sixty of their buildings were torn down. During these episodes, one of Booth's earliest converts—Susannah Beaty—was struck in the head by a thrown rock. When she fell to the ground, she was viciously kicked in the stomach and died.

Police and magistrates tended to ignore these attacks and sometimes actually assisted the mobs in their destructive actions. The Salvationists never retaliated, but Booth knew he must do something and applied pressure on higher-ups, including Prime Minister Gladstone. At last the police cracked down on the thugs. Booth also happened to convert a burly boxer, who began accompanying him in the East End and usually scared off any troublemakers.

Equally disturbing were the verbal attacks by other Christians. William and Catherine were convinced that if these critics took a closer look at what the Booths were doing, and realized how badly the poor had been neglected by established churches, they would welcome their work. Of course, as was ever the case, jealousy of the Booths' success was often at the root of some of these attacks.

◆ ◆ ◆

Both William and Catherine suffered from various illnesses during these years, including, for William, nervous exhaustion and depression. When he was ill, Catherine preached on his behalf and also kept the books for the Mission.

The Mission continued to grow in 1869, and its workers—there were now sixty William could depend on—found their way to the most derelict parts of London. New converts were immediately put to work, helping with services and other activities. That Christmas, the Booth family made 150 plum puddings and delivered them to the poor. Even today, a hundred fifty years later, the Salvation Army continues to make holiday puddings, selling them to provide the less fortunate with meals.

William and Catherine brought in additional income by selling a songbook William had put together and a pamphlet Catherine wrote titled *Female Ministry; or, Woman's Right to Preach the Gospel.* They also took in lodgers.

At home, the children were encouraged to keep animals as pets. As one biographer put it, "Caring for animals, moreover, was training in that thoughtfulness for others which is the very essence of Salvationist principles."[28] When he was at home, William enjoyed playing with his children. Booth child number seven, Evelyne,[29] was born in 1865 on Christmas Day, and their eighth and last child, Lucy, came along in 1868.

With everything else she was doing, Catherine somehow also managed to homeschool her children and encouraged them in outdoor games such as tennis and cricket. When Catherine wasn't busy with the children, she preached to the wealthy in London's West End, bringing in income the family badly needed, since East Enders obviously couldn't afford to pay for William's preaching. Over time, some notable figures saw the tremendous effects of what the Booths were doing. Among the most prominent was Samuel Morley, a wealthy member of Parliament who supported the Booths' work until his death.

The poor continued to be converted in large numbers, thanks to William's inspired preaching. As one biographer noted, "The spirit of The Christian Mission was a reflection of the character of William Booth himself." That spirit "preached the most arresting form of the Christian Gospel, but prescribed an extreme tenderness with the broken-hearted. It denounced sin with an energy that was almost violent, but sought the sinner with a loving-kindness that was entirely beautiful."[30]

By 1870 the number of "preaching stations" had jumped to fifty-seven. The Booth children were put to work rather early in life, leading meetings, preaching, giving testimonies, and visiting the poor.

The Booths eventually tamped down on religious emotionalism, preferring instead to judge whether someone's conversion was genuine by their subsequent actions. William urged people to "go and do something," believing that "true godliness is practical benevolence." As for his fellow preachers, he wanted them to preach simply, not allowing themselves to become overly theological. Their message must be understood by the simplest people, with the goal being to "convert the sinner, raise up the saint, and put the saint to work."[31]

Thanks to Catherine's influence, increasing numbers of women were now preaching too—or "Hallelujah Lassies," as they were sometimes called.

The Booth ministry spread beyond the East End to Edinburgh and Croydon, and in 1870 the Mission took a dramatic step forward, opening a building in London capable of seating fifteen hundred.

The Booths believed the greatest good they could do for the poor was to point them toward Christ. But they realized "it was not enough to preach the gospel to the poor . . . that preaching had to be complemented by taking care of the physical needs of the poor."[32] There were other groups that did this, but the needs were tremendous, and the Booths felt they needed to be part of helping in this way.

As William put it, "What is the use of preaching the Gospel to men whose whole attention is concentrated upon a mad, desperate struggle to keep themselves alive?"[33]

They needed Christ, that was certain—but they also needed blankets and boots and food for their bellies.

William opened Food for the Millions shops in 1870, which offered healthy, low-cost meals for the poor, ultimately placing the ministry in the hands of his eldest son, Bramwell, who began administering it when he was just fourteen.

When William spotted homeless men trying to sleep under a bridge one freezing night, he immediately ordered Bramwell to rent a warehouse, find a way to warm it up, and give the men blankets.

They also sold inexpensive meals from shops down by the West India Dock. Each shop "had a long dormitory attached to it where for four-pence a man could get hot water, soap, and a towel, as well as a good night's sleep in a warm hall."[34]

In an effort to lift converts out of poverty, Booth's Mission offered reading and writing classes and made efforts to get alcoholics to stop drinking.

In 1878, thirteen years after the Mission was founded, something happened that would profoundly alter how the organization was known—and how it saw itself. Booth was dictating a letter when his son Bramwell—then twenty-two—overheard his father refer to the Mission as "a volunteer army."

Bramwell instantly retorted, "Volunteer! I'm no volunteer! I'm a regular!"

William saw the point and instructed his assistant to cross out the word *volunteer* and substitute the word *salvation* instead. The line thus read, "The Christian Mission is a Salvation Army."

The idea and the phrase caught on, bringing a renewed zeal to things. *Salvation Army.* It simply and clearly communicated the ideas behind the organization. So the name was officially changed, and the organization has been known as the Salvation Army ever since.

Nearly everything soon changed to fall in line with this new concept. Their magazine was called *Salvationist*, and in it they explained the centrality of the idea behind the first word of their newly named organization: "We are a salvation people," it said. "This is our specialty—getting saved and keeping saved, and then getting somebody else saved, and then getting saved ourselves more and more until full salvation on earth makes the heaven within, which is finally perfected by the full salvation without, on the other side of the river."[35]

Because they now called themselves "the Army," they explicitly imported a military structure and flavor to things, with rules and regulations. They designed their own flag and songs and required all office holders to refrain from alcohol. William was soon known as

"General Booth," and other leaders were referred to as officers, while laypeople who worked with them were "soldiers." In keeping with the theme, uniforms were created, for both men and women; the women's bonnets, though not quite helmets, were nonetheless designed to be sturdy enough to provide some protection when mobs threw garbage at them.

Salvation Army "cadets" were put through a Bible training program —one that didn't require them to learn subjects such as Latin and Greek, which Booth considered unnecessary to their central work. After all, East End street preachers were usually recent converts who were decidedly uneducated. When some fussy religious leaders caviled about this, Booth explained, "We try to train the mind so that it is a little ahead in intelligence and information of the people to whom they minister. This means we teach cadets who need it reading, writing, and arithmetic and the basics of history and geography."[36]

And he added, in typical blunt, Booth style: "Most Christians would like to send their recruits to Bible college for five years. I would like to send them to hell for five minutes! That would do more than anything else to prepare them for a lifetime of compassionate ministry."[37]

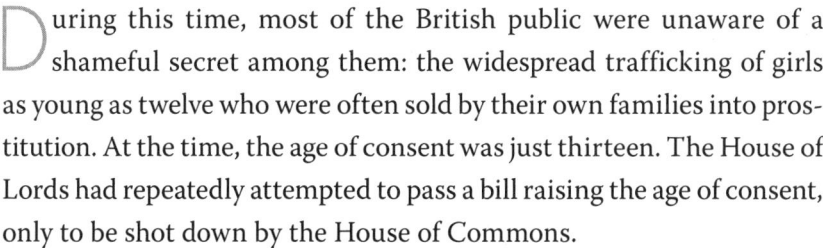

During this time, most of the British public were unaware of a shameful secret among them: the widespread trafficking of girls as young as twelve who were often sold by their own families into prostitution. At the time, the age of consent was just thirteen. The House of Lords had repeatedly attempted to pass a bill raising the age of consent, only to be shot down by the House of Commons.

Members of the Salvation Army who encountered these distressed young girls were outraged at what the British government seemed to tolerate. And they were determined to do something about it. One Army worker named Elizabeth Cottrill encountered some of these girls at Salvationist revival meetings and knew she could never send these sweet young people back to their brothels, or allow them to be trafficked across the Channel to the Continent. So beginning in 1881, Cottrill took these girls into her own home. One day Bramwell encountered a young woman asleep on the steps of the Army's international headquarters in London—she had managed to escape from her brothel—and he too became dedicated to this cause.

Bramwell, who was now married, joined his wife, Florence, in investigating what was called the "white slave trade," and the couple discovered, to their utter horror, that thousands of young girls were caught up in it. Some had been tricked into prostitution, believing they were applying for decent jobs. Even more horrific, some had been drugged and shipped to cities all over Europe inside coffins with air holes. As for those who somehow managed to escape from London brothels, Bramwell and Florence opened the first home for them in 1884.

As a result of the Army's leadership in fighting human trafficking, other religious and social leaders joined them to fight this evil head-on, working together in what became known as the Purity Crusade of 1885. Members enlisted the help of a journalist friend of the Booths, William Thomas Stead, who came up with a daring and brilliant plan to bring attention to this issue.

In what is likely the earliest case of activist, participatory journalism, Stead suggested that he and some other fighting trafficking purchase a child and then sell her to "demonstrate that it was indeed possible to procure a twelve-year-old girl from her parents for the purpose of prostitution in England."[38] Of course they created safeguards so that the child would never be in any real danger, and soon the plan was set into motion.

A former prostitute and procurer named Rebecca Jarrett purchased a child named Eliza Armstrong from her mother. The girl was taken to a brothel, where Stead had rented a room, and a female Salvation Army officer—posing as a "fallen" woman desiring to work at the brothel—subsequently removed Eliza from the premises, after which she was spirited to safety in France.

But now Stead went to work in earnest, writing an explosive series of ten articles on what had happened for *The Pall Mall Gazette.* All England was shocked and horrified, from Queen Victoria on down. The City of London, in an effort to protect prominent men who were involved in this vile trade—including members of Parliament—fought to suppress the stories, declared the articles indecent, and even arrested a dozen paperboys for selling the newspapers. In response to this outrage, London playwright George Bernard Shaw grabbed an armload of the papers and sold them himself. Incredibly, the circulation of the *Gazette* exploded from twelve thousand readers to over one million, and Stead's stories were carried to America and Europe as well.

The British public, now rightfully up in arms at what was being winked at by their own government, demanded that something be done. Catherine Booth herself wrote letters to the Queen and to Prime Minister Gladstone regarding an age-of-consent bill about to be introduced in the House of Commons. The Dowager Duchess of Roxburgh responded on Victoria's behalf, saying that "Her Majesty, fully sympathizing with Mrs. Booth on the painful subject to which it refers, has already had communication thereon with a lady closely connected with the Government, to whom Mrs. Booth's letter will be immediately forwarded."[39]

The Salvation Army also collected nearly four hundred thousand signatures on a petition demanding that Parliament pass a bill raising the age of consent to eighteen and prosecuting those who procured young girls for immoral purposes. On August 14, 1885, the Criminal Law Amendment Act was passed, raising the age of consent to sixteen years, a great improvement from what had previously existed. Afterward, "a thanksgiving meeting was held in the Exeter Hall," where "thousands of Salvationists and other citizens throughout England rejoiced over what many perceived to be a grand moral victory."[40]

Ironically, members of the government—mortified over the exposure of their foul deeds—now viciously prosecuted Stead for the "crime" of abducting a child. They found a man to pose as Eliza's father, who claimed he had not been informed that his "daughter" was to be sold.

Bramwell Booth was also charged in the crime. He was acquitted, but Stead was forced to serve a three-month prison term, something he did proudly and defiantly. For her role in this heroic affair, Rebecca Jarrett was sentenced to six months and sadly died in prison during that time.

The Salvationists next took on the match-making industry, in which four thousand Londoners—mostly women and children—labored sixteen hours a day to make matches under what we now call "Dickensian" conditions, inasmuch as it was Dickens's writing that first drew widespread attention to these practices. The hours and working conditions alone were bad enough, but there was more to be outraged over: factory owners kept costs down by rejecting "red phosphorous match heads in favor of the cheaper yellow phosphorous."[41] The problem was that "the red chemicals were harmless, and the yellow ones, deadly," leading to phosphorous poisoning, necrosis of the jaw-bone, and a painful, lingering death.[42]

Booth's response to this diabolical greed was to open his own clean, well-lit match factory in 1891, where 120 people made "Lights in Darkest England" matches—with red phosphorous, of course. Booth paid his workers considerably more than other match factories, and they even were allowed tea breaks. "Within a year, the factory was turning out more than a million boxes of matches."[43]

The Salvation Army match factory had effects far beyond putting a few dozen poor people to work in safe conditions. Politicians and journalists visited the factory, and "as they did so, seeds were planted that would eventually lead to laws governing conditions in the workplace."[44]

As the years passed, the Salvation Army spread beyond England to other countries, with branches forming in Canada, the United States, Australia, India, South Africa, and many European nations. William and Catherine's many children grew up and married and had children of their own; and rather impressively all of them and their spouses were active in Salvation Army work. As if this weren't enough, the Booth sons-in-law proudly took the Booth name, hyphenating it with their own.

William spent increasing time traveling to other countries to oversee the Salvation Army's work. In 1888, after returning home from one of these trips, he discovered that Catherine was ill, and a specialist soon confirmed she had breast cancer.

"I was stunned," William later wrote. "I felt as if the whole world was coming to a standstill. . . . I could say nothing. I could only kneel with her and try to pray."[45]

But at Catherine's insistence, William continued to work. Catherine's health continued to fail, and on October 4, 1890, she was—as they say—"promoted to glory." She "lay in state in the Army's Clapton Congress Hall," and her fame had become such that "an estimated fifty thousand people filed past her coffin."[46]

"And now I am restarted on the same path, the same work," William wrote ten days later. "A large part of my company has gone before, and I must travel the journey, in a sense that only those can understand who have been through it, alone."[47]

That same month, with the help of journalist William Stead, Booth published a hugely popular book titled *In Darkest England and the Way Out*, an exposé of England's social problems and how they could be solved. His suggested "schemes" were intended to help the poorest 10 percent of the population, people "whose lives were enslaved by poverty, vice, prostitution, and any number of circumstances that kept these people from the security of work, income, home, family, or safety."[48]

For example, Booth suggested, destitute city dwellers could be taken to farms to learn agricultural skills. One of those educational working farms, Hadleigh Farm in Essex, England, is still in operation today, still owned by the Salvation Army. Other people were taught to sew clothing or learned to make such things as shaving mugs and tea caddies.

Impressed with Booth's success, other countries began similar programs, donating buildings to the Salvation Army on the condition that they "house the unemployed and create work for them."[49]

In 1883 in Melbourne, Australia, the Army opened a halfway house for freed prisoners; and in 1886 in Toronto, Canada, it "opened the first institution to give attention to alcoholic women."[50] In 1897 a day-care center opened its doors in one of the "slum posts" of London so that working mothers had a safe place to leave their children. Shelters were opened up for men and women alike. In India, a medical clinic was organized in 1903. By 1891 ten thousand Salvation Army officers served in twenty-six countries.

By 1890 the Army's social programs operated under what became known as the Social Reform Wing of the Salvation Army, but Booth never took his eye off what he considered his ultimate goal: "I must assert in the most unqualified way that it is primarily and mainly for the sake of saving the soul that that I seek the salvation of the body," he wrote. "It will be a very small reward for all your toils if, after bringing them into condition of well-being here, they perish hereafter."[51]

◆ ◆ ◆

After Catherine's death, as he entered his sixties, William Booth returned to his first love—evangelism. He handed over the daily operation of the organization he and his wife had created to his eldest, Bramwell, but continued to keep a close eye on Army activities.

Catherine's death meant that her mediating influence between the rather autocratic William and his children was now gone. Bramwell too now increasingly came across as autocratic in they way he treated his siblings, creating bitter resentment. It was one thing to take orders from their father and quite another to take them from their brother. Unfortunately, this tension soon led to conflicts that were "destructive both to the life of the family and to the mission of the Army."[52]

Things came to a head in 1895 when Bramwell quite imperiously decided to reassign several of his siblings to postings in other countries, having consulted no one in doing this. Herbert, then serving in Canada, was ordered to Australia; sister Kate and her husband were ordered to leave France, where they had served for ten years, to take over the Army in Holland; while Lucy and her husband were told to leave India to take over the work in France. Second son Ballington and his wife, Maud, were ordered to leave America to "trade posts with Emma and Frederick Booth-Tucker, who were serving as joint foreign secretaries of the Salvation Army."[53]

Not surprisingly, the siblings were furious at Bramwell's high-handed decisions, which also seemed to make no sense. So they sent telegrams to their father—then in India—expressing their feelings in no uncertain terms. But sadly, William didn't mediate between Bramwell and his siblings but simply agreed with Bramwell, feeling that obedience to authority overrode every other consideration.

"The Salvation Army does not belong to the Booth family," he wrote. "It belongs to the Salvation Army. So long as the Booth family are good Salvationists and worthy of commands, they shall have them, but only if they are. I am not the 'General' of a family, I am the General of the Salvation Army."[54]

The result was that Ballington and Maud Booth resigned from the Army, taking with them a full third of the Army's officers in America, and formed an American counterpart to the Salvation Army, called the Volunteer Army, which was run along more democratic lines.

William was deeply angered by this split and saw his son and daughter-in-law as traitors. Then in January 1902, Kate and her husband also announced their resignations; and a few months later, Herbert and Cornelie Booth did the same. Their father bitterly regarded them all as traitors to the cause.

More unhappiness came to William when, in 1903, daughter Emma was killed in a train crash, leaving behind a husband and six children.

But along with these great sorrows and disappointments now came honors to an old man whom England recognized as one of its greatest sons. When traveling in America, Booth received an honorary doctorate of civil laws from President William McKinley. And in 1904 King Edward VII invited Booth to Buckingham Palace, where he commended Booth for the impact the Salvation Army had in the lives of so many.

The General was quick to take advantage of modern technology—including a brand-new invention called an automobile—that allowed him to visit many towns far from the railway lines. In 1904, when he was seventy-five years old, Booth set out in a six-car motorcade, with his signature long white beard flapping in the wind. He covered 1,224 miles in a single month and spoke at a staggering 164 meetings in factories or outside village shops. The old man was still able to preach electrifying sermons; and at one factory, seven hundred converts knelt and prayed.

The following year, Booth traveled to visit Salvation Army missions in Australia and New Zealand, visiting the Holy Land along the way. That fall, London's city fathers conferred on William a tremendous honor, called "The Freedom of the City of London," as well as a cash award of one hundred guineas. And William's birthplace—the city of Nottingham—also awarded him a "Freedom of the City" honor.

In 1907 Booth visited his daughter Eva (Evelyne)—now Commander Eva—in America and learned of the great work the Army had done after the San Francisco earthquake, helping thousands of people who had lost everything.

Returning to England, Booth embarked on further motor tours. But he was forced to cut one of them short to see an eye specialist, who diagnosed Booth with cataracts and proposed surgery. Booth agreed to the surgery, but it left him blind in one eye. Still, William refused to rest, and in 1909 he visited King Gustav V of Sweden and King Haakon VII of Norway.

When Booth's vision deteriorated further, Salvation Army staffers would read documents aloud to him so that the General could know what his far-flung troops were up to. He was delighted to hear from the indefatigable Eva in New York, who had inherited her father's flair for drama. She had declared Thanksgiving Day 1910 "Boozers' Day," with the intention of helping fellow New Yorkers understand the seriousness of alcoholism. Since no public buses ran on the holiday, Eva rented "the green double-decker buses that normally drove up and down

Fifth Avenue. Members of the Salvation Army manned the buses."
They followed a man dragging a huge papier-mâché whiskey bottle
while "girls banged tambourines and men blew tubas."[55]

Whenever they came to a bar, "Salvation Army officers would
leap from the buses to 'invade' the drinking establishment, where they
begged, pleaded with, and cajoled drunks to board the buses and the
wagon and go to the Army's memorial hall with them."[56] Twelve hundred drunks took them up on the offer, and once at the Salvation Army
hall, they were served strong coffee and doughnuts. After they sobered
up, they were invited to turn their lives over to the God who could help
them overcome their addictions. That day two hundred men accepted
the offer, with some of them "destined to rank among the Salvation
Army's best soldiers."[57]

By 1912 eighty-two-year-old Booth needed another eye operation.
Before entering the hospital, he spoke to seven thousand of his officers
at the Albert Hall in London. It was the last sermon he would preach.

"When women weep as they do now, I'll fight," he said. "While little
children go hungry as they do now, I'll fight; while men go to prison,
in and out, in and out, I'll fight; while there yet remains one dark soul
without the light of God, I'll fight—I'll fight to the very end!"[58]

The surgery didn't succeed in restoring Booth's sight, and he
became totally blind. Not long after this—in April 1912—he received
further bad news. His brave journalist friend, William Stead, along with
several Salvation officers, had lost his life in the sinking of the *Titanic*.

Booth's health began to fail seriously, and by mid-August he was
"drifting in and out of consciousness, barely aware of what was going
on around him."[59] On the evening of August 20, 1912, in the company of
three of his children and several Salvation Army officers and soldiers,
William Booth, age eighty-three, was himself "promoted to glory."

At midnight William's coffin was taken by car to Clapton Congress
Hall. News of his death had spread throughout the city, and members
of the press followed the hearse. As the vehicle passed each city police
station, "detectives, inspectors, and constables stood bareheaded in a

silent tribute to the general who had commanded a worldwide army" for forty-seven years.[60]

The next morning, Londoners saw a banner hanging in the window of the Salvation Army, reading, "The General Has Laid Down His Sword." Over a three-day period, some 150,000 Britons filed past his casket, grieving the man who had devoted his life to the poorest among them; and heads of state, including King George V and President William Taft, sent wreaths and messages of sympathy.

"Only in the future," King George wrote to Bramwell Booth, "shall we realize the good wrought by him for his fellow creatures. Today there is universal mourning for him. I join in it."[61]

Booth's funeral took place on August 27 at Olympia Hall, where "only the first forty thousand people could be seated."[62] Ten thousand Salvation Army members, proudly wearing their blue uniforms, along with forty bands, accompanied the hearse after the service. William was buried next to his beloved wife, Catherine, at Abney Park Cemetery.

General Booth's efforts live on and continue to expand in what must be described as a truly staggering legacy. Today there are 2,739,191 soldiers, band members, singers, and Sunday school members in 130 countries. They run 2,735 community development programs, 495 hostels for the homeless, 214 residential addiction dependency programs, 232 children's homes, 160 homes for the elderly, 43 mother and baby homes, 114 refugee centers, 661 daycare centers, 77 disaster rehabilitation schemes, 59 hospitals, services to the armed forces and to prison inmates, and many, many more programs, all the way from Australia to Zimbabwe.

As did the first Salvationists, these modern soldiers fight the sale of human beings around the world. And like William and Catherine Booth, they don't hesitate to reach out to those in power and influence for help, including recently meeting privately with another William and Catherine, the Duke and Duchess of Cambridge, to discuss ways to combat human trafficking.

Salvation Army officers, soldiers, and volunteers are so good at what they do that within thirty minutes of the reports of the first plane hitting the World Trade Center on September 11, 2001, the Salvation Army was there—the first relief agency to arrive at Ground Zero. It stayed for nine months, with thirty-nine thousand officers and volunteers "providing pastoral support and refreshments to those involved in rescue and recovery efforts." They were also involved in "the larger rebuilding projects until 2006."[63]

Jesus told us to love our neighbors, to visit those in prison, to help the widow and the orphan, to feed the hungry, and to clothe the naked. William Booth not only did these things, he exhorted millions of others to do the same, and his question to them he asks us too: "Will you go to His feet and place yourself entirely at His disposal?"

FIVE

Sergeant Alvin York

1887–1964

I'm a-telling you the hand of God must have been in that fight. No other power under heaven could save a man in a place like that. Men were killed on both sides of me and all around me and I was the biggest and the most exposed of all. Without the help of God I jes couldn't have done it.

—SERGEANT ALVIN YORK

I f you were to try to come up with the ideal background for creating the perfect Great War soldier, you could scarcely do better than having him grow up in the Cumberland Valley in Tennessee; and as it happened, that's where Alvin York was born in 1887.

He was the third child of William and Mary York and was raised along with his ten brothers and sisters in a one-room log cabin on the family's seventy-five-acre farm, not far from Pall Mall. Alvin wasn't quite born with a gun in his hand, but he was shooting at an extraordinarily young age—when he was "knee high to a duck," as York himself would put it.[1] There was nothing Alvin loved more than going on hunting trips with his father and bagging foxes, raccoons, turkeys, wild hogs, possums, squirrels, and even skunks—all of which landed on the York dinner table or were turned into pelts the Yorks would sell.

As he grew, Alvin followed in his father's footsteps by becoming an expert with both rifles and pistols and like his father was known for his marksmanship, often winning turkey shoots. It was said he could shoot with either hand while riding his mule and hit a target from a great distance.

Life was difficult but happy for the hardworking York family. From an early age, Alvin helped his mother by caring for the younger children and bringing in water and kindling for the stove. The family raised chickens and hogs and grew corn, and before he was six, Alvin was helping chop weeds out of the cornfield and taking care of their animals. When Alvin's father wasn't hunting, he worked as a blacksmith, which Alvin later helped him with. York's heroes were Daniel Boone, Davy Crockett, and Jesse James, all of whom were celebrated marksmen.

On Sundays the York family attended church meetings, which often lasted all day, and now and then itinerant circuit preachers rode into the mountains on horseback to conduct revival meetings.

Though it's not a surprise given where and how he grew up, Alvin didn't receive much of an education. The local school was open only two and a half months each year during the summer, and even during that time, it was closed for two to three weeks so children could help their parents bring in the crops. York later estimated that he actually attended school about three weeks a year for five years—enough for him to learn how to read and write, but little else. All his life, York regretted his lack of education. But a skill he learned outside of school—how to creep through woods unseen and unheard—would one day come in handy on a foreign battle field.

In 1911 tragedy struck the family when Alvin's father died of typhoid fever. Distraught, Alvin fell apart. Drunk on moonshine whiskey, he once got into a knife fight over a girl.

York's mother watched and worried, her heart aching for her son as he bounced in and out of jail. But no matter how drunk he was or how much he'd gambled away, she never stopped believing in him. Mother York never let Alvin forget his father's good example—of how he never drank, cussed, or gambled. She prayed for her son and reminded him of the parable Jesus told about a shepherd leaving his flock to go after the one sheep that had wandered off.

Gradually, York's heart softened. He began to realize he was wasting his life. He knew he would likely die young if he didn't change his ways. He started praying as he walked the mountain paths, and he thought and struggled, knowing how difficult it would be to give up his many bad habits.

As York was thinking and praying, an Indiana preacher, Rev. Melvin Russell, visited the valley and held revival meetings at the Wolf River Church. A huge crowd attended the services each night, with many conversions taking place.

On January 1, 1915, at the age of twenty-eight, Alvin was in church listening closely to Rev. Russell's message based on Romans 6:23: "The wages of sin is death, but the gift of God is eternal life in Jesus Christ our Lord."

It was just the inspiration York needed.

When Rev. Russell gave the invitation, York approached the "mourners' bench," where Russell led York in prayer and welcomed him into the body of Christ.

And there, York noted, "I felt that great power which the Bible talks about and which all sinners feel, when they have found salvation."[2]

His mother was overjoyed.

The change in York was instant and remarkable. He instantly gave up tobacco, drinking, gambling, cursing, and brawling. And York never backslid, even later on when he was in the army, where his fellow soldiers urged him to join them in drinking and carousing. York now joined the church and led the singing and helped with Sunday school classes.

And York faithfully read his Bible. He believed firmly in what the Scriptures taught, including the sixth commandment: "Thou shalt not kill."

There was another big change on the horizon: some time before his conversion, York had noticed that a dark-haired, blue-eyed girl he'd known all his life, Gracie Williams, had grown up. He had sought her out while he was hunting squirrels, accidentally on purpose meeting Gracie when she was bringing in the cows on her family's farm. But Gracie's father took a dim view of allowing a well-known heathen such as York to associate with his daughter and refused to allow him to court her. And although she liked Alvin, Gracie never would have considered marrying an unbeliever.

After York's conversion, however, this impasse was removed, and two and a half years later, the two were engaged.

◆ ◆ ◆

Winston Churchill once remarked that looking back on his life experiences, he realized that everything that happened to him seemed a preparation for leading England to victory in the Second World War. The same might be said of Alvin York regarding the First World War. Growing up, he'd been taught to work hard and had become an excellent shot. And now he was a firm believer in God's leading in his life. He gained experience resisting temptation, even as his friends urged him to return to his old lifestyle, and learned how to deal with mockery by his peers.

In April 1917, the United States declared war on Germany and Uncle Sam joined the Great War. Up until this time, York had been indifferent to the fighting in Europe, believing it had nothing to do with own life in the Tennessee mountains. But shortly after the United States entered the war, York received a card in the mail instructing him to register for the draft.

He suddenly faced a serious dilemma: How could he reconcile his belief that people were not to kill one another with the attitude of his government that he should do so—and must? He felt compelled to respond but couldn't reconcile the dilemma.

Seeking answers, York spent much time in prayer and consulted a man he deeply trusted: his minister, Pastor Rosier Pile. Go ahead and register for the draft, Pile advised, but request an exemption as a conscientious objector. This York did, writing simply and bluntly, "Don't Want to Fight."

Not surprisingly, perhaps, York's exemption was refused, and he was ordered to report for a physical exam. He obeyed this order as well, but he filed for an exemption a second time—this time with Pastor Pile's help—explaining that he was a member of a well-recognized sect, or organization, that forbade war.

The draft board turned him down a second time for two reasons: first, the board didn't consider the church York belonged to—the Church of Christ in Christian Union—a well-recognized sect. Second, the board pointed out that the church's only creed was the Bible, which members interpreted themselves.

Deeply troubled, York walked the mountains night after night, praying that he would not be called up and that God would intervene in the hearts of the draft board members. He also prayed for a clear answer from God regarding what he should do.

Adding to York's inner turmoil was the knowledge that several of his ancestors had proudly fought in wars and that he himself had been brought up to believe in serving his country.

York again talked the matter over with Pastor Pile and prayed with him. But York couldn't get past what the Bible said in the Ten Commandments, "Thou shalt not kill." So he appealed the decision of the county draft board to the State of Tennessee draft board. The appeal was denied. So was a fourth appeal for exemption. York was ordered to be ready to be called up on very short notice.

Now all York could do was pray he would not be called up. But on November 14, 1917, a card arrived telling York to report to the local draft board in Jamestown, Tennessee. He briefly considered hiding in the mountains but decided against it. Pastor Pile offered him comfort, telling York that if he remained faithful to God's Word, he need not worry about the future.

The next day, York began the long journey to Camp Gordon in Atlanta, where he was assigned to the 157th Depot Brigade. Here he encountered, for the first time, people of different ethnic groups and religious beliefs: Slavs and Italians, Greeks and Jews, Poles and Armenians and Irishmen.

Despite his heavy heart, York obeyed every order and never complained. The homesick Tennessean kept his antiwar views to himself but had to endure hearing other soldiers brag about how many Germans they were going to kill, while others didn't brag at all because they were immigrants who couldn't yet speak English.

York's feelings of alienation were lifted somewhat when he discovered that Camp Gordon offered a number of Bible studies. He took part in them, happy to meet and mix with fellow Christians. And he met a man who would become his best friend in the army: Private Murray Savage.

York kept a record of his army life and thoughts in a small red notebook. As he drilled and marched and learned everything from how to salute to how to wear a gas mask, York knew his training with bayonets and rifles was intended to teach him how to kill other human beings in the most effective manner. If, after his basic training, York was assigned to a noncombat unit—for example, one involving clerical work—his problem would be solved.

But after finishing three months of basic training, on February 9, 1918, York was assigned to the 328th Infantry Regiment, 82nd Division, which was also located at Camp Gordon. It was a fighting division, one that would be sent to France as soon as the soldiers finished training.

He knew that unless something changed he would have to kill.

As he continued to train, York kept praying for the right moment to approach his superiors and explain his beliefs about killing. Meanwhile, the army was discovering just how good a soldier it had in Private Alvin York.

The ability to shoot well was highly valued in the soldiers of the First World War. Out on the rifle range, the tall, gangly, red-haired

Tennessean proved to be the best shot in his battalion. Impressed, his officers invited him to teach his entire platoon how to hit their targets.

They badly needed training. York was amused as many obviously hadn't used guns before.

York was wise to put off telling his officers about his religious beliefs until after he had impressed them with his cooperation, good character, and excellent shooting. He also knew by now that many of them were, like he was, devout Christians. One day he approached his company commander, Captain E. C. B. Danforth, and explained his beliefs to him.

"I told him I belonged to a church that was opposed to war and . . . I knowed I was in the army and would have to obey. I would continue to be a soldier if I had to. I would go overseas. I would go in the front-line trenches. I would even kill Germans if I was ordered to. But I told him I wanted him to know I didn't believe in killing nohow, and that it worried me a-plenty."[3]

Danforth knew there were a number of phony "conscientious objectors" at Camp Gordon who simply didn't want to serve in the army. But he believed York was sincere. He told York he would think about it and see what he could do.

Danforth spoke to the battalion commander, Major G. Edward Buxton, who, like Danforth, was a Christian. A few days later, Danforth brought York to Major Buxton's quarters for what would be one of the most important conversations of York's life. York prayed for guidance beforehand and brought his Bible with him. Buxton invited York to sit down and told him he wanted to discuss York's concerns not as a battalion commander to an officer and a private but as an ordinary citizen who cared about the same things.

Why, Buxton asked, did York object to going to war? York explained that he belonged to a church that taught that fighting and killing were wrong. Buxton asked him what the creed of the church was. York said the only creed was the Bible—the inspired Word of God and the final authority for all people.

Buxton asked what York found in the Bible that was against war. York said, 'Thou shalt not kill.' Buxton considered a moment and then asked if York believed everything in the Bible as fully as that commandment. York said yes, he did.

Buxton quoted other passages in the Bible illustrating his point that under certain conditions, a Christian could fight and kill in a war without offending God. He mentioned Luke 22:36: "He that hath no sword, let him sell his cloak and buy one." In response, York reminded him that Christ also said, "If a man smite you on one cheek, turn the other to him" (Luke 6:29).

Yes, Jesus did say that, Buxton acknowledged, but he asked York if he believed that "the Christ who drove the money changers from the temple with the whip" would do nothing to help the Belgians from being "driven from their homes."[4]

Buxton also discussed Luke 20:25, in which Jesus says, "Render therefore unto Caesar the things which are Caesar's and unto God the things that are God's," and introduced York to Augustine's just war theory. Buxton "drew parallels between the German aggression, its atrocities against Belgium, and the obligations of government to protect the liberties and freedoms of people."[5]

For an hour the men went back and forth, without anger and without raising their voices. They considered many references, and to each passage opposing war, Major Buxton responded with passages that argued for justice. "I believe the Lord was in that room," York wrote. "That-there Major Buxton knowed his Bible right smart."[6] What Buxton does not seem to have said, which might have made things simpler, is that "Thou shalt not kill" is better translated "Thou shalt not murder," since the Bible is full of places where killing is indeed justified, while out-and-out murder is not. In any event, even without making this simplest of points, Buxton seems to have gotten his point across.

York was now more confused than ever. Buxton had opened his eyes to another view of Scripture, although York was still not entirely convinced it would be permissible for him to fight and kill.

He considered Buxton's arguments, praying inwardly. Guessing what was going on in York's mind and heart, Buxton sat back, smiled, and suggested that if York still believed it was wrong to kill, he might be allowed to transfer to a noncombat job, or even be allowed to take off his uniform and go home.

York told Buxton he would like some time to think the matter over. Buxton agreed to this and told York to come back and see him when he'd made up his mind.

Back in his own quarters, York spent the entire night praying but still couldn't come to a decision. He wanted to go somewhere he could be alone to think the matter through.

The news that York held antiwar beliefs had leaked out, leading to threats and accusations of cowardice. Amid the constant noise of camp and the crowds of soldiers, York desperately wanted to go home to think and pray about this all-important decision—home to the mountains, home to Tennessee.

York applied for leave and was given a ten-day pass. He took the train as far as it would go and hiked the last twelve miles over the mountains. Once home, he spoke several times with Pastor Pile and thought and prayed—and remained bewildered. But Buxton's arguments were beginning to change York's outlook.

"I knowed that if it was His will He would even use war as an instrument in His hands," York noted in his autobiography.[7]

Struggling to sort out the chaos in his mind, York climbed up the mountainside in the company of his beloved hounds. He knelt down and prayed all afternoon, through the night, and the next morning, pleading for God's wisdom.

He prayed that God would take pity on him and show him the light. As he fasted and prayed for comfort and direction, a great peace came over him, and a calm assurance entered his soul. He said, God "knowed I had been troubled and worried, not because I was afraid, but because I put Him first, even before my country, and I only wanted to do that which would please Him."[8]

York didn't fully understand why it was God's will for him to go to war and kill others, but it didn't matter. He knew it was God's will and that was good enough. Rising from his knees, he thanked his Lord and walked home, singing a hymn as he went.

Back at the cabin, York announced to his mother that he was going to fight, and that as long as he believed in God, not a hair on his head would be harmed.

Back at Camp Gordon, York told Captain Danforth of his decision and asked him to explain in greater detail what they were fighting for. Danforth described how Germany—in what became known as the Rape of Belgium—had overrun Belgium, killing many innocent civilians. They would continue to do so, if they were not stopped, until they overran the world.

York could see they had to stop them and his battalion was the one to do it. Slowly, he understood the role he and his fellow soldiers were meant to play. Into his mind came the words of Jesus from the Sermon on the Mount: "Blessed are the peacemakers" (Matthew 5:9).

❖ ❖ ❖

On April 19, York's regiment traveled to Camp Upton, New York, by train. After drilling for nine days, they traveled to Boston and boarded a ship headed for France, joining a convoy of sixteen ships. It was York's first sight of open sea—and his first experience with seasickness. As they rode the waves, their training continued. In their free time, York and his friend Murray Savage continued to study the Bible together.

They arrived in Liverpool on May 16 and five days later crossed the English Channel on a ship that was "more like a bucking mule than a boat."[9] They landed in Le Havre amid the cheers of the French people. The men continued to train, and to fight among themselves—since they couldn't yet get at the Germans, York recalled. He continued to read his Bible, pray, write in his diary, and follow orders. But he worried about the time, soon to come, when he would be asked to kill.

Even though York knew they were fighting for peace, he still felt strange thinking he might have to "cut up human beings."[10] It was still wrong to him—terribly so—to take a person's life.

York's regiment left Le Havre by French troop trains and traveled about eighty miles northeast to the village of Eu. Two days later, York wrote in his diary, they were in Floraville, where they stayed for a few days, billeting mostly in barns.

The British Expeditionary Force taught the Americans how to use bayonets, machine guns, and hand grenades. They learned to "navigate through wire entanglements, properly react to incoming artillery, and prevent death and injury from gas attacks."[11]

The men also did a great deal of marching—so much so that the weary Americans were beginning to wonder whether they were ever going to see the front.

In June, York's division was sent to Toul. Before hitting the trenches, the men were allowed a few days of R & R. York himself avoided drinking and usually avoided the bars, but here he did go along with his friends and watched his comrades drink and carouse.

He recounted that as soldiers, they seemed as good at finding "pretty French girls" as he was at hunting game back home. For his part, York continued to read every day from the Bible.

As the men hiked roads crowded with troops, they saw deserted trenches, gun emplacements, and many graves topped with wooden crosses. Those sights brought home to them the gravity of what they were doing.

In late June the 82nd Division took a train to Rambucourt. As they marched toward the frontline trenches, York could hear guns in the distance that sounded like thunder.

Approaching the front, the men now ducked as stray bullets whistled overhead; and then, under cover of darkness, the men took over the frontline trenches for the first time. It was far from the glorious battle some had anticipated. Instead, they were "shocked by the reality of war, . . . the smell of death and decay," and "the condition of the trenches, which often were filled knee-high in water," one biographer wrote.[12] The men endured hour after hour of watch, gas warnings, and patrol of no-man's-land, all of which "wore the men out mentally and physically."[13] During his free time, York continued to read his New Testament, taking comfort in its words.

York impressed his officers as a soldier who could be relied on to stay steady under fire and do what he was told. It wasn't long before York was promoted to corporal and given command of an automatic weapons squad. York led his men on several raids into no-man's-land. He prayed constantly, even as German bullets buzzed overhead.

Over the next two months, the Americans "rotated in and out of the Lagny Sector trenches, slowly gaining experience." On August 10, the 82nd was ordered to "the Marbache Sector in the town of Pont-a-Mousson," putting "the division on the eastern edge of the St. Mihiel salient, where it would support the first American army offensive on the Western Front."[14]

On September 12, the Allies (fourteen US divisions and four French), attacked the Germans with artillery and tanks and by air. It began with terrible noise from the big American guns, which shook the ground.

On the second day of the Saint-Mihiel offensive, York's battalion captured Norroy, with the men leaping out of their trenches and charging "across an expanse of wire and craters," enduring intense German fire.[15]

Squad leader York was astonished at the behavior of his men when the attack began. They were supposed to follow him into battle, but he couldn't seem to go fast enough for them. He'd speed up and the men would continue on even faster, just to get at the German army. They were so "full of fight that wild cats shore would have backed away from them."[16] The men called out and swore at the Germans for fleeing.

After capturing Norroy, York and his men searched houses for German soldiers. The 82nd then "advanced 1.25 miles north to seize Vandieres . . . against heavy German resistance."[17]

A few days later, the men of the 82nd hopped aboard some one hundred trucks and traveled sixty-two miles west "to support the Meuse-Argonne Offensive," which was "the first of four Allied attacks that spanned some two hundred miles of the Western Front"[18] designed to finally end the war. As military historian Douglas Mastriano writes of this offensive, General Pershing believed the Americans "had the most difficult task," as they "had to fight against some of Germany's best divisions, across impossible terrain that threatened the heart of their vital Western Front command and control network: the Sedan-Mezieres rail line."[19]

An astounding 1.2 million Americans took part in this offensive—the largest in American history. York was now just days away from the battle that would make him famous. Knowing they would soon be called into combat, York prayed and thought about what they were about to get into.

York soon discovered that just as war could turn men into angry animals, it could also draw out a deep affection and even love for the people who went to battle at your side. Incredibly, York claimed it wasn't until he was a military man that he realized how much he loved his fellow man. He couldn't bear imagining any of them being hurt or killed, and yet somehow he seemed to know they were heading into something horrible in those woods.

On October 3, the men spent the night in the Zona Woods. The next day, York recorded that they went into the Argonne Woods and stayed overnight.

Each night they camped in the cover of the trees and encroached on the German line a bit at a time. On October 5 he noted that while the Germans were shelling the road and airplanes buzzed overhead, with dead horses and men and shells falling around him, he felt moved by the thought of how God's power could help any man if only he would trust.

York looked heavenward and prayed,

> O Jesus, the great rock of foundation
> Where on my feet were set with sovereign grace;

Through Shells or Death with all their agitation
Thou wilt protect me if I will only trust in thy Grace
Bless thy holy name.[20]

On Sunday, October 6, the men of the 82nd listened as their battalion chaplain, Daniel S. Smart, preached a sermon based on 2 Timothy 4:1–8, struggling to be heard over the sound of artillery and German planes flying above. This passage includes the words, "I have fought a good fight, I have finished my course, I have kept the faith" (v. 7 KJV).

It was the last sermon many of the soldiers would ever hear, and the last Smart would preach before his own death on the field of battle.

October 7 was a day of horror. York wrote of how he saw men blown up by German shells raining down all around them. The order came to take Hills 223 and 224 on the following day. The men passed the wounded being carried on stretchers groaning and convulsing, and the dead lying all along the road, mouths open and eyes staring out at nothing. Seeing them as he hiked along in the mud and in the rain, York longed for home.

On October 8, 1918—the day that would make Alvin York the most famous soldier of the Great War—Captain Danforth told the men they were to move on to Hill 223 at daybreak, the origination point for the attack. The plan was to reach the Decauville Railroad about three kilometers northwest, in the middle of the Argonne Forest. Their goal: to destroy the railroad, which would prevent the Germans from bringing in fresh troops and supplies.

The men started their march across a little bridge above the Aire River, through the town of Chatel-Chéhéry, and on up to Hill 223. It was rough going in the dark; the noise of the big guns was horrific, and their progress was very slow.

When dawn came, they could finally see where they were going— but so could the Germans, who immediately launched a savage assault, which wounded or killed nearly every man. The air was also full of gas. But the Americans kept going, stumbling their way to the hill while

German snipers fired on them. The Americans had been told to reach the top of the hill by 6:10 a.m. and continue into the valley, working their way across the ridges to the railroad. Two platoons were ordered to advance first, and another two would follow a hundred yards after. York was in the left supporting platoon, which was supposed to keep in contact with the 28th Division, but they got separated and didn't show. York figured they were held up in another area of the battle, and yet at 6:10 a.m., his men fixed bayonets and went over the top of the hill as ordered. The expected support barrage never arrived, so they had to go on without one.

As the men started over the top, "the germans was Putting their machine guns to working all over the hill in front of us and on our left and right. . . . I could see my pals getting picked off until it almost looked like there was none left."[21]

York would never forget what came next.

"The Germans met our charge across the valley with a regular sleet storm of bullets. I'm a-telling you that-there valley was a death trap . . . with steep ridges covered with brush, and swarming with machine guns on all sides. I guess our two waves got about halfway across and then jes' couldn't get no further nohow. The Germans . . . jes stopped us in our tracks. Their machine guns were up there on the heights overlooking us and well hidden, and we couldn't tell for certain where the terrible heavy fire was coming from."[22] York watched in horror as he watched his fellow soldiers being mowed down from all sides.

The men lay flat on the ground, unable to go farther without the help of a barrage. York's lieutenant, who was leading the platoon, was struck with a machine gun fire, which shattered his legs. Almost unbelievably, he dragged himself along the ground, shouting encouragement to his men. But then a German shot him through the head, taking his life.

The German machine guns had halted the Americans in their tracks.

Now Platoon Sergeant Harry Parsons was in command. Parsons

realized it would be impossible to get through to the railroad until the German machine guns were silenced. It was equally clear that there was no possible way the machine gun nests could be taken out by a frontal attack. But it was essential that they be taken out of action somehow.

Sergeant Parsons, who had repeatedly exposed himself to enemy fire in his effort to locate the guns, ordered half the platoon to back up and attempt to work their way "down around on the left" and attempt to make their way through the protective shrubbery and attack the machine gunners from behind. There were just seventeen men left.

Walking single file, the men advanced as quickly and quietly as they could through the brush, keeping well to the left as they headed toward the vicious *rat-a-tat-tat* of machine gun fire.

They managed to skirt the side of the valley without losing any men and approached the same ridge where the machine gun nests were placed. When they realized this, the men paused to figure out what to do next. They decided to keep going until they had gotten behind the German lines, and then "move behind and around the flank of the German machine guns on the center hill that were holding up the attack in the valley."[23]

The Americans dodged from bush to bush and encircled the Germans, going behind them without their enemies learning of their presence. As they fell in behind the machine guns, they spotted two Germans with Red Cross bands on their arms. The Americans ordered them to stop, hoping to capture them before they could give the alarm, but the Germans broke into a run. The Americans opened fire on them—and missed.

The Americans now realized from the sounds of gunfire that they were directly behind the machine guns. As they crossed a stream, they suddenly stumbled across fifteen or twenty Germans—orderlies, stretcher bearers, runners, and a few officers—who had evidently just finished their breakfast. The surprised Germans surrendered instantly, assuming that there far more Americans than there actually were. York saw no reason to correct this misapprehension.

But then, without warning, the German machine gunners, who had spotted the Americans, swung their guns around, shouted to their comrades to drop to the ground, and opened fire, killing six Americans and wounding three. York was horrified to see that his close friend Corporal Savage was among those killed, his body riddled with more than a hundred bullets.

York estimated that more than twenty machine guns were firing on them continuously, filling the air with death. Because everyone senior to York was now dead or wounded, he was suddenly in charge—but only of eight men because three of his soldiers had been wounded and six more killed. There was no time for York to give orders.

"Whatever misgivings York had about fighting vanished upon seeing the death of Savage," Colonel Douglas Mastriano wrote in his biography of York. "With the burden of command now upon him, York determined to stop the killing."[24]

As the machine guns continued to fire, some of the Americans huddled behind the captured Germans to protect themselves while others crawled under cover or hid behind trees. The six-feet four York was caught out in the open, to the left and in front of the group of prisoners and some twenty-five yards away from the machine guns on the hillside above.

And now, York put his mountain man skills to work. Each time he spotted a German, he "just teched him off," as he put it, from a prone position.

At first York was shooting from a prone position, just as he did when taking part in shooting matches back home. Given his skill, he could hardly fail to miss at such close range—especially since the targets were far larger than the turkeys he was accustomed to picking off. If they lifted their heads in order to learn where York was, he'd shoot them. If they kept their heads down, they would be unable to return fire.

Miraculously, despite the fact that York was out in the open, none of the machine gunners were able to hit him.

York had no way of knowing what the others eight men were doing or even if they were still alive. He later learned that as he was fighting off the Germans, they had not fired a single shot.

As soon as he was able, York stood up and began shooting with his army rifle, using several clips. The barrel of his gun was heating up, and his rifle ammunition was running low, but York kept firing.

Suddenly, twenty-five yards away, six Germans leaped out of a trench and charged York with fixed bayonets. York, knowing he had only about half a clip in his rifle, grabbed his pistol. This was where his Tennessee hunting experience came into play. He shot the sixth German first, then the fifth one, the third one, the second one, and finally, the one in front—just as if they were a flock of wild turkeys.

After the last charging German fell to the ground, York switched back to his rifle and went after the machine gunners, knowing that if he kept his head down and didn't run out of ammunition, he had them. Not wanting to kill any more Germans than he had to, York shouted at them to give up. The Germans ignored him, so York shot two more of them and again yelled at them to give themselves up.

Either the Germans couldn't hear him, didn't understand English, or simply didn't want to surrender, York never knew. By now the Tennessee mountain man had killed more than twenty enemy soldiers.

In the midst of the fight, one of the Germans being held prisoner, Leutnant Paul Vollmer, stood up and approached York.

"English?" he yelled.

"American," York replied.

"Good Lord!" Vollmer exclaimed. "If you won't shoot any more I will make them give up."[25] York covered Vollmer with his automatic, threatening to kill him next if Vollmer didn't keep his word. Vollmer had no doubt that York would do as he said and blew a whistle, signaling to his men to come out, thrown down their weapons, as hold up their hands

But one of the Germans wasn't quite ready to surrender. As he approached York, he threw a grenade at his head. It missed York and wounded one of the prisoners. York promptly shot him dead, and had no further difficulties with his prisoners.

York and seven other Americans were now guarding about a hundred German prisoners. The question now was, What was York going to do with them? There was another line of Germans they had to get through to get back to American lines. When a German officer— now probably wondering if he'd surrendered too soon—asked how many Americans were holding them, York stretched the truth a bit: He pointed his pistol at him and told him he had plenty of men.

Using Vollmer to translate orders, York lined the prisoners up by twos, placing himself in front of the first Germans in the line. He ordered Vollmer to walk ahead of him, and his own men to walk on either side of the column, with one guarding the rear.

Two more of York's men—Corporal Cutting and Sergeant Early— were wounded. York told them to follow the column of German prisoners. Other American soldiers were too badly wounded to walk, so York ordered the prisoners to pick them up and carry them. He had no intention of leaving his fellow soldiers out there to die of their wounds.

York poked Vollmer in the back with his Colt and ordered him to get moving. Vollmer, still attempting to salvage the situation, suggested that York hike down the gully. York immediately realized that he was being misled; he told Vollmer he wanted them to head straight through the German front-line trenches back to the American lines. And that's just what they did.

York now faced yet another challenge. A German platoon led by Leutnant Kübler was just ahead of them. As Mastriano writes, "Kübler realized that it was too quiet behind the lines and to his left and told his second in command, Sergeant Major Haegele, 'things just don't look right.' Kübler ordered his men to grab their weapons and follow him to the battalion command post. As they approached, he and his men were immediately surrounded by several of York's men. Kübler and his platoon surrendered and joined the prisoners."[26]

In an effort to alert troops nearby, commanded by German

Leutnant Thoma, Vollmer loudly ordered Kübler's men to drop their weapons and equipment belts. Hearing Vollmer, Leutnant Thoma turned around. He saw several of York's men moving up the road. Thoma ordered his men to follow him with their bayonets fixed and ran in the direction of York and the one hundred plus German prisoners, yelling, 'Don't take off your belts!'"

As Thoma's men prepared to fight, York shoved his Colt into Vollmer's back. Tell Thoma to surrender, he ordered.

"You must surrender!" Vollmer shouted.

"I will not let them capture me!" Thoma shouted back.

"It is useless, we are surrounded," Vollmer yelled.

"I will do so on your responsibility!" Thoma replied.

"I take all responsibility," Vollmer returned.[27]

Thoma and his men surrendered and joined their fellow prisoners. On they marched, but as they crossed the valley, Lieutenant Joseph Woods, the battalion adjutant of York's unit, spotted them. Thinking it was a German counterattack, he prepared to fight, but a second look revealed that the Germans were unarmed. He also spotted York, who, upon reaching Hill 223, stopped and saluted.

"Company G reports with prisoners, sir," York said.

"How many prisoners have you, corporal?"

"Honestly, lieutenant," York said, "I don't know."[28]

Woods told him to take the prisoners back to Chatel-Chéhéry and counted the Germans as they walked past him. There were 132 of them.

York and his men were still not safe. A German soldier, observing "the large formation of troops . . . called for artillery fire. As the shells began to land, York ordered the Germans to double time out of the valley."[29]

Brigade commander General Lindsey stopped York and his prisoners near Chatel-Chéhéry. In Vollmer's pocket, Lindsey discovered orders "to counterattack and seize Castle Hill."[30]

Then Lindsey addressed himself to York.

"Well, York, I hear you have captured the whole damned German army."[31]

"No, sir," the literal York replied. "I only got 132."

At Chatel-Chéhéry, the wounded Germans and Americans were taken to the aid station. But York and his men were told to walk the remaining prisoners back to Varennes, some six miles away, as the regimental holding area couldn't handle so many. They'd captured so many prisoners no one seemed willing to take them off York's hands.

As they marched, York and his prisoners were constantly under shell fire. York did his best to get the Germans through safely. They'd surrendered, so York felt it was his duty to ensure they remained unharmed.

When they reached Varennes, York's men and the prisoners were given a meal and then began marching to yet another village—Boureuilles—where the Allies had the facilities to hold the many captives.

The actions of York and his platoon forced the Germans to give up more than thirty machine guns. Consequently, "the 2nd Battalion, 328th Infantry Regiment, was able to resume the attack. They continued up the valley to reach their objective, the Decauville Railroad and the North-South Road. . . . The German line was broken, and the 120th Landwehr would never recover from the loss."[32]

York took part in other battles over the next few days. In one, he came close to being killed. A shell struck the ground just in front of his unit, sending many soldiers into the air. Miraculously, no one was hurt.

On about November 1, York was promoted to sergeant, and on November 11 the armistice was signed, and the war was suddenly over. While his fellow soldiers, both American and French, celebrated noisily, York, on leave in Aix-les-Bains, walked into a church and prayed.

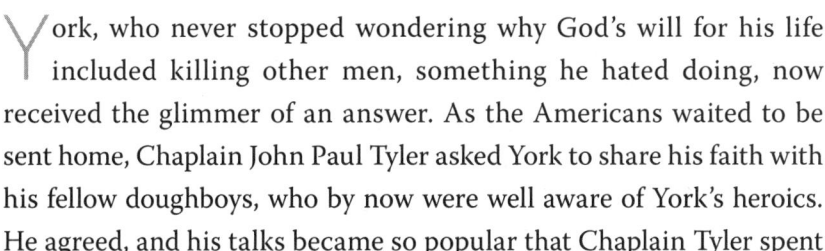

York, who never stopped wondering why God's will for his life included killing other men, something he hated doing, now received the glimmer of an answer. As the Americans waited to be sent home, Chaplain John Paul Tyler asked York to share his faith with his fellow doughboys, who by now were well aware of York's heroics. He agreed, and his talks became so popular that Chaplain Tyler spent six weeks taking York over the length and breadth of France to share his Christian testimony with thousands of soldiers.

On November 3, after an investigation into York's actions in battle, he was awarded the Distinguished Service Cross. But then Captain Danforth requested that York's award be upgraded to the Congressional Medal of Honor, the highest award any soldier may receive.

In February 1919, additional investigations into York's actions were carried out in the snow-covered Argonne by Colonel Richard Wetherill, York's regimental commander; Brigadier General Lindsey, his brigade commander; and Major General George Duncan. A *Saturday Evening Post* writer named George Pattullo was also on the scene—and it was he who would ultimately turn the simple mountain man into an international celebrity.

Hearing York explain what had occurred, and having spoken with his men, none of the investigators could believe their eyes and ears. It was clear that York simply should not have survived.

"York, how did you do it?" Lindsey asked

"It was not man-power but it was divine power that saved me," York explained, adding, "Before I went to war I prayed to God and He done gave me my assurance that so long as I believed in Him not one hair of my head would be harmed; and even in front of them-there machine guns He knowed I believed in Him."

"York," Lindsey responded, "you are right."

Wetherill agreed as well. "It is not human to do what you have done," he told York.

Other members of the investigation team suggested York's survival was down to luck or the skills he had honed in the mountains of Tennessee.

York would have none of it.

"I'm a-telling you the hand of God must have been in that fight. It surely must have been divine power that brought me out. No other power under heaven could save a man in a place like that. Men were killed on both sides of me and all around me and I was the biggest and the most exposed of all. I have got only one explanation to offer, and only one: without the help of God I jes' couldn't have done it. . . . There can be no arguments about that."[33]

Reporting on this battlefield visit later, George Pattullo wrote, "At last I said, 'I cannot understand, even now, how any of you came out alive.' York replied, simply but earnestly, 'We know there were miracles, don't we? Well this was one. I was taken care of—it's the only way I can figure it.'"[34]

On April 18, Major General Duncan presented York with the Medal of Honor "for conspicuous gallantry and intrepidity above and beyond the call of duty. . . . Fearlessly leading seven men, he charged with great daring a machine gun nest, which was pouring deadly and incessant fire upon his platoon. In this heroic feat, the machine gun nest was taken together with four officers and one hundred and twenty-eight men and several guns."[35]

Immediately after York was given the medal, France's Marshal Ferdinand Foch, overall Allied commander, awarded him the French Médaille Militaire, as well as the Croix de Guerre and the Legion of Honour, telling York that his actions were "the greatest achievement accomplished by a common soldier in all the armies of Europe!"[36]

◆ ◆ ◆

York arrived back in the US on May 22, 1919, traveling on the *SS Ohioan*. He was delighted to see the Statue of Liberty and the New York skyscrapers, comparing them to the mountains back home. Because of heavy fog, the ship docked in Hoboken, New Jersey.

York didn't know it, but the month before, George Pattullo's story about his heroics had appeared in the *Saturday Evening Post*, at that time the most popular magazine in the US. Americans were proud of the mountain man who had gone into Argonne Forest and emerged a modest hero, giving the credit to God alone.

The Tennessee Society of New York was determined to give York a welcome-home reception he would never forget (whether he wanted it or not). York was granted a five-day furlough to attend events in both New York and Washington.

Observing the huge number of people on the Hoboken dock waiting to greet him, the shy Tennessean, who wrote that he was "plumb scared to death,"[37] hid on the ship until most of the other soldiers had disembarked. It did no good: the Tennessee Society welcome committee boarded the ship to greet York and escort him off the *Ohioan*. As York and the committee headed for their car, reporters surrounded York, firing questions at him about his actions in France and the fact that he'd once been a conscientious objector.

York's answer was simple. "It was the hand of God that guided us all and brought about the victory. . . . I feel it was through Him that I accomplished what I did."[38]

York was the recipient of a ticker tape parade. Papers and ticker tape and confetti came from the windows of skyscrapers. He said it looked like a blizzard, with thousands waving from New York skyscrapers and sidewalks. York—who had certainly never seen a ticker tape parade—marveled at the fuss that was being made. He had no idea that all this celebrating was for him alone; he thought New Yorkers did the same thing for every soldier who came back.

Following the parade, York was taken to the Waldorf Astoria, where he was given the presidential suite. He attempted, unsuccessfully, to call his mother at Pastor Pile's store. That evening, he was the guest of honor at a banquet where he was confused by place settings that were far more elaborate than what he was accustomed to at home.

During the many speeches glorifying the young soldier, York daydreamed of going home to his log cabin, his mother and Gracie, and his dogs. The Tennessee Society attempted to get York to talk of his heroics, which he politely declined to do, and then handed York a two-thousand-dollar Victory Note.

Sadly, York never got to sleep at the Waldorf: Congressman Hull took him on a train to Washington to visit the White House, the War Department, and the House of Representatives. York responded graciously to all the people who wanted to shake his hand, but he began to wonder whether he'd ever get back home. Not yet, it turned out: he was taken back to New York City to see the stock exchange.

When he was finally asked whether there was anything he especially wanted to see in New York, the mountain man said he wanted to see the subway system. The president of the Interborough Rapid Transit Company took York on a grand tour. His final visit was to a musical review, where the man from Tennessee was shocked at how little clothing female performers wore.

Americans delighted in this unassuming hero—his modesty, his folksy way of talking, and the fact that he continually gave the credit to God rather than his own bravery and shooting ability. The whole country, it seemed, understood who Alvin York was—everyone, that is, except members of the entertainment world, who immediately made plans to put York in films, vaudeville, the *Ziegfeld Follies*, and on cereal boxes. They scrambled over one another, offering York enormous amounts of money if he would only sign their contracts. Their offers amounted to a staggering $250,000—more than $4.5 million in today's currency.

York didn't need time to think about it. He declared his life was not for sale. Accepting money for his wartime heroics would be to commercialize his soldiering and betray his uniform. He hadn't gone to war to get into films, he noted; he'd gone to help make peace. He'd only done his duty to God and to his country, as every man should. And this is what he told anyone who questioned him about his service in France. Hearing of this, Americans admired Alvin York even more.

His leave finished, York was demobilized and began the long journey home, taking the train to Crossville, Tennessee—the closest the train could get to Pall Mall. Here another welcoming committee awaited him, including his old friend Pastor Pile. York climbed into one of the six waiting cars and headed for Jamestown, where his mother and siblings eagerly awaited him. With tears in her eyes, Mother York said with great dignity, "Hello, Alvin."

"Hello, Ma," he replied.

The Yorks piled into a mule-drawn wagon that took them to Pall Mall, thirteen miles away. York couldn't get enough of his beloved mountains. Along the way, friends and neighbors called up greetings and asked him how he was.

"Oh, fair to middlin," he replied. "How's the hogs and crops?"[39]

Clearly, Alvin York had already left the war behind.

Back at home, his hounds raced out to greet him, leaping on Alvin and licking his hands. And then he went to see Gracie, and the two decided to marry and did so before the week was out.

The next morning, York set out for the same mountain he had climbed more than a year before to fast and pray about God's will regarding his military service. All alone in the peaceful silence, York gave thanks to God.

Nothing at home had changed, but a restless Alvin York knew *he* had changed. He had seen things in the outside world, and the experience of combat had permanently altered him. Thinking about it, York realized for the first time that while the mountains had kept out many of the iniquities of the world, they had also kept out many good things, such as good roads, schools, medical clinics, libraries, modern homes, and up-to-date farming methods. Alvin began to believe that everything he had experienced during the war had prepared him to serve his mountain neighbors.

York's fame went a long way in helping him achieve his goals. First, York asked the State Highway Department to build a badly needed road through the mountains. The road was soon built.

Next he set up the York Foundation to raise funds to build schools so that his neighbors' children would receive the education York lacked. He began a speaking tour across the country to raise funds for his charitable work, always dodging any talk of his experiences in France.

In 1928, to raise the large sums to achieve his ambitious goals, York decided to do something he had for ten years declined to do: write his autobiography. *Sergeant York: His Own Life Story and War Diary* became a bestseller, raising a great deal of money for his many projects.

York's wife, Gracie, also kept busy, caring for the couple's eight children.

York continued to resist having a film made of his life. But the rise of Hitler in the late 1930s caused him to change his mind. York believed the United States would eventually have to join this war, and if a film about his life would help bring that about, he was willing to agree to it. It would be an uphill battle; a 1941 poll revealed that 80 percent of Americans wanted to stay out of another war. Many were bitter over the sacrifices made during the First World War, which—as Germany again began saber-rattling—they now believed had been a waste of time, money, and precious lives.

In 1939 film producer Jesse Lasky met with York several times to discuss filming the story of his life. York eventually agreed and decided to use his share of the profits to finish building a local Bible school.

York was pleased when Gary Cooper was chosen to portray him. He insisted that the actress portraying his wife, Gracie, not be "any cigarette smoking actress" but a nice, wholesome girl.[40] Sixteen-year-old Joan Leslie (who had never smoked) got the role, and Walter Brennan was chosen to play Pastor Pile.

The film was to include the story of York's upbringing in Tennessee, his conversion, his struggle with his conscience after he was drafted, and his military service. The screenplay would follow as accurately as possible York's actions in the Argonne.

Sergeant York was slightly less accurate in other respects. For instance, regarding his conversion experience, York had written that he felt as though he had been struck by lightning. Screenwriters decided that in the film, York should *literally* be struck by lightning while traveling by horseback to revenge himself on a man who'd cheated him.

Screenwriters were also concerned that the film would not have enough appeal to nonreligious viewers. They solved that problem by having York's Major Buxton talk with him about American history as well as Christianity.

Sergeant York was released on July 4, 1941, premiering in both New

York and Washington. It was a runaway hit and garnered an Academy Award for Gary Cooper.

Five months later the Japanese attacked Pearl Harbor. Now few people required convincing that the United States needed to enter the war. But the film about York's life is credited with helping to prepare "America morally and mentally for the need to go to war."[41]

Two of York's sons served in the Second World War, and both, like their father, returned home safely. York, now fifty-five, overweight, and suffering from various health problems, volunteered to serve in a combat unit but was turned down for health reasons. But the War Department recognized that York's celebrity could be exploited. He was commissioned as a major in the Army Signal Corps and traveled the country, speaking at training camps and helping with war bond drives.

But instead of making the sort of patriotic speeches the War Department likely expected, York urged young soldiers and sailors to avoid alcohol and to put their faith in God.

In 1949 York's health began to fail. He suffered two strokes and developed colitis. The following year was no better: York caught pneumonia and was hospitalized with high blood pressure and heart disease.

In 1954 a cerebral hemorrhage and stroke ended York's hunting and shooting days; he was bedridden for the last ten years of his life.

On September 2, 1964, at the age of seventy-six, Alvin York died. Over eight thousand mourners attended his funeral. His First World War division, the 82nd, had not forgotten his heroism forty-five years earlier: it sent to the funeral both an honor guard and a band to honor the hero of the Argonne.

York was buried on the grounds of the same church where he had accepted Christ nearly fifty years before. If ever anyone lived out his faith in a way from which we might all learn, that person is the humble backwoods Tennessean named Alvin York, whose phenomenal display of bravery in the Argonne forest that day over a hundred years ago lives on in books such as this and in hearts and minds such as yours and mine.

SIX

Alexander Solzhenitsyn

1918–2008

The line dividing good and evil cuts through the heart
of every human being. And who is willing to destroy
a piece of his own heart?

—ALEXANDER SOLZHENITSYN

On June 8, 1978, Harvard University students, parents, professors, and administrators stood beneath a sea of umbrellas, waiting to hear a speech by one of the most famous men in the world. Lengthy applause and a standing ovation followed his introduction, after which Alexander Solzhenitsyn—celebrated Russian dissident, poet, playwright, and Nobel Prize–winning novelist—stepped forward. But his commencement address—delivered in Russian and translated into English—wasn't what his audience expected. And by the end of it, outraged members of the audience booed him. Why? Because Solzhenitsyn, who had spent much of his life condemning communism and Soviet power, had dared to criticize the West.

◆ ◆ ◆

Alexander Solzhenitsyn was born in Kislovodsk, Russia, on December 11, 1918, fourteen months after Russia's October Revolution, five months after Lenin murdered Czar Nicholas and his entire family, and four months after the Bolsheviks began the Red Terror, rounding up their enemies and murdering them by the thousands.

Alexander's mother, Taisiya Zakharovna, was of Ukrainian descent; his father, Isaakiy Semyonovich Solzhenitsyn, was a decorated young artillery officer in the Imperial Russian Army of Cossack, but six months before his son was born, he was killed in a hunting accident.

While Alexander slept peacefully in his mother's arms, civil war raged across Russia between the White Russians (who opposed the Bolsheviks) and the Red Army, which, after two years of vicious fighting, ultimately prevailed.

Thanks to Soviet policies, deep poverty was widespread, and Alexander and his mother faced brutally hard circumstances. When he was six, his mother, who had trained as a stenographer, took him to live in Rostov, which was on the shores of Lake Nero, 125 miles northeast of Moscow. They rented a converted stable without running water. There was never quite enough food, and the two often shivered in the cold.

Although Alexander's mother had abandoned her Christian faith, she now reembraced it, as did many others during the painful years of the Red Terror. But it was Alexander's grandmother who taught him to say his prayers, and in his earliest years, he drew comfort from an icon hanging in his room, the last thing he saw before falling asleep.

During this time, the Bolsheviks viciously persecuted the Orthodox Church, stealing its valuables and absurdly claiming to sell them to feed the starving populace. Church leaders who protested were tried and shot, "all of which went to prove that what was important was not to feed the starving but to make use of a convenient opportunity to break the back of the church," Solzhenitsyn later wrote.[1]

From an early age, Alexander loved reading, and he devoured the Russian novels he found in his aunt Irena's home when he visited each summer. He also enjoyed hiking through the nearby countryside.

This deeply devout aunt played a role in the boy's religious education, taking him to church, where he absorbed, "perhaps unconsciously, the rhythms and rituals of the ancient Russian faith, and hearing from [her] how central orthodoxy was to the history and identity of Russia itself."[2]

Among his earliest memories was the shock of seeing Soviet soldiers brutally bursting into the church where he and his mother were worshiping, and imperiously halting the service. He remembered spending much of his childhood standing in line for bread and meal, but he later wrote that he didn't make the connection between food shortages and the Soviets' actions. Nor was he aware that, night after night, his neighbors were being arrested and jailed, because his classmates fearfully kept silent about the disappearance of their fathers.

During the 1920s the situation deteriorated so that an estimated eight million children wandered the streets in packs like animals, searching for food and often selling their bodies to get it.

While Alexander was taught Bolshevik propaganda at school, at home he listened attentively as family members expressed opinions deeply critical of the government. Alexander was highly intelligent and excelled in his studies. Already at an early age, he decided he wanted to be a writer, and he filled notebook after notebook with stories.

But Alexander's faith slowly eroded during these years. He recalled how, at age ten, boys belonging to the atheistic Young Pioneers yanked from his neck the cross he had worn all his life. After two years of mockery and torment, Alexander joined the organization.

Far worse than having his cross taken away, however, was the sight of the secret police arresting a family friend, Vladimir Fedorovsky—another victim of Stalin's cruel purges. Nevertheless, Alexander continued to enthusiastically accept the Soviet view of things.

By the time he was eighteen, Alexander had determined what he would write about: "the tragic cycle of revolution and tyranny that was to be Russia's experience throughout most of the twentieth century."[3] He began by researching Russia's role in the First World War.

Solzhenitsyn's high grades earned him a place at Rostov University, where he studied mathematics and physics rather than literature (in part because Rostov didn't offer it and also because it would have been dangerous in that time and place to embark on a writing career). He continued to study Marxist-Leninist texts, "increasingly convinced of the correctness of their view of life." As for the horrors Stalin inflicted, Solzhenitsyn was "convinced that it was only Stalin's diversions from Leninist doctrine that had brought about the crueler and highly questionable aspects of Soviet life."[4]

Because both Solzhenitsyn and his friend Vitaly Vitkevich lived far from Moscow, they enrolled as external students in Moscow's Institute for the Study of Philosophy, Literature, and History. And in any time he had to spare, Solzhenitsyn devoured more Marxist-Leninist writings.

It was at Rostov University when he was just seventeen that Solzhenitsyn met a young, vivacious chemistry major named Natalya Reshetovskaya. This was in 1936. The two were soon seeing much of each other, attending parties and concerts. Because Solzhenitsyn was simultaneously earning degrees at two colleges, he spent nearly all his time studying, sometimes even forgoing sleep to finish his work. Still, he managed to find the time to become editor of the school newspaper. His academic excellence earned him a Stalin scholarship, and he eventually earned a first-class degree in mathematics and physics at Rostov and then sat for his second-year examinations at the Moscow Institute for the Study of Philosophy, Literature, and History.

Despite his considerable fear that marriage—and possible children —could interfere with the great work he intended to do, Solzhenitsyn and Natalya secretly married on April 27, 1940.

——— ◆ ◆ ◆ ———

A year later something happened that would push Solzhenitsyn's life in a new direction. On June 22, 1941, Hitler's Germany invaded the Soviet Union. Like many of his fellow students, Solzhenitsyn tried to volunteer for the draft, but because of a childhood injury, he was deemed ineligible for military service. Disappointed, Solzhenitsyn became a teacher in the village of Morozovsk, as did his wife.

But as the Germans continued their deadly advance into Russia over the next months, desperate Soviet leaders drafted every able-bodied man available. Solzhenitsyn found himself drafted "into a rear-area unit responsible for military transportation using horses."[5] And so the brilliant young man was put to work cleaning manure from stables. Feeling not fully utilized in this assignment, and tormented by fellow soldiers who had taken a dislike to the highly educated village school teacher, he got himself reassigned "as the courier of an official packet to the nearest main military headquarters of Stalingrad on the Volga"[6] and later talked his superiors into making him an artillery officer, despite the inconvenient fact that he wasn't an officer. He was sent to attend the Third Leningrad Artillery School's course and learned "the newly emerging art of artillery instrumentation through acoustics."[7] He graduated that October as a second lieutenant, and his unit took part in the intense, three-week-long battle for Kursk and then the battle for Orel, another three weeks of nonstop fighting.

Solzhenitsyn entered Orel with the victorious Russian army and ten days later was awarded the Order of the Patriotic War, second class, for "a speedy and successful training of battery personnel, and for [his] skilled command in determining the enemy's artillery groupings."[8]

Solzhenitsyn took part in more battles on the Eastern Front, including the June 1944 assault on Belorussia, for which he received the Order of the Red Star. When he encountered Russian soldiers fighting ferociously for Germany, he was shocked, not yet realizing what had driven them to do so.

Solzhenitsyn later wrote of the shame he felt when he saw a Russian soldier who had apparently joined the Germans being lashed viciously by a Soviet security sergeant. Solzhenitsyn knew he, as an officer, should stop the "senseless torture." But "I was afraid. . . . I said nothing and I did nothing," because, one biographer noted, he "had learned to fear the consequences of questioning the rising tide of brutality he was witnessing."[9]

But the stream of horrors he saw changed him, and he wrote of his feelings in a poem titled "Prussian Nights," describing the gang rape of a young girl by soldiers.

In January 1945 Solzhenitsyn was awarded the Soviet's second highest military order, the Order of the Red Banner, for "heroism in combat."[10]

In his spare time, Solzhenitsyn, now promoted to captain, worked on his manuscripts, even while living in a dugout, and sent letters to both his wife and his university friend Vitaly Vitkevich. These letters to Vitkevich were to change his life. That's because—rather astonishingly, considering his extraordinary intelligence—Solzhenitsyn did something extraordinarily reckless. In these letters he wrote freely and critically of Stalin, even though he knew military censors were reading his letters. Though Solzhenitsyn was still a committed Marxist-Leninist, he had learned enough about the "incompetence and corruption of Communist Party life in the Soviet era to grasp that life in his country would never significantly improve unless political changes took place," and he even dared to draft a political manifesto in which he imagined a future political party.[11]

On February 9, 1945, as the Soviets prepared for an attack on Berlin, Solzhenitsyn was summoned to the office of his commanding officer, who unhappily instructed Solzhenitsyn to hand over his revolver, which the confused young captain did. Two officers then stepped toward him.

"You're under arrest!" they shouted.

"Me?" Solzhenitsyn said. "What for?" He was dumbfounded.[12]

The soldiers didn't answer but tore off his officer's insignia and his belt. But the general, who was fond of Solzhenitsyn, managed to get a message to him as the soldiers led him away.

"Have you a friend on the First Ukrainian Front?" he asked meaningfully.[13]

At last Solzhenitsyn understood. His letters to Vitaly were the cause of his arrest and of the events that would forever and dramatically change his life.

◆ ◆ ◆

Solzhenitsyn described the first few days of life in the Lubyanka prison in excruciating detail in his books *The Gulag Archipelago* and *The First Circle*: the humiliating strip searches, the cold, the endless questions, the slop that passed for food. His entire body was shaved, and he was forced to stay awake day and night. Things got a little better when Solzhenitsyn was assigned to a different cell and was given a mattress, a pillow, and a blanket. He was now allowed to sleep, if he could manage to do so under the light of a two-hundred-watt bulb that burned all night.

Then came four days of interrogation. Of his interrogators, Solzhenitsyn wrote, "Their branch of service does not require them to be educated people of broad culture and broad views—and they are not. Their branch of service does not require them to think logically—and they do not. Their branch of service requires only that they carry out orders exactly and be impervious to suffering—and that is what they do and what they are."[14]

In *The Gulag Archipelago*, Solzhenitsyn described unspeakable horrors of life in the prison camp system of the Soviet Union: interrogators spitting at the prisoners, shoving their faces into full spittoons, dragging priests around by their long hair, and urinating in prisoners' faces. He wrote of loathsome attacks on female prisoners.

Solzhenitsyn was informed that he had been charged with producing anti-Soviet propaganda. He was then sent to a cell that he shared with three other prisoners—a happy turn of events, as he now at least had people he could talk to. Two he immediately befriended; the third turned out to be an informer. Conversations with his two new friends—an "Old Bolshevik" named Anatoly Ilyich Fastenko and a lawyer from Estonia named Arnold Susi—opened Solzhenitsyn's eyes to the inherent problems of communism.

May 9 was Victory in Europe Day; Solzhenitsyn and his fellow soldiers listened from behind prison walls as Russians celebrated the end of the war with Nazi Germany, dancing in the streets and shooting off fireworks.

In June, Solzhenitsyn was transferred to yet another prison, Butyrki, also in Moscow. And here it was that he met a young man named Boris Gammerov. The former sergeant had served in an antitank unit and was in poor health as a result of shrapnel wounds in his lung that had not fully healed. But Solzhenitsyn learned that Gammerov's faith was as strong as his body was weak. President Roosevelt had died not long before, and one day the two of them were discussing one of the late president's prayers. Solzhenitsyn remarked that it was "hypocrisy, of course."

Gammerov disagreed and asked, "Do you not admit the possibility that a political leader might sincerely believe in God?"[15]

Solzhenitsyn was startled. As far as he knew, only the elderly believed in God; people of his own age had "progressed" beyond irrational beliefs.

"Do you believe in God?" he asked Gammerov.

"Of course," Gammerov replied.[16]

Solzhenitsyn was mulling over his friend's words when he was summoned from his cell. Was he going to be given amnesty? There had been hopeful rumors that Stalin would offer a widespread amnesty for all who had fought in the war. But Solzhenitsyn's happy anticipation swiftly spiraled into despair: he was informed that for his "crimes" he would have to serve an eight-year sentence in the labor camps.

He was staggered at the horrific news. "Eight years! What for?" he asked.[17] The only response to his question was the order to move along so the next prisoner could be brought in.

Solzhenitsyn wrote to Natalya, telling her the bad news and offering her "complete personal freedom"[18] as long as he remained behind bars. Over the next months and years, while he and Natalya continued to write to each other, Solzhenitsyn slowly underwent a spiritual transformation, one that would cause even greater separation between him and his wife. Even at the beginning of his Gulag experiences, Solzhenitsyn "was beginning to discern that a man's spirit was not determined by his material circumstances but could rise above them."[19]

Days after learning of his lengthy sentence, Solzhenitsyn was taken to the Krasnaya Presnya transit prison. It was hideously crowded, with one hundred prisoners—hardened criminals as well as political prisoners—packed into one cell, which made it unbearably hot. On his first night, Solzhenitsyn was forced to sleep on the floor beneath the bunks, where a gang of child prisoners immediately stole the precious food package Natalya had sent.

An outraged Solzhenitsyn angrily spoke to the "godfather" of the cell—who had ended up with the food—telling him that if he was going to steal his provisions, at least he could see to it that Solzhenitsyn was allowed to sleep on a bunk. The godfather agreed and forced another prisoner to give his bunk to Solzhenitsyn.

But just as Saint Augustine grieved for the small sin of stealing a neighbor's pears, so Solzhenitsyn later grieved at the shame of having put his own comfort before that of a fellow prisoner. "Only then did awareness of my own meanness prick my conscience and make me blush. (And for many years thereafter I blushed every time I remembered it)," Solzhenitsyn wrote.[20]

On August 14, 1945, he was transferred to the New Jerusalem prison thirty miles outside Moscow. Here Solzhenitsyn was forced to work "in the digging brigades in the clay-pits," work he was ill-equipped to perform. As he wrote to his wife, "The work-loads of an unskilled labourer are beyond my strength. I curse my physical underdevelopment."[21]

But he was at least working alongside his Christian friend, Boris Gammerov. As they worked, they discussed Vladimir Solovyov, a Christian mystic, and told jokes. But not long afterward, Gammerov died from a combination of tuberculosis and simple exhaustion. Solzhenitsyn mourned him deeply.

In *The Gulag Archipelago*, Solzhenitsyn wrote of how hunger gnawed at the bellies of the inmates: Hunger, "which compels the most unselfish person to look with envy into someone else's bowl, and to try painfully to estimate what weight of ration his neighbor is receiving. Hunger, which darkens the brain and refuses to allow it to be distracted by anything else at all, or to think about anything else at all, or to speak about anything else at all except food, food, and food." He wrote of how the prisoners would wait for the dishwasher to bring out "the slops in the dishwasher. How they throw themselves on it, and fight with one another, seeking a fish head, a bone, vegetable parings."[22]

On September 9, 1945, Solzhenitsyn was transferred yet again, this time to Kaluga Gate in Moscow, where he spent the next ten months engaging in forced labor. In July 1946 he was taken back to Butyrki and assigned to cell 75, designed to hold twenty-five men but which Solzhenitsyn had to share with eighty others. Here the men suffered in the intense summer heat, the incessant buzzing of flies constantly interrupting their sleep.

Solzhenitsyn was awakened, as well, whenever another prisoner had to step over him to use the latrine. Still, it was a vast improvement over the agonies of the labor camp.

He wrote of this time: "I was happy! After camp, which had already seemed endless, and after a ten-hour workday, after cold, rain, and aching back, oh, what happiness it was to lie there for whole days on end, to sleep, and nevertheless receive a pound and a half of bread and two hot meals a day."[23]

Solzhenitsyn also made friends. They played chess, read what books were available, and took part in discussion groups. Solzhenitsyn's political and religious education continued; he argued with an Orthodox priest, Evgeny Divnich, who denounced Marxism. Solzhenitsyn argued the subject but found that somehow his heart was no longer in it.

"Even a year ago I would have confidently demolished him with quotations; how disparagingly I would have mocked him!" Solzhenitsyn wrote. But long months in prison had gradually changed his thinking.[24]

Solzhenitsyn had escaped the labor camp through a bit of trickery.

He had recently read a book about America's nuclear testing and had heard rumors that the Soviets—realizing they had locked up some brilliant minds—were creating special institutes for scientific research. Not only did such prisoners not have to engage in hard labor, they also enjoyed many perks unavailable to other prisoners: mattresses, sheets and blankets, access to libraries, and even free time to exercise. Above all, the food was a huge improvement over the gruel prisoners were used to. These research institutes were called *sharashkas*.

When Solzhenitsyn filled out a camp registration form, he identified himself as an "atomic physicist," which he certainly wasn't. But he knew that with his Rostov University degree in mathematics and physics, he could fake it.

Solzhenitsyn was recategorized as a special assignment prisoner, and in July 1946 he was sent to a facility in Rybinsk to work on the design and construction of jet engines. He and his new friends debated philosophy and politics with no fear they might be sent to prison, since they already *were* in prison. Privately, Solzhenitsyn continued to write.

A few months later, Solzhenitsyn was transferred to Marfino, another *sharashka* just outside Moscow. This was the setting for his autobiographical novel *The First Circle*. Here (as in Rybinsk), he wrote, "there was meat for dinner and butter for breakfast. You didn't have to work till the skin came off your hands and your fingers froze. . . . At [Marfino] you slept sweetly under a nice clean sheet."[25]

Solzhenitsyn spent three years working in the *sharashkas*.

Just before Christmas of 1948, Natalya was allowed to visit her husband. She told him that unless she divorced him, she would lose her job. Solzhenitsyn understood but was nonetheless devastated.

When discipline was tightened in the *sharashka*, Solzhenitsyn and his friend Dimitri Panin revolted, refusing to work on Sundays and complaining to the authorities. So eventually the authorities struck back by transferring both men in 1950 to "the deepest and most unforgiving recesses of the Gulag," the Ekibastuz labor camp in Kazakhstan.[26] Solzhenitsyn was back to a life of intense cold, gruel, and brutal labor, this time as a brick layer. Thousands of prisoners died under this treatment. Inmates were stripped of their names; they were instead called by numbers. Once again Solzhenitsyn made friends with other prisoners.

◆ ◆ ◆

In January 1952 Solzhenitsyn learned he had a malignant tumor on his groin. He could scarcely believe that, after enduring seven vicious, hungry years in the Gulag, mostly working in the freezing cold, he would die of cancer. He was thirty-three.

Solzhenitsyn was admitted to the camp hospital, where he waited two weeks for an operation that was conducted under local anesthesia.

He might later have speculated that the reason for his transfer to this terrible labor camp, and the appearance of this deadly disease, might have been the work of God—the final step in the long journey from atheism to Christianity and the answer to the question of why God allows bad things to happen to people he loves.

"Following an operation, I am lying in the surgical ward of a camp hospital. I cannot move," Solzhenitsyn relates in *The Gulag Archipelago*. "I am hot and feverish, but nonetheless my thoughts do not dissolve into delirium—and I am grateful to Dr. Boris Nikolayevich Kornfeld, who is sitting beside my cot and talking to me all evening."[27]

Kornfeld wasn't Solzhenitsyn's physician, so it was kind of him to visit with Solzhenitsyn. Sadly, this would be the last conversation of Kornfeld's life—and possibly the most important, although he couldn't have foreseen how famous this young man would one day become and how far-reaching his influence would be.

In this final conversation of his life, Kornfeld spoke to Solzhenitsyn of his conversion from Judaism to Christianity. This amazed Solzhenitsyn. "I am astonished at the conviction of the new convert," he wrote, "at the ardor of his words."[28]

The next morning, Kornfeld was carried into the operating room; he had been struck on his skull while he slept. He didn't survive the assault.

But his words to the prisoner the night before didn't go unheeded. Solzhenitsyn began to reexamine his life, to consider the twists and turns it had taken, and he wrote his thoughts down in verse to remember them.

"It was only when I lay there on rotting prison straw that I sensed within myself the first stirrings of good," Solzhenitsyn recalled. "Gradually, it was disclosed to me that the line separating good and evil passes not through states, nor between classes, nor between political parties either—but right through every human heart."[29]

Thinking of the vileness of high-ranking Soviet bureaucrats and executioners, "I remember myself in my captain's shoulder boards and the forward march of my battery through East Prussia, enshrouded in fire, and I say: 'So were *we* any better?'"[30]

"It was granted to me to carry away from my prison years on my bent back, which nearly broke beneath its load, this essential experience: how a human being becomes evil and how good," Solzhenitsyn wrote. "In the intoxication of youthful successes I had felt myself to be infallible, and I was therefore cruel. In the surfeit of power I was a murderer and an oppressor.

Since then I have come to understand the truth of all the religions of the world: They struggle with the evil inside a human being (inside every human being). It is impossible to expel evil from the world in its entirety, but it is possible to constrict it within each person."[31]

"That is why I turn back to the years of my imprisonment and say, sometimes to the astonishment of those about me: 'Bless you, prison!' I . . . have served enough time there. I nourished my soul there, and I saw without hesitation: 'Bless you, prison, for having been in my life!'"[32]

Commenting on this event in Solzhenitsyn's life, biographer Joseph Pearce wrote, "In facing death, he had gained an immeasurably greater understanding of life. It was an eternal paradox, at the very heart of life and death, which is encapsulated in the Gospels: he who loses his life shall find it."[33] And now the man who once eagerly embraced atheism "had ceased seeing life in terms of dialectical materialism and was beginning to perceive it in the light of theological mysticism."[34]

Solzhenitsyn identified his near-death from cancer, his service during the war, and his arrest as the "most important and defining moments" of his life.[35]

"When at the end of jail, on top of everything else, I was plagued with cancer, then I was fully cleansed and came back to a deep awareness of God and a deep understanding of life. From that time, I was formed essentially into who I am now."[36]

As he told an interviewer in 1976, "First comes the fight for survival, then the discovery of life, then God."[37]

Solzhenitsyn now sympathized with those who were being persecuted for their faith, as many of his fellow prisoners had been. In an astonishing feat of mental effort and discipline, he continued to write down his thoughts on scraps of paper, memorized the words, and then burned the papers. He befriended another poet, Anatoly Vasilyevich Silin, who also committed much of his writing to memory in the form of poetry. Silin quoted some of the twenty thousand lines of verse he'd memorized to Solzhenitsyn. By the time he left prison, Solzhenitsyn himself had memorized some twelve thousand lines of verse.

On February 13, 1953, after eight long years in the Gulag, Solzhenitsyn was released. He was taken by train to Dzhambul, near Kazakhstan, to begin what he thought would likely be permanent internal exile, far from his former wife and home. Nevertheless, Solzhenitsyn was overjoyed to be out of the hell of the Gulag.

Looking around him, he saw "amiable donkeys with little carts" that made way for them, "and from one yard a camel turned slowly and contemptuously to look at us. There were people, too, but we had eyes only for the women—those unfamiliar, forgotten creatures."[38]

That night—his first night of freedom—Solzhenitsyn walked in the moonlight, enjoying the fresh air. "Every fibre in me sings: I am free! I am free!"[39]

His first order of business, after celebrating his freedom, was to find a place to live. He moved into a hut with a roof so low he couldn't stand fully upright. It had no electricity and a dirt floor. He borrowed two boxes, which became his bed.

Two days later Solzhenitsyn arrived in town to hear, over a loudspeaker, the "sad" news that Stalin, the sadistic tyrant who had murdered at least twenty million people, had died. Little could have delighted Solzhenitsyn more, and he imagined the "unconcealed rejoicing" of his friends back in the prison camp. "I could have howled with joy there by the loudspeaker; I could even have danced a wild jig!"[40] Instead, he fixed a mournful expression on his face, pretending to grieve as the townspeople were doing.

Not long afterward, Solzhenitsyn joyfully resumed the work he had performed before the war: he became a village schoolteacher, teaching physics and mathematics. He made friends in his new town—but carefully. He knew the authorities were keeping a close watch on him. Solzhenitsyn became particularly close to fellow political exiles Nikolai and Elena Zubov.

Nothing was more important to Solzhenitsyn than his writing. The act of writing down his stories of life in the Gulag was illegal, and Solzhenitsyn hid his manuscripts in various places, even including inside a champagne bottle he buried.

Later in the year, his cancer returned, causing great abdominal pain. In January 1954 Solzhenitsyn entered the Tashkent Medical Institute and, over the next six weeks, endured "55 sessions of radiotherapy, during which the tumor was bombarded with 12 roentgens of radiation."[41] His autobiographical novel *Cancer Ward* was based on his experiences at the hospital. In this novel, he wrote, "This autumn I learned from experience that a man can cross the threshold of death even when his body is not dead. Your blood still circulates and your stomach digests, while you yourself have gone through the whole psychological preparation for death—and lived through death itself."[42]

With this round of cancer, at least—while he would prefer to live—Solzhenitsyn was comforted by his belief in the afterlife. Solzhenitsyn recovered from his cancer, an event he attributed to God's active intervention. There was simply no other rational way to understand it.

"With a hopelessly neglected and acutely malignant tumor, this was a divine miracle; I could see no other explanation. Since then, all the life that has been given back to me has not been mine in the full sense: it is built around a purpose."[43]

Leaving the hospital for the last time in the spring, Solzhenitsyn spotted a Tashkent church. To his surprise, the doors were open. He entered the church and thanked God for saving his life. But why had God spared him? Was it to tell the story no one else would tell, of the grotesque evil of the Soviet communist system—from someone who had experienced it personally? Had God allowed him to suffer as he had so that the world could know the truth?

◆ ◆ ◆

Over the next two years, Solzhenitsyn continued to teach during the day and write in secrecy at night. In February 1956 Soviet leader Nikita Khrushchev made his famous "secret speech" denouncing Stalin's crimes. The speech astonished the communist world. Two months later, it was announced that millions of former political prisoners, including Solzhenitsyn, would be given amnesty. This meant Solzhenitsyn no longer had to live in exile.

This amnesty brought about a surprising reunion with Natalya, who had been living in a common-law relationship with another man. Solzhenitsyn traveled to Ryazan, where Natalya lived, and now courted her for the second time, and eventually she agreed to remarry him.

Solzhenitsyn began teaching physics and astronomy at a Ryazan high school. But almost immediately, his relationship with Natalya took a downward turn. Prison had changed Solzhenitsyn dramatically, as might be expected. He no longer felt it was right to spend much time attending concerts and the ballet or visiting friends. He had a job to do that was infinitely more important than his own pleasure. So instead of doing these things, he spent nearly all his free time writing.

This devotion to his work frustrated Natalya, who wanted to enjoy life. Nonetheless she assisted him, copying drafts of his work, including several plays and early drafts of the manuscript that would become his masterwork and principal legacy, *The Gulag Archipelago.*

Despite the amnesty, however, Solzhenitsyn still had to keep his work utterly secret, so he shared what he was doing with only a handful of trusted friends.

In 1959 Solzhenitsyn wrote the novel that would change his life. It was a semiautobiographical novel titled *One Day in the Life of Ivan Denisovich,* describing a typical day at the Ekibastuz labor camp in Kazakhstan, detailing the merciless treatment of the prisoners and the arbitrary attacks by those in charge.

Solzhenitsyn showed the novel to his friend, a fellow political exile named Veniamin Teush, who in turn showed the work to another friend. Both were deeply impressed with what Solzhenitsyn had accomplished in writing it. But it might never have seen the light of day had it not been for Khrushchev's surprising speech, which "galvanized the Soviet cultural and intellectual elite out of its fearful passivity."[44]

In 1961 Khrushchev began an effort to "loosen the tight restraints upon society," leading the intelligentsia—including Solzhenitsyn—to wonder whether they could at last begin to write truthfully about life under Stalin.[45]

Solzhenitsyn now shared his novel with his friend Lev Kopelev; the two agreed that the monthly literary journal *Novy Mir* might be willing to publish it. The manuscript landed on the desk of the journal's editor, Aleksandr Trifonovich Tvardovsky, who took it home to read. He was deeply affected by the power of Solzhenitsyn's able storytelling. He cabled Solzhenitsyn, inviting him to Moscow to discuss the manuscript. The big question was, Might the Communist authorities possibly permit such an exposé of their evils to be published?

Tvardovsky sent copies to twenty-three Soviet authorities, including Khrushchev himself. The leader's secretary made a number of editorial changes before giving it his approval, and in October 1962, history was made. No fewer than one hundred thousand copies of *Novy Mir* hit the newsstands.

Solzhenitsyn's story was greeted with thunderous acclaim, although some commentators, knowing Khrushchev had approved it, believed Solzhenitsyn was merely "advancing the party's own cause of doing away with Stalin's personality cult."[46]

But ordinary Russian readers saw the author's truth-telling for what it was. *One Day in the Life of Ivan Denisovich* broke through decades of Soviet deceit, telling the truth about life under Communist rule. *Novy Mir* ultimately printed a staggering additional 750,000 copies for Russians eager to read it.

News of the novel sped around the world, and it was translated into several languages and read all over Western Europe. The royalties were such that Solzhenitsyn quit his teaching job to write full time. He bought a cabin in Rozhdestvo, some one hundred miles east of Moscow, where he wrote in solitude.

Tvardovsky and others demanded more of Solzhenitsyn's work, and the author obliged with two autobiographical short stories, titled "An Incident at Krechetovka Station" and "Matryona's Place," which Tvardovsky considered "a bit too Christian."[47] The story, which describes a woman who insists on returning good acts for evil ones—in effect, turning the other cheek—was deeply critical of Stalin's policies.

Solzhenitsyn had a feeling this openness would not last, that the time would come when he would no longer be able to publish works critical of the Soviet system—and he was right. Within just one year, the winds of literary freedom ceased to blow, and Communist Party members attacked Khrushchev for allowing Solzhenitsyn to publish his work. So he was denied permission to publish his manuscript of *The First Circle*. Then in 1964 Khrushchev himself was deposed and was replaced by Leonid Brezhnev.

Solzhenitsyn continued to write—he was now working on *The Gulag Archipelago*—and he continued to hide his work, now using a camera and microfilm to make copies of it. And his relationship with Natalya continued to deteriorate.

Meanwhile, Soviet authorities had their eye on Solzhenitsyn and again cracked down on him and other dissidents. To Solzhenitsyn's horror, the KGB raided the home of his friend Veniamin Teush, seizing three copies of Solzhenitsyn's novel *The First Circle* and other work that had not yet been published, "including two stridently anti-Soviet plays, *The Feast of the Victors* and *The Republic of Labor*."[48]

The loss of these works deeply distressed Solzhenitsyn. Concerned that he would be arrested and sent back to the camps, he went into hiding in the homes of friends. And like a man on a mission—which he certainly was—he continued to write. He didn't realize at the time how closely the Soviet government was watching and listening to everything he said and did. The KGB listened in on his conversations with Teush as Solzhenitsyn expressed his deep hostility to communism and his prediction that this system of government would collapse, along with the Soviet federation, before too many more years passed.

When the "Solzhenitsyn files"—secret documents the Soviets kept on the writer—were released, it became clear that the Politburo of the Communist Party viewed Solzhenitsyn as a dangerous threat.

To Solzhenitsyn's disappointment, a wary *Novy Mir* declined to publish *Cancer Ward*, which the writer had finished in 1966. But Solzhenitsyn went on the offensive in a shocking way. In November 1966 the Lazarev Institute of Oriental Studies invited Solzhenitsyn to read from his works. At this meeting he attacked the KGB for making "use of excerpts from my papers, taken out of context, to launch a campaign of defamation against me."[49] His fearlessness in doing this is hard to fathom, as though he was a prophet of God who existed only to speak the truth.

The response by his audience to this truth-telling was extraordinary and amazed him. "This was perhaps the first time, the very first time, that I felt myself, saw myself, making history," he wrote exultantly. "Almost every sally scorched the air like gunpowder! How these people must have yearned for truth. Oh God, how badly they wanted to hear the truth!"[50] With this speech, Solzhenitsyn—clearly no longer afraid—had gone from writing about the horrors of the communist system to openly condemning those who imposed it.

He spent the next two months frantically working to finish the second draft of *The Gulag Archipelago*, writing for sixteen hours every day. With *Novy Mir* refusing to publish any more of Solzhenitsyn's work, the author now considered another tack: somehow publishing outside the Soviet Union.

In 1967 trusted friends smuggled out microfilms containing *The First Circle* and much of Solzhenitsyn's other work. The following year, British and American publishers released both *Cancer Ward* and *The First Circle*, "causing an uproar in the Soviet literary establishment that reverberated all the way to the top of the Communist Party's political hierarchy."[51] But in the West, critics wildly praised *The First Circle*, comparing Solzhenitsyn to such Russian giants as Chekhov, Dostoyevsky, and Tolstoy. He was now "a novelist of international stature who was forcing both the Soviet Union and Western audiences to come to regard him as a person of rising personal authority in his own country."[52]

◆ ◆ ◆

Among the many people Solzhenitsyn trusted to help him with his work was a young mathematician named Natalya (or "Alya," as she preferred to be called) Svetlova. She was the divorced mother of a six-year-old son. At this point, Solzhenitsyn and his wife were seeing very little of each other, in part because Natalya disliked the publicity that now pursued her husband. Their marriage had been marked with impossibly long separations—the four years of the Second World War, the eight years in the Gulag, and then three more years while Solzhenitsyn lived in exile. By now their relationship had deteriorated to the point that even when they were in the same house, they slept in separate rooms.

So what Solzhenitsyn really thought of his relationship to his wife at that point is hard to say. With all that had transpired between them, he likely felt they were no longer obligated to each other. After all, she had lived with another man for some time before they came back to each other, and they had continued to grow further and further apart. Legally, however, he was still married. Nonetheless, not long after meeting Alya Svetlova, the two fell in love. She was just twenty-eight years old; Solzhenitsyn was forty-nine.

In 1970 Svetlova gave birth to Solzhenitsyn's son, a boy they named Yermolai. Another son, Ignat, was born in 1972, and a third son, Stephan, was expected in September 1973. At this point, Solzhenitsyn's wife finally agreed to give him the divorce he'd wanted for years. He and Alya were married in April 1973.

"In the interim, one can only guess to what degree Solzhenitsyn fought to suppress the voice of conscience," wrote Pearce.[53] Solzhenitsyn viewed his new wife as his soulmate. She was an Orthodox Christian, vibrant and intelligent, and deeply committed to helping her new husband with his work.

Solzhenitsyn spent 1969 working to finish *August 1914*, the first section of a planned multivolume novel he called *The Red Wheel*. This book explores the events that led to the 1917 Revolution.

It was that year, to Solzhenitsyn's shock, that the Soviet Writers Union expelled him. Angrily, he wrote, "At this time of crisis you are incapable of offering our grievously sick society anything constructive and good, anything but your malevolent vigilance, your 'hold tight and don't let go!'"[54]

But his loud protests went nowhere. Meanwhile, Soviet leaders had had quite enough of Solzhenitsyn and his incendiary scribblings. A wary Solzhenitsyn now began living in the home of a famous Soviet cellist, Mstislav Rostropovich. The musician's prestige was likely responsible for the fact that Solzhenitsyn wasn't arrested as other dissidents were at this time.

Then in October 1970, staggering news: Solzhenitsyn learned he had won the Nobel Prize for Literature. But he wasn't willing to travel to Sweden to receive the award because he feared he would not be allowed back into Russia. And quite shamefully, the Swedes refused to hold the ceremony in their embassy in Moscow, for fear of offending the Soviets.

In 1971 the KGB raided Solzhenitsyn's cabin in the woods. Outraged, the writer sent a letter to KGB chairman Yuri Andropov, telling him he had "borne in silence the lawlessness of your employees: the inspection of all my correspondence, the confiscation of half of it, the tracking down of my correspondents, their persecution at work and by state agencies, the spying around my house, the shadowing of visitors, the tapping of telephone conversations, the drilling of holes in ceilings. . . . But after the raid yesterday I will no longer be silent."[55]

The irony, of course, is that Solzhenitsyn had not been silent for some time, and Soviet higher-ups were at a loss as to what to do with this thorn in their side. His fame in the West prohibited their simply sending him to a prison or a mental hospital, as they had done with other troublemakers they wished to punish and silence. He was causing problems at a time when the Soviet Union was trying to negotiate "trade, cultural, and arms control agreements with the United States. It could no longer play Stalin's role of neighborhood thug in international affairs," biographer David Aikman observed.[56] Should they simply throw this infuriating so-and-so out of the country?

But the satanically devious KGB were never without options for long. In September 1973, they arrested one of Solzhenitsyn's assistants, Elizaveta Voronyanksaya, who broke down under vicious interrogation and revealed the location of a copy of *The Gulag Archipelago*. It was "one of the most damaging exposés of the reality of Soviet totalitarianism that had ever been written," based, as it was, on the memories of 227 survivors of the Gulag, plus Solzhenitsyn's own damning memories of his eight years behind bars.[57] If it were released to the world, it might well help to bring down that hellish Potemkin village known as the Soviet Union.

But Solzhenitsyn was as clever as his tormentors and had wisely sent a copy of *The Gulag Archipelago* to France. He knew the time for action had come and ordered, through his emissaries, that the French publish it immediately. Three months later, the book hit bookstores in Paris—and its devastating message exploded onto the global stage. Worldwide, readers learned, to their horror, how newly arrested Soviet prisoners were treated. They learned of the various forms of torture they endured when being questioned. They learned that inmates were shuttled to other locations in bread vans to prevent their fellow citizens from realizing just how many people were being rounded up. It was like reading George Orwell's *1984*—except almost unbelievably it wasn't fiction. In no time the Western world's views of the Soviet Union changed forever, which began the inevitable dismantling of what Ronald Reagan famously called "an Empire of Evil." And it began with a book, written in secret by a man who knew that, as an old Russian proverb said, "one word of truth outweighs the world." God had chosen him to be the brave truth-teller, had allowed him to suffer horribly and yet to survive, and had given him not just the terrible experiences but the gifts as a writer to tell this story that must be told and that would forever change the history of the world.

The Gulag Archipelago "stripped away the last fig leaf of pretense that the Soviet Union was anything other than a monstrous structure of lies and coercion," wrote Aikman.[58] No longer could leftist Western writers, so quick to defend communism, get away with claims that the Soviet system was an improvement on more democratic forms of government. The truth was that it was difficult to imagine a much worse form.

The humiliating publication of this book was predictably the last straw for Soviet leaders. Solzhenitsyn, they agreed, had to go—just as soon as they could find a country willing to take this peevish troublemaker. But first they would do all they could to destroy his reputation through the press, slamming him as a traitor, "a Maoist, a Judas, a blasphemer, an ally of hawks in the Pentagon."[59] *The Gulag Archipelago* was lies, they declared, all lies. But who would believe the claims of a regime built on lies from the beginning?

Solzhenitsyn swiftly fired back. *"Pravda* lies when it says that the author 'sees with the eyes of those who hanged revolutionary workers and peasants.' No! With the eyes of those who were shot and tortured."[60]

In February 1974, West German chancellor Willy Brandt announced that his country would be happy to take Solzhenitsyn off the Soviets' hands. The Soviets lost no time in taking him up on his offer.

To Solzhenitsyn's shock, on February 12, six KGB agents showed up at his apartment and arrested him. He packed a bag for what he expected to need in prison and kissed his wife goodbye, making the sign of the cross over her as he did so. The agents escorted Solzhenitsyn down three flights of stairs and into a car. They took him to Lefortovo Prison, where he was treated exactly as he had been treated nearly three decades previously: he was strip-searched and forced to share a small cell with two other men.

The next day, the Soviet deputy prosecutor-general informed Solzhenitsyn that he was a traitor and would be stripped of his citizenship and forced to leave his country. The author was then driven to a nearby airport and put on a plane. Where it was headed, he had no idea. Only when the plane landed did Solzhenitsyn look out the window and realize where he was. He was in Frankfurt, West Germany. He was free.

A few weeks later, his wife and children were allowed to join him in Zurich (where Solzhenitsyn had moved) for a life in exile. While it pained both Solzhenitsyn and his wife to leave Russia, their new life outside it meant that, at last, Solzhenitsyn could say and write what he pleased without the threat of prison. So he immediately went to work on *The Oak and the Calf,* his autobiography, which was published the following year. While he now enjoyed the freedom to write what he liked, he withheld publication of a portion of the book (which he titled

Invisible Allies) for two decades so as not to put at risk friends still living under Soviet rule.

Solzhenitsyn further outraged Soviet leaders by publishing *Lenin in Zurich*, an exposé of Lenin's collaboration with the Germans during the First World War.

Understanding freedom better than most in the free world, Solzhenitsyn admired Swiss democracy precisely because the country "was organized in small local units, such as the village and the canton," and unlike other western democracies, in which power was centralized, the Swiss emphasized "local self-determination and the active participation of the entire population."[61] Solzhenitsyn would later choose to live in a similar village in Vermont.

Meanwhile, *The Gulag Archipelago* was translated into English to cataclysmic acclaim, becoming an international bestseller. The book was, noted historian George Kennan, "the most powerful single indictment of a political regime ever to be leveled in modern times."[62] The dissident had exposed to the world the brutal murder of millions upon millions of people.

Solzhenitsyn traveled to Stockholm in December 1974 to belatedly accept his Nobel Prize, and it was here that he astonished the world by telling journalist and fellow Christian Malcolm Muggeridge that he fully expected to return one day to a Russia free of communist oppression—something that struck many as absurd, given how powerful the Soviet Union was at that time.

Solzhenitsyn traveled to Washington, DC, in June 1975 to deliver a speech to the American Federation of Labor and Congress of Industrial Organizations—one that would irritate the US government. This was because his speech was, in part, an attack on "the American policy of détente [easing hostility among nations through diplomacy], which he believed was a betrayal of his dissident friends in the Soviet Union and amounted to nothing less than a shameful compromise with evil."[63] Secretary of State Henry Kissinger, the author of détente, was especially annoyed, as was President Gerald Ford, who declined to invite the world-famous dissident to the White House. But Solzhenitsyn knew speaking the truth about moral courage—and moral cowardice—was far more important than dining with morally compromised leaders for a photo opportunity. God would be his judge. What others thought was infinitely less compelling.

Of course Solzhenitsyn liked the United States, and in July 1976—around the 200th anniversary of the birth of the freest country in the world—he decided to move his family to a home near the quiet village of Cavendish, Vermont. Here, on fifty acres of land, they would live for the next eighteen years in seclusion in a large two-story house set among the woods and mountain streams. A chain-link fence surrounded the property, with a television monitor perched above the electric gate. Their neighbors protected their privacy, both from curious tourists and from visitors who might have darker motives than simply spotting the bearded Russian, refusing to give directions to the Solzhenitsyn home and calling the police if they spotted a car with out-of-state plates.

In addition to Solzhenitsyn's wife and three sons, his secretary lived in the house, along with a Russian tutor for the children, Alya's mother, and Alya's son from her first marriage, who visited during school vacations.

Christian faith was deeply important to the former atheist and his family. A cross dangled from the neck of each of the Solzhenitsyns, and the family faithfully observed religious holidays, particularly Lent and Easter. Their home boasted an Orthodox chapel, and whenever a priest visited the family, he performed services there.

Early each morning, the family prayed together, particularly that Russia's people would ultimately prevail over their oppressors. And then, after downing a cup of coffee, Solzhenitsyn would head for a little summerhouse not far from the main house, where he could write undisturbed.

When his sons grew older, Solzhenitsyn tutored them in mathematics and physics, while their mother taught them Russian literature. It was important to the parents that their children know what was going on in Russia, and they immersed them in Russian culture in anticipation of returning to their homeland. After this grounding, the boys attended local American schools.

Solzhenitsyn became more and more concerned with the spiritual renewal of his people, believing that political change would not occur without it.

In 1978 the fifty-nine-year-old was invited to give the commencement speech at Harvard University—which turned out to be, in the opinion of many, one of the greatest speeches of the twentieth century. Solzhenitsyn titled it "A World Split Apart," and in giving it, he managed to enrage much of the American press, the socialist intelligentsia, and a good many Harvard parents in a speech that was, as my old friend Chuck Colson put it, "a no-holds-barred condemnation of western secularism" and decadence. With his beard and fearless proclamation of difficult-to-hear truths, Solzhenitsyn was like an Old Testament prophet come to life, and the spoiled Harvard audience hardly knew what to make of it.

"The Western world has lost its courage," he thundered, "both as a whole and separately, in each country, each government, each political party, and, of course, in the United Nations. Such a decline is particularly noticeable among the ruling groups and the intellectual elite, causing an impression of loss of courage by the entire society. . . . Should one point out that from ancient times declining courage has been considered the beginning of the end?"

He noted that the "defense of individual rights has reached such extremes as to make society as a whole defenseless against certain individuals. It is time, in the West," he announced, "to defend not so much human rights as human obligations."

The writer pointed out that "destructive and irresponsible freedom has been granted boundless space," resulting in a society that "appears to have little defense against the abyss of human decadence, such as, for example, misuse of liberty for moral violence against young people, such as motion pictures full of pornography, crime, and horror. It is considered to be part of freedom and theoretically counterbalanced by the young people's right not to look or not to accept," he noted. But he pointed out that "life organized legalistically has thus shown its inability to defend itself against the corrosion of evil."

Solzhenitsyn then turned his attention to the Western media, bemoaning that there was "no true moral responsibility for deformation or disproportion." Journalists intruded on the privacy of famous people (such as himself), then claimed that the public had the right to know, he charged. "This is a false slogan. . . . People also have the right not to know, and it's a much more valuable one. The right not to have their divine souls stuffed with gossip, nonsense, vain talk."

With many journalists still reeling, Solzhenitsyn struck again. Hastiness and superficiality, he said, "are the psychic disease of the twentieth century, and more than anywhere else this disease is reflected in the press. How many hasty, immature, superficial, and misleading judgments are expressed every day, confusing readers, without any verification?" he asked. And why were so many journalists content to simply follow intellectual fashions?

Solzhenitsyn, it seemed, understood American freedom infinitely better than those on whom it had been showered. He now looked to America's birth, suggesting that our Founding Fathers would be shocked at the idea that "an individual could be granted boundless freedom simply for the satisfaction of his instincts or whims." They would, instead, have expected that individual human rights be given "in the assumption of his constant religious responsibility."

His audience should not assume that his fellow Russians longed to live in the West, Solzhenitsyn went on; those who spent decades suffering under Communist rule would hardly desire the shallow, materialist lifestyle of the West, because "through deep suffering, people in our country have now achieved a spiritual development of such intensity that the Western system in its present state of spiritual exhaustion does not look attractive" because "the human soul longs for things higher, warmer, and purer than those offered by today's mass living habits, introduced by the revolting invasion of commercial publicity, by TV stupor, and by intolerable music."

If humanists could be believed, he continued, our only purpose in life is to be happy. But if that were the case, we would not be born to die. But since we are "doomed to death, [our] task on earth evidently must be of a more spiritual nature: It cannot be the search for the best ways to obtain material goods and then cheerfully get the most of them. It has to be the fulfillment of a permanent, earnest duty so that one's life journey may become an experience of moral growth, so that one may leave life a better human being than one started it."

Solzhenitsyn left his audience with a warning: "All the glorified technological achievements of progress, including the conquest of outer space, do not redeem the twentieth century's moral poverty," he argued. "On the way from the Renaissance to our days we have enriched our experience, but we have lost the concept of a Supreme Complete Entity which used to restrain our passions and our irresponsibility. We have placed too much hope in political and social reforms, only to find out that we were being deprived of our most precious possession: our spiritual life."[64]

After the pit bulls of the press on both sides of the Atlantic had sunk their teeth into him, Solzhenitsyn wryly wrote, "What was mainly expected of me . . . was the gratitude of the exile to the great Atlantic fortress of Liberty, singing praises to its might and virtues, which were lacking in the USSR."[65]

Ordinary Americans, reading of his remarks in their newspapers, wrote Solzhenitsyn to express tremendous enthusiasm for his views. Many wondered how such a fresh voice had managed to escape the deep rut of clichés they read day after day. To them it was a miracle and a gift, and in the decades since he delivered the speech, it has inspired count-less others in whose souls the powerful truth of his words has resonated.

With this historic speech at last behind him, the writer now spent long hours every day working on his books, including the completion of the five-thousand-page *Red Wheel*.

In 1983 Solzhenitsyn traveled to London to accept the Templeton Prize. In his address at Buckingham Palace, titled "Men Have Forgotten God," he warned against the dangers of atheism. He also met with Prime Minister Margaret Thatcher and attended services at the Russian Church in Exile.

In March 1985, Mikhail Gorbachev became general secretary of the Soviet Union. Under his leadership, things changed, albeit slowly; and Soviet dissidents campaigned for Solzhenitsyn's return. But then the worm turned; the hardliners fought back. Vadim Medvedev, newly appointed as the Politburo member responsible for ideology, vetoed publication of Solzhenitsyn's books in the Soviet Union on the basis that they were "undermining the foundations of the Soviet state."[66]

But the forces of liberalization would not be stopped. Communist Party liberals formed the Democratic Union, the first organized opposition movement to emerge since 1921; Gorbachev banned its meetings. Then Estonia defiantly broke away from the Soviet Union; and Latvia and Lithuania boldly published Solzhenitsyn's essay "Live Not by Lies." The Soviet Union was foundering, and its leaders knew it. As Shakespeare had said four hundred years earlier, "The truth will out."

In March 1989, Soviet citizens were, for the first time in many years, allowed to choose from more than one candidate, including some who were not Party members. Boris Yeltsin and Andrei Sakharov—another Gulag survivor—were elected to the Soviet parliament, along with other reformers.

In April, delegates—including fellow writer Yury Karyakin— demanded that Solzhenitsyn be given back his citizenship. "Let us restore Soviet citizenship to the man who was the first person to tell the truth about Stalin!" Karyakin exclaimed.[67]

In October, despite efforts to block its publication, *Novy Mir* published portions of *The Gulag Archipelago*. The totalitarian Soviet dam at last was breaking.

In Red Square there were counterdemonstrators during the annual

October Revolution celebrations. Meanwhile, the Berlin Wall had fallen, and the Velvet Revolution was taking place in Czechoslovakia. The year 1989 was, to borrow from Queen Elizabeth, the Communists' *annus horribilis.*

In December, they finally gave up and sourly told Solzhenitsyn to apply for citizenship if he wanted to. But he wasn't about to leap back into their arms. So he rejected the offer because, as Alya told the press, "It's shameful, after all that they have done to him, that the Parliament doesn't have the simple courage to admit that they were wrong. . . . They kick him out and after that they want him to come and bow and ask permission to enter. . . . We've waited a long time. We will wait until they become wise."[68]

But Gorbachev didn't become wise; he sent tanks into Azerbaijan in an effort to smash that country's independence movement, killing over one hundred people and further outraging Soviet citizens. But whatever the Soviets did now was whistling in the dark. Their day had come and gone.

In the elections of March 1990, Soviet republican nationalists "swept the board, paving the way for the declarations of independence that followed," Pearce wrote, adding that "in Russia, the anti-communist Democratic Platform gained majorities in the powerful city councils of Leningrad and Moscow"; by month's end, a triumphant Boris Yeltsin was elected chairman of the Russian parliament. And on June 12, Yeltsin declared "Russian independence from the Soviet Union in imitation of the Baltic states."[69]

The Soviet Union was no more. Watching events from faraway Vermont, the Solzhenitsyns were overjoyed.

Would Solzhenitsyn return to the place of his birth? Yes, he announced—but only when "all the judicial procedures that had been taken against him [were] annulled." What was the rush? Knowing he had the upper hand, he also demanded that his books be sold openly in Russia; and by September 1991, both wishes had come true. Soviet prosecutor Nikolai Trubin announced that the charges against Solzhenitsyn at the time of his 1974 arrest were "baseless." And in 1990 alone, an astonishing seven million copies of his books were sold in Russia.

Solzhenitsyn and his wife and son Yermolai went home to Russia in May 1994. It was a triumphal return, complete with dozens of journalists and cheering crowds. After landing in Khabarovsk, the family traveled triumphantly by train across the country, stopping to chat cheerfully with various people, while Solzhenitsyn took notes of everything he saw and heard.

The former dissident settled in a large house in the woods not far from Moscow with his family and continued to write. For a few months, he hosted a biweekly television program titled *A Meeting with Solzhenitsyn*. When talking with journalists, he seemed as irritated with the flaws of his own postcommunist country as he was with the West, especially the "former members of the communist elite, along with Russia's new rich, who amassed instant fortunes through banditry."[70]

He spoke with journalist David Aikman about Russia's "fatigue of culture, its emaciation," and its "need for repentance . . . for the terrible wrongs committed there under the rule of Communism."[71] And Solzhenitsyn shocked many by expressing his gratitude to God for having been a resident of the Gulag, "because in those circumstances human nature becomes very much more visible. I was very lucky to have been in the camps—and especially to have survived" to tell not only his own story but the stories of so many others he had met there.[72]

In 2007 Russia awarded Solzhenitsyn the State Prize of the Russian Federation. Yury Osipov, president of the Russian Academy of Sciences, lauded Solzhenitsyn as "the author of works without which the history of the 20th century is unthinkable."[73]

On August 3, 2008, fourteen years after returning to the land he loved, at the age of eighty-nine, Alexander Solzhenitsyn died at home of heart failure and was buried three days later in the Donskoy Monastery. He had outlived the Soviet system by eighteen years.

The Nobel Prize winner will always be remembered as the man who exposed the horrors of the Soviet labor camps, which destroyed the lives of some sixty million people, and who played an undeniably dispositive role in the collapse of the Soviet Union. But he should also be recalled as a man who made a triumphant, unlikely leap from atheism to a rich faith in God.

A few months prior to returning to Russia, a journalist asked Solzhenitsyn if he feared death.

"Absolutely not!" Solzhenitsyn replied, smiling. "It will just be a peaceful transition. As a Christian, I believe there is life after death, and so I understand that this is not the end of life. The soul has a continuation, the soul lives on. Death is only a stage, some would say even a liberation. In any case, I have no fear of death."[74]

SEVEN

Billy Graham

1918–2018

I am convinced the greatest act of love we can ever perform for people is to tell them about God's love for them in Christ.

—BILLY GRAHAM

t was September 14, 2001—three days after the September 11 attacks robbed nearly three thousand people of their lives. A service of prayer and remembrance was taking place at the National Cathedral in Washington, DC. After prayers and hymns, including "O God, Our Help in Ages Past," a hush fell as an elderly man with a mane of white hair stood up. A church official helped him up the steps to the pulpit. From there, the man gazed through his spectacles at an audience that included every living former president, along with the current one, George W. Bush. It was to Bush that the eighty-two-year-old known as "America's pastor"—Billy Graham—addressed his first words, thanking him for calling a national day of prayer and remembrance, which the country badly needed.

His next words were for his fellow Americans—the thousands seated in the pews and the millions watching at home on their television sets—who desperately needed comfort and hope after the evil and horrible attacks earlier that week.

"We come together today," Graham said, "to affirm our conviction that God cares for us, whatever our ethnic, religious, or political background may be."

His message may have surprised some—especially those who had suffered the loss of loved ones on 9/11 or those whose feelings about Muslims had hardened into hate. He reminded his audience, quoting Psalm 46:1–2, that "God is our refuge and strength, an ever-present help in trouble. Therefore we will not fear, though the earth give way and the mountains fall into the heart of the sea."

He understood that many were angry with God for allowing the loss of so many lives at the hands of evil men. God understands this anger, he said, and we should remember that he "can be trusted, even when life seems at its darkest."

The attacks were a reminder of "the mystery and reality of evil" and of our need for one another. And as difficult as it may be for us to understand, Graham noted, the attacks "can give a message of hope . . . for the future" because of God's promises.

Graham spoke of his own hope for his earthly life and for the life to come and reminded his audience that many of those killed in the attacks were now with God, enjoying the glories of heaven so much that they would not desire to return to earth. This, he announced, is the hope for everyone who puts his faith in God.

Then Graham briefly gave the witness that made it into every sermon he'd ever given since he'd first begun preaching in 1937 as a teenage boy. And then he prayed that all who heard his voice would feel God's loving arms around them, understanding that, if they put their trust in God, he would never forsake them.

As Graham made his way back to his seat, there was silence at first. Then the congregation rose to its feet and gave a standing ovation.

◆ ◆ ◆

When we read the words of Jesus, who commanded his followers to go into the world to preach the good news to every creature, we don't get the idea that we are to do this by ourselves. But William Franklin Graham Jr. probably came closer to achieving this magnificent goal than anyone who has lived since Jesus spoke these words. Over a career spanning seventy-six years (1937–2013), the evangelist preached the gospel *in person* to almost 215 million people in 185 countries. He reached hundreds of millions more through radio, television, newspaper columns, magazines, books, films, and webcasts.

Many younger people don't remember Billy Graham, or if they do, they remember him as an old man with a shaky voice. They probably don't picture him as a skinny teenage boy milking cows on his parents' farm or a tall, good-looking, and popular high school student going out on dates in his father's Model T Ford. They don't envision a young man trying to figure out what to do with his life—and then coming to the conclusion that he wanted to devote himself, heart and soul, to . . . baseball. But that's a fact.

◆ ◆ ◆

William Franklin Graham Jr. was born on November 7, 1918, four days before the armistice that ended the First World War. His father was a dairy farmer, William Franklin Graham Sr.; and his mother was Morrow Coffey Graham.

Billy—called Billy Frank by his family—was raised to believe in hard work. The 1929 stock market crash led to his father losing his entire savings, $4,000 ($58,000 in today's money), when the Farmers' and Merchants' Bank of Charlotte failed; the Great Depression followed, and the Graham farm nearly went under when the price of milk dropped to five cents a quart. But no matter how bad things got, Graham's father never lost his sense of humor. Billy recalled that neighbors enjoyed coming to the Graham home simply to hear his dad crack his jokes.

When Billy was two, his sister Catherine was born. Four years later brother Melvin came into the world, and the family moved to a two-story brick house that—unlike their first home—featured indoor plumbing. In 1932 sister Jean arrived.

As a boy, Billy rode his bike down the road, followed by goats and dogs, and enjoyed riding one of the family's mules, which quietly tolerated the Graham children standing upright on its back. Treats took the form of ice cream or soft drinks at the drugstore now and then on a Saturday evening or a film starring the aw-shucks wisdom of Will Rogers or the shenanigans of whatever incorrigible rogue Wallace Beery was playing at the time. Billy and his brother worked in their mother's garden and in the fields of corn, wheat, rye, and barley.

The hardest work—because it meant getting up at 2:30 a.m.—was milking twenty cows every morning. This took two hours, after which Billy was allowed to have breakfast. The same task awaited Billy when he got home from school that afternoon, followed by shoveling out the manure, refilling the feed troughs, and lugging the milk cans to the milk-processing house.

As a boy, Graham was taught to obey his parents without questioning their orders, and it never would have occurred to him to lie, cheat, steal, or destroy property. As for laziness—that was considered a great evil in a home where honest labor was viewed as honorable.

Billy, who became an early opponent of segregation, received his earliest lesson in the equality of all people through his father's friend Reese Brown, an African American former army sergeant who worked as the foreman on the Graham farm for fifteen years. Graham's father paid him three to four dollars per day, making him one of the highest-paid farmhands in the county, which earned Billy's father some criticism from other farmers who were shocked a black man made so much. Young Billy played with the Brown children and fondly remembered Mrs. Brown's "fabulous" buttermilk biscuits. Billy, along with everyone else he knew, had great respect for Reese. In Billy's view, there was nothing Reese couldn't do if he put his mind to it.

When it rained, Billy liked to go to the hay barn, lie on a pile of straw, and listen to the rain. He kept the habit, in a sense, for the rest of his life. Whenever the noise of big cities became too much for him, Graham escaped into a quiet church to meditate.

His early-morning responsibilities on the farm meant Billy often didn't sleep more than three or four hours per night—a factor, he believed, in his doing poorly in high school. But he enjoyed reading adventure books at home, especially Tarzan stories. By the time he was ten, his mother had taught him to memorize the Westminster Shorter Catechism. When Billy was as young as eight, Reese Brown taught him to drive a truck so that by the time he was twelve, he was driving the family's Model T Ford.

Billy began borrowing the car when he was in ninth grade, to attend a basketball game or go on a date. As with most kids in that time and place, nothing happened on those dates beyond hand-holding and kissing. He shared the same kind of thoughts and desires as any other teenage boy, but God used the love, faith, and discipline of his parents— not to mention their excellent example—to keep the boy out of trouble.

The Grahams attended an Associate Reformed Presbyterian church on Sundays, often going to both morning and evening services, although Billy was mostly bored by the sermons. If they missed the evening service, Billy's mother made up for it by telling her children Bible stories.

The Graham parents were teetotalers and were determined that their children should be too. One day, when Billy was about fifteen, his father sat him and his sister Catherine down and forced them each to drink a bottle of beer, convinced the taste would cure them forever of wanting more. It did. Whenever any of their friends tried to get them to imbibe, the elder Graham said, Billy and Catherine could truthfully tell them that they'd already tasted alcohol and didn't like it.

As a high school student, in addition to the considerable farm-work, Billy practiced baseball, did his homework, and went hunting and fishing with his friends. But baseball was his favorite pastime, and he played on his high school team.

Billy gave his first speech when he was about twelve, portraying Uncle Sam in a school pageant. He practiced the speech over and over again until he was word perfect. Despite this, when the time came, he went through exquisite agony, his hands perspiring and his knees shaking. Graham vowed to himself that he would never become a public speaker.

Billy began to take his faith more seriously when he was sixteen. An itinerant evangelist named Mordecai Fowler Ham Jr. arrived in town, spending eleven weeks preaching morning and night in a tent on Pecan Avenue. Billy stayed away because he had heard things about Ham that antagonized him. He thought Ham's approach to the gospel sounded like "a religious circus."

But his parents attended the meetings and spoke well of them. Still, Billy wasn't interested. He was particularly irritated when he read in the newspapers that Ham had spoken about immoral conduct by students at the local high school. Angry students made plans to demonstrate on the platform where Ham stood, and Billy thought he might go and see whether something interesting happened. He became even more interested in going when his friend Albert McMakin urged him to "come out and hear our fighting preacher."[1]

Ham was a fighter? Well, that was different! Albert allowed Graham to drive his truck—filled with both blacks and whites—to the meeting. They joined thousands of others, sitting in the back of the auditorium. As Graham remembered, Ham opened his Bible and began speaking directly from the text. Decades later, Graham could no longer recall the subject of Ham's preaching, but he was "spellbound." Ham was getting through to him, and as Graham listened, he heard the voice of the Holy Spirit.

Graham eagerly attended the next night—in fact, he attended every single meeting for the next few weeks. He may have picked up a sermon trick from Ham, of beginning his sermon with an exciting topic, such as the second coming, infidelity, or the reality of hell. Years later, Graham would often do the same.

Ham's manner of preaching fascinated Graham. As a result, he became deeply convicted about his sinfulness and rebellion.

Ham spoke with embarrassing frankness about various sins and ordered his listeners to mend their ways lest they end up in hell. One night, Graham was so sure that Ham was speaking directing to him that he did his best to hide behind a woman sporting a wide-brimmed hat. Despite his discomfort, Graham found it impossible to stay away.

It dawned on the teenager that he really did not know Jesus Christ for himself. While his parents were Christians, Graham knew faith couldn't be inherited "like the family silver."[2] Nor could regular church attendance or his own efforts to do better earn him any merit. He was spiritually dead, and he knew it.

Everything changed when Dr. Ham finished his message and invited his listeners to accept Christ. He quoted Romans 5:8 (KJV): "But God commendeth his love toward us, in that, while we were yet sinners, Christ died for us." This was followed by two hymns, "Just as I Am" and "Almost Persuaded, Now to Believe."

As the second hymn ended, Graham joined hundreds of others in walking to the front of the auditorium. Billy experienced no emotional reaction, which bothered him. He considered going back to his seat when a friend of the family named J. D. Prevatt approached him, weeping. Embracing Graham, Prevatt helped him understand God's plan for his salvation, and urged him to accept Christ in order to become a child of God.

Prevatt prayed for Billy and guided his young friend to pray as well. Having heard Ham's message, Billy felt an inner compulsion to go forward and publicly commit himself to Christ. Intellectually, Graham accepted Christ to the extent that he acknowledged what he knew about him to be true. But on the emotional level, Graham wanted to love Christ "in return for His loving me."[3] But was Graham willing to turn his life over to God and allow him to rule in his life?

Graham checked "recommitment" on the card he was given, believing that his baptism and confirmation had been professions of faith as well. The difference was that now he was "doing it on *purpose*, doing it with *intention*."[4] Graham believed that this was the moment that he truly committed himself to Christ.

But there were no bells and whistles, no palpitations. His father hugged him, and back at home his mother told him how happy she was with his decision.

Upstairs, preparing for bed, Billy dropped to his knees and prayed, "Lord, I don't know what happened to me tonight. *You* know. And I thank You for the privilege I've had tonight."[5]

Back at school, Billy invited friends to attend Ham's meetings with him, and they went a few times but made no commitment. He endured his first dose of persecution when one of his teachers mocked him, saying in front of the class, "I understand we have Preacher Graham with us today."[6]

While he still didn't fully understand what had happened to him, Graham now enjoyed attending church activities, and he prayed and read the Bible with real joy. He even sang hymns, despite being a terrible singer. But his bovine audience was gracious and simply continued chewing their cud as Billy milked them. Family members noticed a difference in Graham. For one thing, he felt he must break up with his girlfriend because she didn't believe as he did, and he did.

Billy still enjoyed working on the farm and playing baseball, but he realized his life lacked genuine purpose. If he couldn't be a Major League Baseball player—which seemed painfully to be the case—he assumed he would become a farmer, like his father. Was that God's plan?

But then one day he preached something like a sermon. An evangelist named Jimmie Johnson drove Graham to a nearby jail and then told the prisoners that Graham would be happy to tell them what it was like to convert to Christianity. With his knees knocking, Graham spoke for perhaps three minutes. This experience reinforced his conviction that becoming a preacher was the last thing he would ever do.

Billy began attending a Tuesday night Bible study called the Fellowship Club at the home of "Mommy" Jones, who taught the Bible on her screened front porch.

Then two evangelists who stayed at the Graham home, including Jimmie Johnson, convinced Billy that he should attend college. After evangelist Dr. Bob Jones Sr. spoke at Billy's high school, Graham's parents decided it would be a good idea for him to attend the college Jones had founded in East Tennessee, not knowing it was unaccredited. Grady Wilson, a high school friend of Billy's who would work at Graham's side for the rest of his life, decided to attend as well. His older brother, known as T.W., was already enrolled.

After graduating from high school, to earn tuition money, Graham went to work for the Fuller Brush Company, selling brushes door-to-door and earning a then-whopping seventy-five dollars a week.

When he began college at Bob Jones that fall, Billy still didn't know what he wanted to do with his life. And he discovered, to his dismay, that the college's rules were extremely rigid, as was Billy was bothered by the fact that Bob Jones allowed no one besides himself to interpret doctrine, ethics, and academics. Why was no one permitted to reason matters out or consider other viewpoints?

A friend urged Billy to join him at the Florida Bible Institute near Tampa (now Trinity College of Florida). When he visited Florida with his family over Christmas vacation, he was delighted with the warm weather and orange groves and in January 1937 began classes at the Institute, earning money by working in the kitchen and on the grounds. He also had a chance to meet famous evangelists, for whom he sometimes caddied on the golf course.

In the classroom, he enjoyed exposure to diverse viewpoints, "a wondrous blend of ecumenical and evangelical thought that was really ahead of its time," Graham noted.[7] His instructors represented many different denominations and backgrounds, and exhibited to their students the harmony that could exist "where Christ and His Word were loved and served."[8] Contrary to Jones's approach, students here were encouraged to think matters through for themselves, never forgetting to undergird their thinking with scriptural authority.

Students were also sent out to talk about Jesus at churches, trailer parks, street corners, and jails. Billy felt that it came more naturally than it had before and sometimes preached six times a day. He even thought God might want him to spend his life preaching. But it wasn't a career choice he was especially excited about. Nonetheless, he practiced giving sermons by borrowing sermon outlines from books, paddling out to an island, and preaching to every creature he encountered, from alligators to birds. He remembered that "fellow students would line the opposite bank at my return to cheer me on with comments like, 'How many converts did you get today, Billy?'"[9]

During that first year at school, Billy met a lovely dark-haired girl named Emily Cavanaugh—and promptly fell in love. Though just eighteen, he proposed to her during summer vacation, in a letter. Emily said she needed time to think about it. By that fall she indicated that she would say yes to his letter but began having second thoughts. By the end of the school year, she confessed she was in love with someone else.

Billy was devastated. But he realized that an even bigger problem was figuring out what God wanted for his life. He loved sharing the gospel but had no interest in spending the rest of his life doing it. But he couldn't shake the idea that this was what God wanted him to do. When he preached in one of the trailer parks, the crowds ranged from two hundred to a thousand, and many people responded to his sermons by turning to Christ.

When Billy finally made his decision to serve God fully, it was on a nearby golf course—a telling setting, given how much time he would spend playing golf in his lifetime, often with presidents. While taking a walk on the course one balmy evening, he dropped to his knees, prostrated himself, and sobbed, "Oh, God, if you want me to serve you, I will."[10]

Ironically, as soon as he made this decision, the preaching invitations seemed to evaporate. Eventually, that summer he was invited to speak at the West Tampa Gospel Mission to a group of Hispanic teenagers. Afterward he went out and preached seven more sermons on street corners, something he continued to do each weekend for the next two years, usually in front of bars.

Other preaching offers began to arrive. And then came an exciting opportunity to preach every evening for a week at East Palatka Baptist Church, where eighty souls accepted Jesus. He was also invited to preach live every morning over the airwaves at radio station WFOY in St. Augustine.

Around this time, Graham officially joined the Southern Baptist denomination and was ordained.

In the summer of 1939, Graham was invited to preach at a two-week evangelistic series at Florida's Welaka Baptist Church, the longest he had preached at one place. While the fishing village had a reputation for having a rough clientele, the Lord, through Graham, drew large crowds and converts.

Graham was next asked to replace a pastor at a large church, the Tampa Gospel Tabernacle, for six weeks, where his congregation was mostly Cuban immigrants. Graham had amusing memories of those weeks when he lived in the church parsonage. For instance, during his rehearsals on Saturdays, the church's janitor didn't hesitate to critique his sermons and offer helpful tips for improving them.

One night, Graham woke up to the sound of someone breaking into the parsonage. He grabbed his old .22-caliber rifle, loaded it, and fired it through the bedroom door into the next room. The bullet lodged harmlessly in the ceiling, but the noise clearly made an impression on the intruder, who instantly fled out the back door.

Graham graduated from the Institute in 1940, and when a friend, after hearing Billy preach, offered to fund a year of schooling at Wheaton College, Graham, now twenty-one, gladly accepted. Among his classmates were the first blacks he had ever shared a classroom with. He was sure his classmates were amused by his "Li'l Abner appearance," he remembered. "I felt like a hick."[11] Nor could some of his fellow students make hide nor hair of what he was saying through his Southern drawl.

Billy majored in anthropology and took classes in everything from classical Greek to economics to geology, hoping to gain as broad a liberal arts education as possible. As a student, he was invited to speak at the United Gospel Tabernacle a number of times.

In 1941 he accepted a position as pastor of the Tabernacle, where he had to preach two sermons per week in addition to running a Wednesday night prayer meeting.

But after the Japanese attacked Pearl Harbor on December 7, 1941, Graham attempted to become a military chaplain. But the War Department said that as he was lacking both a college degree and seminary courses, he was unqualified. But God had other plans for Graham at Wheaton. They involved a young woman named Ruth Bell, whom he described as a "slender, hazel-eyed movie starlet." But Ruth was the daughter of a missionary doctor and had spent most of her life in China and Korea. After their first date—to a production of Handel's *Messiah*—Ruth later wrote that she returned to her dorm room, dropped to her knees, and told God that she would consider it the greatest privilege imaginable if she could spend the rest of her life serving him as Graham's wife. For Billy's part, he fell instantly in love with this beautiful, devout girl.

On a subsequent date, the two walked to a graveyard and read the tombstones. When Ruth informed him that she believed God was calling her to the mission field in Tibet—and wanted Billy to go with her—he was shocked. He felt no such calling. Meanwhile, they continued to enjoy the social events and activities Wheaton offered. When he proposed marriage, Ruth didn't give him an immediate answer. The two were separated that summer, but in July Ruth sent Billy a letter in which she told him she believed God wanted her to marry Graham. So she accepted his proposal. But they agreed not to marry until they had graduated.

Already during their engagement, Ruth was frustrated at how much time her fiancé spent traveling to preach. What, she wondered, was life going to be like once she had married this hard-charging evangelist?

January 1943 brought an offer for Billy to pastor Western Springs Baptist Church, not far from Wheaton. Graham, who thought the pastorate would help him achieve his then-goal of becoming an army chaplain, accepted the offer.

That June, Ruth and Billy graduated from Wheaton and married in August. After a honeymoon in the Blue Ridge Mountains, they returned to Chicago to a furnished apartment. Shortly after their arrival, Ruth came down with a high fever and sore throat. This was when she realized how committed her new husband was to preaching. Needing to travel to Ohio for a weeklong engagement, he took Ruth to the hospital, kissed her goodbye—and drove off.

It was an odd beginning to their life together, but the couple quickly recovered. They were "typical lovebirds," as Graham recalled, and loved going out for hamburgers together or listening to murder mysteries on the radio while eating at home.[12] Ruth helped Billy research his sermons and went with him to visit parishioners, and church attendance grew rapidly.

And then came the first big turning point in the lives of the newlyweds: a minister named Torrey Johnson asked Billy to take over a forty-five-minute Sunday night radio program he no longer had time for. After Graham discussed the matter with Ruth and his deacons, and prayed about it, he accepted.

Members of the Wheaton women's glee club agreed to sing on the show. But Billy, who knew few listeners had heard of him, determined to get someone on the show they *had* heard of: George Beverly Shea, who was working at Moody Bible Institute's WMBI station in Chicago. Billy visited Shea in his Chicago office and convinced him to sing on his new program.

Ruth helped Billy write scripts for the program, which involved Billy telling three-minute stories focused on the day's news, followed by a song, after which Graham would preach. The show was broadcast from the basement of Graham's church and immediately became popular. Fan mail poured in.

By the following spring, Graham's popularity was growing, and he was becoming restless with his church duties. He wanted to be moving, traveling, and preaching. In turn, his church was frustrated at Graham's seemingly endless out-of-town engagements.

And now Torrey Johnson stepped backed into his life. He wanted to start Christian rallies for soldiers and other young people flooding into Chicago every weekend, who usually headed for the taverns and other unsavory places. The rallies would feature gospel music, testimonies, and short, youth-oriented sermons. Johnson planned to call it Chicagoland Youth for Christ. And he wanted Billy Graham to be part of it.

Graham accepted, preaching for the first time on May 27, 1944, at Chicago's Orchestra Hall to nearly three thousand people. When he gave the invitation, forty people stepped forward. When Youth for Christ rallies were founded in other cities, Graham preached at those as well.

He received flattering offers from various churches, but Graham knew he couldn't accept an offer unless he felt God was behind it.

With the war still raging, Billy was finally accepted into the army chaplaincy program, but he suddenly came down with a severe case of the mumps, with serious complications. Two months later he was still in bed and had become so weak and underweight that the only job the army would consider giving him when he was released was a stateside desk job. Evidently God had different dreams for Billy than Billy did, so he requested and received a release from his commission.

While still recovering, Graham again encountered Torrey Johnson, who said he hoped to expand his rallies across the United States, Canada, and Europe. Johnson wanted to call the rallies Youth for Christ (YFC) International, and he wanted Graham to help organize them. An enthusiastic Billy talked with Ruth, prayed about it, and said yes, after which he resigned his pastorate.

Graham began work with YFC early in 1945 in Chicago. It wasn't long before invitations to start rallies around the country came in. Realizing that Ruth would likely be alone as Billy traveled around the country, the couple decided to move from Chicago to the home of

Ruth's parents in Montreat, North Carolina. Ruth was now expecting the couple's first child, and Billy was comforted knowing her family could look after her as he traveled.

Within a short time, there were YFC organizations in three hundred cities, and Billy was often on the road. In fact, the night his daughter Virginia, "Gigi," was born—September 21, 1945—Billy was speaking in Mobile, Alabama.

In March 1946, Graham traveled with a small team to Europe for several months to organize YFC there and hold large evangelism meetings. The war had been over less than a year, and in London, the team was shocked at the extent of the bombing damage. Europeans, who had suffered so much, were hungry for the gospel. Graham found this especially true in Norway, whose citizens had not yet recovered from Nazi occupation. He preached several times a day to capacity crowds in churches, public halls, and movie houses. Back home in April 1947, Graham preached all summer at YFC rallies all over the country. This kind of evangelism, he believed, was where his future lay.

◆ ◆ ◆

Although Graham was now well known in evangelical circles, he was about to be catapulted into national fame. He accepted a three-week preaching campaign in Los Angeles in September 1949 at the "Canvas Cathedral" (a circus tent). He had been invited by a group of businessmen representing about two hundred churches that called themselves Christ for Greater Los Angeles. This campaign grew naturally out of Graham's YFC work and was heavily advertised. Unlike the YFC rallies, people of all ages were invited. Graham insisted that the businessmen broaden church support, involving as many denominations as possible and putting the public leadership in the hands of local clergy. Graham believed this approach was vital not only to attendance but also to the follow-up of new Christians. Every day before the beginning of the crusade, dozens of people prayed for its success.

But the initial results were disappointing. Three to four thousand people attended each night and on Sunday afternoons—but this was far from capacity. Worse yet, most of the guests were already Christians. Nonetheless, feeling that interest was growing, Graham extended his engagement even though counselors and choir members were getting tired.

During this crusade Stuart Hamblen, the most popular radio host on the West Coast, was converted and talked about it on the air, urging others to attend the crusade. Suddenly, the press took interest. The powerful publisher William Randolph Hearst telegrammed his Los Angeles editors, saying simply, "Puff Graham." In other words, give him good press. Suddenly, the tent was jammed with the ladies and gentlemen of the press.

The wire services and major news-magazines covered the crusade too. "Blond, trumpet-lunged North Carolinian William Franklin Graham, Jr. . . . dominates his huge audience from the moment he strides onstage. . . . His lapel microphone, which gives added volume to his deep, cavernous voice, allows him to pace the platform as he talks, rising to his toes to drive home a point, clenching his fists, stabbing his finger at the sky," wrote *Time* magazine.[13] Some 350,000 people attended this crusade—an unusually large crowd for an evangelistic gathering in those days.

For his staccato-rapid delivery, some journalists nick-named him "God's machine gun."

Something was happening that none of the press journalists could explain; nor could the preacher himself. While the Lord may have used Mr. Hearst to publicize his meetings, Graham writes in his autobiography, the credit for their success belonged to God alone. And God, it appeared, had great plans for the young evangelist who now knew that he, and those who worked with him, were on a journey from which, Graham recalls, "there would be no looking back."[14]

The preacher was becoming famous all over the world. But the eight-week Los Angeles crusade took a great deal out of him. Graham lost a good deal of weight and became so tired that he often feared he might topple over while preaching.

In the eighth week of the crusade, Olympic runner Louis Zamperini, who was now suffering emotionally from his agonizing and brutal treatment at the hands of his Japanese captors in a POW camp, accepted Christ. The final meeting on November 20 saw eleven thousand people inside the tent, while thousands of others were unable to get in. Graham recalled of that exciting time, "Hundreds of thousands had heard, and thousands had responded to accept Christ as Savior."[15]

The year 1950 was a busy one for the evangelist. He formed the nonprofit Billy Graham Evangelistic Association and began speaking on his *Hour of Decision* weekly radio program, broadcast on hundreds of stations around the country. And he began World Wide Pictures, devoted to producing Christian films.

Now a nationally known figure, he continued to preach everywhere and often, in cities from coast to coast, with overflow crowds filling huge auditoriums. And then he did something that was surprising for the time. As the civil rights movement heated up, Graham made it a precondition of his preaching that seating at his crusades would not be segregated; and he refused an invitation to preach in South Africa because the country refused to comply with this request. At a New York crusade, he even invited the Reverend Dr. Martin Luther King Jr. to offer a prayer. Taking such a stand garnered some of the most vicious hate mail Graham would ever receive, but he wasn't a man to back down, because he knew it was only what God thought of what he did that mattered.

In 1954 Graham and his team traveled again to England. This time Ruth joined him, leaving behind their family, which had now grown to three daughters—Virginia, Anne, and Ruth—and a son, Franklin.

The crusade would be remembered as one of the most significant and memorable he would ever hold. It took place in Harringay Arena, which held twelve thousand people. Typically used as a dog-racing track and for boxing matches, the arena was "complete with the full apparatus of gambling," noted journalist David Aikman.[16] As always, many people around the world were asked to pray for the success of the crusade, and much money was spent advertising it. A thousand London churches supported the crusade, which would take place at a time when churchgoing in England was the lowest it had been for a century.

British journalists disdained the idea of an American preacher crossing the pond to "save them." As the Grahams disembarked from their ocean liner in Southampton, they were faced with sarcastic questions by the press. "Who invited you over here, anyway?" one asked. "Don't you think you're more needed in your own country?" asked another.[17]

But ordinary Brits—from customs officials to soldiers to dockworkers—were more welcoming. When the Grahams' train arrived at Waterloo Station, a huge, friendly crowd greeted them and then spontaneously broke into a hymn. The next morning some 150 journalists and photographers gathered at Central Hall in Westminster. Graham learned it was one of the biggest press conferences for anyone in many years.

"I have come to preach Christ," he announced in his bold, distinctly American voice. "You may ask me, 'Do you feel this is a message we need in Britain?' I should answer that it is the message the whole world needs."[18] He told them he was planning to preach a gospel, not of despair, but of hope, and was calling for a revival that would lead the British people to return to their offices and shops to live out Christ's teachings.

The days prior to the crusade flew by. At a luncheon Billy entertained one thousand ministers and was then the guest of honor in the House of Commons. He was also invited to a dinner party by the Lord and Lady Luke of Pavenham.

Despite pouring rain on the first night of the crusade, the arena was packed; and after Graham preached on the subject "Does God Matter?" about two hundred people came forward to accept Christ into their hearts.

The second night, it snowed, causing delays with the public transportation. Graham wondered whether anyone would show up, but over ten thousand did. On the first Saturday of the crusade, the arena was packed—filled to capacity a full hour prior to the beginning of the service. Between 30,000 and 35,000 more stood outside, hoping to get in, leading Graham to begin holding two services on weekends. Ruth Graham was among those who counseled and prayed with those who accepted Christ.

Members of the London crusade committee now wondered whether it was possible for these services to be held outside London too. An ABC network engineer named Bob Benninghoff "found that during World War II, the General Post Office had constructed telephone-type message lines throughout the country—lines that they called landline relays," over which news about the war could be broadcast.[19] The committee got hold of the lines. Local churches and other groups were invited to broadcast Graham's services in public spaces in their own neighborhoods, in public halls and theaters. An astonishing four hundred lines "went out from Harringay, and 400,000 listeners received the audio signal from the Crusade."[20] This was an early effort to use technology to spread Graham's message to as many people as possible.

The final night of the crusade was held at two locations. Graham preached first at the White City Stadium, where sixty-five thousand people came to hear him speak, and then took a bus to Wembley, where one hundred thousand people were jammed into their seats. As he was about to start, he noticed that guards had reopened the gates to allow twenty-two thousand more people to sit on the playing field.

Under the torrents of rain and sleet, Graham preached the final sermon of the crusade, after which around two thousand people came forward.

By the crusade's end—twelve weeks after it began—more than two million people had heard the gospel, and news reports about it were circumnavigating the globe, resulting in invitations for Graham to speak in many other countries and on other continents. This particular gathering was "perhaps the most dramatically attended and nationally significant visit by the BGEA [Billy Graham Evangelistic Association] team in the entire five-decade history of Graham's evangelism," noted Aikman.[21]

As Billy and Ruth were about to leave for a well-deserved vacation in Scotland, a call came from the secretary to Prime Minister Winston Churchill, inviting them to meet with him the next day. He congratulated Graham for the huge number of people his meetings were attracting. Graham promptly gave the credit to God.

"That may be," Churchill responded. "I daresay that if I brought Marilyn Monroe over here, and she and I together went to Wembley, we couldn't fill it."[22]

After the men discussed politics for a few minutes, Churchill said, "I am a man without hope. Do you have any real hope?"

Graham explained the gospel to him and told him about the second coming of Christ. "His eyes seemed to light up at the prospect," Graham recalled. When told his next visitor had arrived, Churchill growled, "Let him wait!" and urged Graham to keep talking. He did for another fifteen minutes, and then the two men prayed together.[23]

◆ ◆ ◆

The following year, Graham returned to Europe, where the team barnstormed through Helsinki, Stockholm, Copenhagen, and Amsterdam, with huge crowds again attending. In Berlin, Billy preached at the same stadium known for the fanatical speeches given by another man some two decades previously: Adolf Hitler. Despite a pouring rain, eighty thousand Germans showed up.

Graham reminded them of those who had, in the past, stood where he was now standing, and spoken to them. But today, he announced, lifting his Bible aloft, "God speaks to you."[24]

Sixteen thousand Germans, including most dramatically many from Soviet East Berlin, filled out decision cards. Graham and his team were overwhelmed by this response—and, as always, gave God the credit and the glory. "For millions in Europe, the crushing devastation of war and the failure of secularism and rationalism to prevent the greatest slaughter in history were creating a new openness to Christ."[25]

The following year Graham returned to the British Isles, preaching in Glasgow for six weeks. On Good Friday, the BBC broadcast on radio and television a sermon Graham had prepared on the meaning of the cross to the biggest audience for a single program since Queen Elizabeth II was crowned. The Queen herself was among the viewers. She invited Graham to preach at Windsor Castle—the first of a dozen friendly meetings between the two.

As his fame grew, reporters asked Graham for his opinion about political matters. In his later years, Graham ruefully acknowledged that he had at times, in all innocence, spoken out on political and foreign affairs that were outside his jurisdiction as a preacher. The preacher also embarrassed himself after meeting with President Harry Truman in 1950, unaware he should not have repeated what was said in their brief meeting. Truman was furious, viewing Graham as a publicity-seeking huckster. But Graham developed a warm relationship with Truman's successor, Dwight Eisenhower, whom Billy had urged to run. He suggested the new president declare a National Day of Prayer, which he did. And Eisenhower delighted Graham with an executive order eliminating racial segregation in the armed forces.

During a visit to the president's farm in Gettysburg, Eisenhower asked Graham if he believed in heaven. Yes, Graham replied; I do.

Eisenhower asked him to explain the reasons behind his belief. Graham opened his Bible and took him through verses that talked about the afterlife. How, Eisenhower wanted to know can someone know he will go to heaven?

Graham explained the gospel to the president, as he had done several times previously. He sensed that the general understood and was reassured by the message that "salvation is by grace through Christ alone, and not by anything we can do for ourselves."[26]

In 1968, a few months before Eisenhower died, he asked Graham to visit him at Walter Reed, where he was hospitalized. The former president took Billy's hand—and asked him to tell him, once again, how he could be certain his sins would be forgiven and that he would spend eternity in heaven. Once again, Graham took out his Bible and read the promises of God regarding eternal life and prayed for Eisenhower.

"Thank you," he responded. "I'm ready."[27]

Graham's relationship with President John Kennedy was far less close, probably because Kennedy knew Graham had wanted his old friend Richard Nixon to win. Graham had gotten to know Nixon during Eisenhower's presidency, when Nixon was vice president. But just before Kennedy's inauguration, Kennedy invited Graham to play golf in Palm Beach, where the new president's father owned an estate. After Graham lunched with Kennedy, his wife, Jacqueline, and a few friends, Kennedy drove him to the golf course.

On their way back to the house, Kennedy suddenly stopped the car and asked Graham, "Do you believe in the Second Coming of Jesus Christ?" he asked.

"I most certainly do," Graham replied.

"Well, does *my* church believe it?"

"They have it in their creeds," Graham responded.

"They don't preach it," Kennedy replied. "They don't tell us much about it. I'd like to know what you think."

Graham went through what the Bible teaches: that Christ died on the cross, was resurrected, and will one day return.

"Very interesting," Kennedy said, adding that he would like to discuss the matter more one day—something that, sadly, never happened, although Kennedy did invite Graham to the White House a few times to ask his advice.[28]

Graham became much closer to Lyndon Johnson, who invited him to stay overnight in the White House several times. Graham frequently prayed with the president in LBJ's bedroom, with the pajama-clad president kneeling by his bed. While Johnson acknowledged that he had done many things he was ashamed of, he told Graham that he believed he was saved and would spend eternity in heaven.

One day, when Graham was visiting Johnson at his Texas ranch, LBJ told Billy he wanted him to preach at his funeral one day. He pointed to the tree he wanted Graham to stand under and where he wanted to be buried in the family cemetery. Johnson knew Graham would read the Bible and preach the gospel—which the former president wanted him to do. But he hoped Billy would also tell folks some of the things he tried to do. Graham followed through on his promise less than two years later.

Graham was also close to Richard Nixon, whom he urged to run for president again in 1968. Nixon invited Graham to preach at a number of services held in the White House. The evangelist was saddened by the events of Watergate, but the two men remained friends until Nixon's death.

Graham came to know Gerald Ford when he became president and urged him to pardon Nixon for any crimes he may have committed, for the good of the country, which Ford did. The two enjoyed playing golf together.

President Jimmy Carter never really warmed up to Graham, miffed at some comments he had made during the campaign.

Both of the Grahams, however, enjoyed a warm friendship with Ronald and Nancy Reagan. Billy had met Reagan when the president was still an actor in Hollywood. Reagan invited the Grahams to several state dinners, including—knowing of Ruth's childhood in China—one for China's president. Both Reagans were interested in understanding the Bible better, especially President Reagan. He often asked Graham about the biblical view on important topics, abortion being one such issue he wrestled with.

One Reagan dinner that stood out in memory was given in honor of Queen Elizabeth and Prince Philip in San Francisco. The Grahams were invited to a reception the following evening on the Queen's yacht, *Britannia*. "As Ruth and I boarded, a man with several stripes on his uniform sleeve saluted and whispered, 'Wembley '55.'" He had been converted the day Billy Graham preached there three decades before.[29]

George H. W. Bush and his wife, Barbara, were also friends of the

Grahams and invited Graham to come to the White House on January 16, 1991—the day before the start of Operation Desert Storm. The quartet prayed about the events occurring in Kuwait and Iraq, of their hope that the war would be a short one with few casualties, and that God's will would be done. The Bushes also invited Graham to conduct Bible studies with their extended family at Kennebunkport, the family vacation home in Maine.

Graham met Bill Clinton when he was still the young governor of Arkansas, but in his autobiography, Graham graciously declined to speak about the scandals of the Clinton years. He wrote, instead, of an informal White House meeting in which he and Clinton discussed the Scriptures and its teachings about God's plans for the lives of his people. Graham recalls it as a time of warm fellowship with a president who has "not always won the approval of his fellow Christians but who has in his heart a desire to serve God and do His will."[30]

Graham got to know George W. Bush at a Bush family gathering in Kennebunkport, when the younger Bush was struggling with a drinking problem. Graham offered to send Bush a Bible. "There was no lecture, no grabbing of the shoulders," Bush recalled.[31] This marked the beginning of Bush reading the Scriptures, beginning a walk with God that continues today.

Many years later it was this young President Bush who invited Graham to comfort the nation at the National Cathedral in the days after the September 11 attacks.

Barack Obama was the first and only president to visit Graham in his own home in North Carolina. The men talked together and prayed for one another.

Billy Graham met Donald Trump at Graham's ninety-fifth birthday party in 2013, but the two never got together after Trump became president. At Graham's memorial service in 2018, Trump fondly recalled that his own father, Fred Trump, had taken him to a crusade in Yankee Stadium many years before, which he remembered as being quite special.

It became clear to Graham, as the years went by, that he didn't know some of his presidential friends as well as he thought he did. He seemed to have forgotten at times that many people—including presidents—turn their best face to clergy and that politicians some-times use religious figures for political ends.

An interesting side point: Graham himself briefly—very briefly—considered running for president. When, in 1952, billionaire H. L. Hunt offered him $6 million to do so, Graham declined. But when he later speculated about the possibility of running if he were drafted to run, the preacher was brought back to earth by his wife. If he traded in the work God had called him to do—evangelism—for politics, Ruth announced, she would divorce him. And she meant it.

◆ ◆ ◆

After the success of the London crusade in 1955, Graham preached all over the world—ultimately to 185 countries. He became acquainted with many world leaders, at times bringing private letters from the American president to foreign leaders. He frequently attacked communism during his crusades in the 1950s and 1960s and many of his overseas visits. Later he backed away from such commentary, stirring huge controversy and accusations that he was a pawn being used by the Communists.

In 1955 Graham prepared for crusades in India, the Philippines, Hong Kong, Taiwan, Japan, and South Korea, which took place in 1956. In India, he told the people he had not come to talk with them about an American or a European, but about "a Man who was born right here in your part of the world . . . where Asia and Africa and Europe meet. He had skin that was darker than mine, and He came to show us that God loves all people."[32]

Graham later recalled seeing their eyes light up as they realized that Christ came for everyone, including them. In a country where the caste system said some people were inherently better than others, this was a powerfully countercultural thing to say.

Graham met Prime Minister Nehru, who commended his work, and later, Generalissimo and Madame Chiang Kai-shek in Taiwan, as well as Japan's prime minister Hatoyama Ichiro in Tokyo. Everywhere Graham preached, great crowds jammed the stadiums, often riding trains for days and sleeping in the streets in their eagerness to hear the evangelist speak. In later years, Graham would return to Asia again and again.

Always looking for new ways to reach people, in the 1950s, Graham began writing a newspaper column titled "My Answer" and began publishing *Christianity Today* magazine. He also wrote a bestselling book titled *Peace with God*, which sold millions of copies.

In 1959 and 1960, Graham and his team struck out for Australia, New Zealand, Africa, and the Middle East. The Australia and New Zealand tours were especially difficult because Ruth—who had recently delivered the couple's youngest child, Ned—and her husband were apart for four months.

As always, the team prepared well, organizing five thousand prayer meetings in Sydney alone. They even developed committees to assist with outreach to all sorts of groups: doctors, college students, trade unionists, Australian Aborginals and the Maori of New Zealand. Many counseling teams were organized, and because immigrants spoke so many languages, the BGEA provided translation via headphones.

For those who lived too far away to attend, the team did something similar to what they had done in England, creating a system of telephone landlines to reach hundreds of distant towns and settlements. These audio meetings reached around 650,000 people, listening in churches, theaters, and cattle ranch bunkhouses. Fifteen thousand people registered commitments.

Graham preached to capacity crowds in Melbourne, Perth, Sydney, Adelaide, Brisbane, and Tasmania; in New Zealand he preached in Wellington. By the end of the tour, well over three million people had attended the meetings in person, including those led by Graham's associates, and 150,000 had become "inquirers."

Graham frequently heard interesting stories about how conversion to Christ had changed lives. For instance, he told the story of a safe-cracker whose gang was planning a theft. For some reason, the safe-cracker decided to attend one of Graham's meetings—and accepted Christ. Of course, he then had to go back to his gang, tell them about his conversion, and let them know he was resigning from his career as a safecracker.

In 1967 Graham traveled to Yugoslavia at the invitation of Yugo-slavian Protestant churches. It was the first communist country he had preached in, and over seven thousand people endured heavy rainfall to hear Graham speak in Zagreb.

In 1973 a crusade in Yoido Plaza in Seoul, Korea, drew over a million people, the largest live audience addressed at one time in Graham's ministry. People everywhere were hungry for the meaning of life and for the hope and good news of Jesus.

The evangelist visited Belfast, Northern Ireland, in 1972, where war raged between Protestants and Catholics. While he couldn't, for security reasons, hold a crusade there, Graham did preach in one church. One day Graham and two others, a fellow American evangelist named Arthur Blessitt and a British businessman, took a walk along Falls Road and Shankill Road, often viewed as the dividing lines between the warring groups. They had brought no security guards with them, and since Graham's picture had been in all the newspapers, everyone on both sides knew who he was. A nervous Graham asked how he knew they were going to accept him.

"Well, if they don't, you'll get a bullet in the back!" Blessitt told him. It was a grim thing to say, but it was true.[33]

Graham stopped to visit with passersby and tell them about Christ's love. In the Catholic area, the men approached a public house, where Sunday morning drinkers recognized Graham and invited them in. Graham talked about God while some joked and whispered. But some of them "seemed to take the words of Jesus Christ to heart," he later wrote.[34] When he finished his talk, the men applauded and offered their best wishes for his safety in their country.

Shortly afterward, a bomb went off. Following the crowd, Graham and his friends encountered the terrible sight of bodies blown apart. Three of the dead were known terrorists who had mishandled the bomb, but others were innocent bystanders. Although he wasn't wearing a clerical collar, Graham was recognized by people who called him "Father" and begged him "to give the last rites to the dead and the dying." Graham understood that this was not a time for theological distinctions. He knelt beside each of the wounded and dying and prayed for them. A Catholic woman told Graham that he was the first Protestant minister she had ever met. Many of the distraught citizens thanked Graham for coming. And then British soldiers showed up and told Graham he had better leave.

I n the late seventies, Graham turned his eyes to the Iron Curtain. In 1977 he preached in Hungary, where Christians tape-recorded Graham's sermons so they could share them with others. He spoke privately with government leaders and preached before a crowd of thirty thousand at a camp outside Budapest (although the government had not allowed them to advertise the meetings). The following year Graham was invited to preach in Poland's four cathedrals. Graham couldn't help wondering why Communist authorities were allowing him to come to their countries. Probably, he concluded, because they hoped to improve their image in the West. In any event, he knew God could and would use the opportunity for his purposes.

In 1981 Graham met with Pope John Paul II. The following year, Graham controversially attended "a patently Soviet-sponsored propagandistic religious event in Moscow," an attempt by the Soviet government to "transform quite genuine support for peace in the West into crudely anti-U.S., pro-Soviet 'peace' propaganda," noted Aikman.[35] The Soviets did everything they could to limit Graham's opportunities to preach to Russian Christians, and his naive-sounding statements about life under Soviet rule infuriated many. Nevertheless, the trip had the positive effect of helping make possible Graham's preaching in other Soviet-bloc countries—including, that same year, Czechoslovakia and East Germany.

Graham returned to Moscow two years later, this time preaching to many thousands of people in four Soviet cities without interference. He returned in triumph in 1992, after the Soviet Union had collapsed, and encountered daily crowds of forty-five thousand, a quarter of whom walked forward to accept Christ.

Some observers believed Graham's visits to these countries contributed to the crumbling of Communist rule in Eastern Europe.

◆ ◆ ◆

Ruth Graham had long desired to return to the country of her birth: China. She returned there with her sisters and brother in 1980 to visit familiar sites from their childhoods. Ruth and Billy prayed that he would one day be able to hold a crusade there. And in April 1988, Graham accepted an invitation from the China Christian Council to preach.

With a television crew documenting the trip, Graham preached in five cities, packing in a flurry of preaching engagements, press interviews, social activities, and—unusual for him—quite a bit of sightseeing. He met with Premier Li and with members of both the official Three-Self Patriotic Movement and the illegal house churches. The evangelist sensed great spiritual vitality. Some fifteen hundred people jammed Beijing's Chongwenmen Church, built to hold seven hundred. Thousands more gathered to hear Graham in Shanghai churches and in Guangzhou, where he made an unannounced visit to a house church and spoke for twenty minutes at the pastor's invitation.

One highlight was a visit with Pastor Wang Mingdao, an elderly man whom the Communists had greatly persecuted for his beliefs. When Graham asked whether he had a word from God for them, Wang replied, "Be faithful, even to the point of death, and I will give you the crown of life" (Revelation 2:10).[36]

Astonishingly, Graham was even able to visit North Korea in 1992 and 1994, speaking before students and government leaders. Billy Graham has met more world leaders than perhaps anybody else, but he says the famous made up only about 2 percent of the people he encountered. While people who live their lives before the public learn to hide their inner thoughts, Graham notes, they have the same questions and problems everyone else has. Over the years, some of them have trusted Graham enough to open their hearts to him. In some cases, their character flaws were known all-too-well, not only to Graham but to the rest of the world. In such cases, the evangelist made an effort to help them, offering biblically-based advice. He never visited the rich and famous without the realization that he was—first and foremost—an ambassador of the King of Kings and Lord of Lords.

Billy and Ruth became acquainted with the perils of bringing up children in the glare of publicity. Strangers didn't hesitate to walk into their yard and peer through the windows or break off bits of wood from the fence or grab rocks to take home. The Grahams eventually bought a property higher up the mountain. Ruth named it Little Piney Cove and designed a comfortable log-and-frame home. A more serious problem was the amount of time Billy spent away from home, missing out on many of his children's special events. Graham writes of this reality with regret, believing that his long weeks and months away from home left both psychological and emotional scars, not only on himself, but on his wife and children, particularly his two boys, who engaged in some rebellious behavior. And near the end of his life, he warned evangelicals just beginning their careers to learn from his mistakes.

Graham also regretted his involvement in partisan politics, recognizing that at times he "stepped over the line" between his calling and his political activities, which inevitably diminished his evangelical impact and compromised his message.

The five Graham children grew up, married, and had children and grandchildren of their own. All of Ruth and Billy's children work in ministry. The best known of these ministries is Samaritan's Purse, run by Franklin.

As Graham reached his eighties, he began slowing down. He preached his last crusade in New York City in July 2005, when he was eighty-six. Various illnesses plagued him, including hydrocephalus, vision problems, and hearing loss. Eventually, he was confined to a wheelchair. Franklin Graham took over leadership of the BGEA in 2002.

Graham grieved deeply when his beloved wife of sixty-four years died in 2007 at the age of eighty-seven.

On his ninety-fifth birthday, friends and family held a party for Graham, who was now very frail.

Billy Graham died at home at the age of ninety-nine on February 21, 2018. He lay in honor at the US Capitol Rotunda and was buried in a simple wooden casket made for him by prisoners at Angola Prison, next to his wife in Montreat, North Carolina, on the grounds of the Billy Graham Library. His son Franklin gave the funeral message, which included an invitation to those in attendance to repent of their sins and be saved. And he repeated a comment his father often made about his death, one that sums up the meaning of his entire life's work: "I'll be more alive than I am now. I'll have just changed addresses, that's all."

Notes

CHAPTER 1: MARTIN LUTHER

1. Quoted in Martin Brecht, *Martin Luther: His Road to Reformation, 1483–1521*, trans. James L. Schaaf (Minneapolis: Fortress, 1985), 5.
2. Quoted in Brecht, *Martin Luther*, 48.
3. Roland Bainton, *Here I Stand* (Nashville: Abingdon, 2013), 45—in this text only *monkery* is a direct quote, doesn't include *sheer*. Other works sometimes include the word *sheer* in the full quote.
4. Martin Marty, *Martin Luther: A Life* (New York: Viking, 2004), 10.
5. Quoted in Heiko A. Oberman, *Luther: Man Between God and the Devil* (New York: Image, 1992), 149.
6. Quoted in Brecht, *Martin Luther*, 184.
7. Martin Luther, *Martin Luther's 95 Theses: With the Pertinent Documents from the History of the Reformation*, ed. Kurt Aland (St. Louis: Concordia, 1967).
8. *Martin Luther's Letter to the Archbishop of Mainz*, 1517.
9. *Martin Luther's Letter to the Archbishop of Mainz*, 1517.
10. Luther, *Martin Luther's 95 Theses.*
11. Luther, *Martin Luther's 95 Theses.*
12. Luther, *Martin Luther's 95 Theses*, number 27.
13. Luther, *Martin Luther's 95 Theses.*
14. Martin Luther, *Luther's Works, American Edition*, eds. Jaroslav Pelikan and Helmut T. Lehman (Philadelphia: Muehlenberg and Fortress and St. Louis: Concordia, 1955–86), 32:114.

15. Bainton, *Here I Stand*, 107.
16. James Aitken Wylie, *The History of Protestantism* (Charleston: Nabu, 2012), 279.
17. Wylie, *The History of Protestantism*, 279.
18. Charles P. Krauth, "The Life and Labours of Martin Luther," *Dickinson's Theological Quarterly* no. 3 (1877): 321.
19. Bainton, *Here I Stand*, 166.
20. Bainton, *Here I Stand*, 166.
21. James Reston Jr., *Luther's Fortress: Martin Luther and His Reformation Under Siege* (New York: Basic, 2015), 21–22.
22. Douglas O. Linder, "The Trial of Martin Luther: An Account," *University of Missouri-Kansas City*: w2.umkc.edu/faculty/projects/ftrials/luther/luther account.html.
23. Linder, "The Trial of Martin Luther: An Account."
24. Bainton, *Here I Stand*, 178.
25. Luther, *Luther's Works*, 32:114.
26. Dennis Bratcher, ed., "Edict of Worms," *University of Missouri-Kansas City*: http://law2.umkc.edu/faculty/projects/ftrials/luther/edictofworms.html.
27. Timothy F. Lull, *Martin Luther's Basic Theological Writings*, ed. Timothy F. Lull and William R. Russell (Minneapolis: Fortress Press, 2012), 289.
28. Martin Luther, ed. Ulrich Nembach, "Eight Sermons at Wittenberg 1522," *Göttinger Predigten im Internet*: http://www.predigten.uni-goettingen.de /archiv-6/eight-sermons-wittenberg.pdf.
29. Luther, ed. Nembach, "Eight Sermons at Wittenberg 1522."
30. Luther, *Luther's Works*, 46:49–55.
31. Marty, *Martin Luther*, 102.
32. Quoted in Bainton, *Here I Stand*, 290.
33. Martin Luther, "Last Will and Testament of Martin Luther Wittenberg, January 6, 1542," *The Nebraska District of the Lutheran Church:* http:// www.ndlcms.org/publication/martin-luthers-will-christian-preamble/.
34. Marty, *Martin Luther*, 162.
35. Marty, *Martin Luther*, 174.

CHAPTER 2: GEORGE WHITEFIELD

1. Thomas S. Kidd, *George Whitefield: America's Spiritual Founding Father* (New Haven: Yale University Press, 2014), 253.
2. Benjamin Franklin, *The Autobiography of Benjamin Franklin*, ed. Charles Eliot (New York: P. F. Collier and Son, 1909), 108.
3. J. B. Wakeley, *The Prince of Pulpit Orators: A Portraiture of Rev. George Whitefield, M. A.* (Wentworth Press, 2016), 226.

4. Henry Scougal, *The Life of God in the Soul of Man* (Grand Rapids: Christian Classics Ethereal Library, 2015), 2.

5. John Gillies, *Memoirs of the Life of the Reverend George Whitefield M. A.* (Wentworth Press, 2016), 38.

6. Gillies, *Memoirs*, 38.

7. Arnold A. Dallimore, *George Whitefield: The Life and Times of the Great Evangelist of the Eighteenth-Century Revival* (Scotland: Banner of Truth Trust, 1970), 483.

8. Samuel Palmer, *St. Pancras: Being Antiquarian, Topographical, and Biographical Memoranda, Relating to the Extensive Metropolitan Parish of St. Pancras, Middlesex; with Some Account of the Parish from Its Foundation* (London: S. Palmer, 1870), 286.

9. Boyd Stanley Schlenther, "George Whitefield (1714–1770)," *Oxford Dictionary of National Biography*: https://www.oxforddnb.com/view/1 0.1093/ref:odnb/9780198614128.001.0001/odnb-9780198614128-e-29281.

10. Schlenther, "George Whitefield (1714—1770)."

11. Franklin, *The Autobiography of Benjamin Franklin*, 108.

12. Franklin, *The Autobiography of Benjamin Franklin*, 108.

13. George Whitefield, *The Revived Puritan: The Spirituality of George Whitefield*, ed. Michael A. G. Haykin (Los Angeles: Joshua Pr, 2000), 35–37.

14. George Leon Walker, *Some Aspects of the Religious Life of New England: With Special Reference to Congregationalists* (New York: Silver, Burnett, 1897), 89–92.

15. Michael J. Crawford, "The Spiritual Travels of Nathan Cole" *The William and Mary Quarterly* vol. 33, no. 1 (Jan. 1976): 89–126.

16. Harry S. Stout, "Heavenly Comet," *Christian History* 38 (1993): 13–14.

17. George Whitefield, *The Works of the Reverend George Whitefield, M.A...: Containing All His Sermons and Tracts Which Have Been Already Published: with a Select Collection of Letters... Also, Some Other Pieces on Important Subjects, Never Before Printed; Prepared by Himself for the Press; to Which Is Prefixed, an Account of His Life, Compiled from His Original Papers and Letters, Volume 3* (Edward and Charles Dilly, 1771), 254.

18. Kidd, *George Whitefield*, 226.

19. *A Sermon by the Reverend Mr. George Whitefield, Being His Last Farewell to His Friends, Preached at the Tabernacle in Moorfields, at Seven in the Morning. August the 30th, 1769, Immediately before His Departure for Georgia* (S. Bladon, 1769), 11.

CHAPTER 3: GEORGE WASHINGTON CARVER

1. "George Washington Carver," *George Washington Carver*: https://www .georgewashingtoncarver.org/.

2. Other sources say George's brother Jim was fathered by a white man, possibly a farmhand named Jim Carroll, who for a time lived with the Carver family.

3. Lawrence Elliot, *George Washington Carver: The Man Who Overcame* (Upper Saddle River, NJ: Prentice Hall Direct, 1966), 13.

4. Elliot, *George Washington Carver*, 13.

5. Elliot, *George Washington Carver*, 14.

6. Elliot, *George Washington Carver*, 20.

7. George Washington Carver, *George Washington Carver in His Own Words*, ed. Gary R. Kremer (Columbia, MO: University of Missouri Press, 1987), 128.

8. Elliot, *George Washington Carver*, 31.

9. Elliot, *George Washington Carver*, 30.

10. Elliot, *George Washington Carver*, 30.

11. Elliot, *George Washington Carver*, 39.

12. Elliot, *George Washington Carver*, 39.

13. Biographer Christina Vella, author of *George Washington Carver: A Life*, writes that the man was thrown to the ground, where his brains were dashed out onto a sidewalk. He was then hanged. After taking his body down, the crowd built a fire, and burned the body.

14. Elliot, *George Washington Carver*, 55.

15. Elliot, *George Washington Carver*, 60.

16. Elliot, *George Washington Carver*, 61.

17. Elliot, *George Washington Carver*, 64.

18. Elliot, *George Washington Carver*, 65.

19. Elliot, *George Washington Carver*, 71.

20. Elliot, *George Washington Carver*, 74.

21. Elliot, *George Washington Carver*, 81.

22. Elliot, *George Washington Carver*, 82.

23. Elliot, *George Washington Carver*, 84.

24. Elliot, *George Washington Carver*, 88.

25. Elliot, *George Washington Carver*, 89.

26. Elliot, *George Washington Carver*, 104.

27. Elliot, *George Washington Carver*, 106.

28. Elliot, *George Washington Carver*, 109.

29. Elliot, *George Washington Carver*, 115.

30. Elliot, *George Washington Carver*, 116.

31. Elliot, *George Washington Carver*, 117.

32. Elliot, *George Washington Carver*, 119.

33. Elliot, *George Washington Carver*, 120.

34. Elliot, *George Washington Carver*, 120.

35. Elliot, *George Washington Carver*, 122.

36. Elliot, *George Washington Carver*, 131.

37. Elliot, *George Washington Carver*, 133.

38. Elliot, *George Washington Carver*, 135.

39. John Perry, *George Washington Carver* (Nashville: Thomas Nelson, 2011), 52–53.

40. Carver, *George Washington Carver in His Own Words*, 101.

41. Perry, *George Washington Carver*, 59.

42. Perry, *George Washington Carver*, 60–61.

43. Perry, *George Washington Carver*, 61.

44. Linda McMurry Edwards, *George Washington Carver: Scientist and Symbol* (New York: Oxford University Press, 1981), 158.

45. Carver, *George Washington Carver in His Own Words*, 172.

46. Perry, *George Washington Carver*, 75.

47. Perry, *George Washington Carver*, 77.

48. Perry, *George Washington Carver*, 77.

49. Perry, *George Washington Carver*, 98–99.

50. Elliot, *George Washington Carver*, 172–173.

51. Elliot, *George Washington Carver*, 173–174.

52. Elliot, *George Washington Carver*, 176.

53. Elliot, *George Washington Carver*, 176.

54. Elliot, *George Washington Carver*, 177.

55. Elliot, *George Washington Carver*, 172.

56. Perry, *George Washington Carver*, 94.

57. Perry, *George Washington Carver*, 98.

58. Perry, *George Washington Carver*, 145.

59. Elliot, *George Washington Carver*, 185.

CHAPTER 4: GENERAL WILLIAM BOOTH

1. Janet Benge and Geoff Benge, *William Booth: Soup, Soap, and Salvation* (Edmonds, WA: YWAM Publishing, 2002), 25.

2. Benge, *William Booth*, 25.

3. Benge, *William Booth*, 25.

4. Benge, *William Booth*, 30.

5. Benge, *William Booth*, 33.

6. Benge, *William Booth*, 46.

7. Benge, *William Booth*, 28.

8. Benge, *William Booth*, 58.

9. Benge, *William Booth*, 59.

10. Benge, *William Booth*, 64.

11. Benge, *William Booth*, 68.

12. Benge, *William Booth*, 68–69.

13. Benge, *William Booth*, 69.
14. Benge, *William Booth*, 70.
15. Roger J. Green, *The Life and Ministry of William Booth: Founder of The Salvation Army* (Nashville: Abingdon Press, 2006), 97.
16. Green, *The Life and Ministry of William Booth*, 100.
17. Benge, *William Booth*, 72.
18. Norman H. Murdoch, *Origins of the Salvation Army* (Knoxville, TN: University of Tennessee Press, 1994), 74–75.
19. Benge, *William Booth*, 72.
20. Benge, *William Booth*, 74–75.
21. Benge, *William Booth*, 94.
22. Benge, *William Booth*, 114–115.
23. Rudyard Kipling, *The Complete Works of Rudyard Kipling: Novel, Short Stories, Poetry & Non-Fiction* (General Press, 2017), Kindle edition.
24. Green, *The Life and Ministry of William Booth*, 108.
25. Green, *The Life and Ministry of William Booth*, 110.
26. "Who We Are: Our History," *The Salvation Army*: https://neo.salvationarmy.org/northeastohio/our_history.
27. By now, The Mission had been renamed the Salvation Army.
28. Green, *The Life and Ministry of William Booth*, 101.
29. She later changed her name to Evangeline.
30. Harold Begbie, "Life of William Booth Founder and First General of the Salvation Army," *Gospel Truth Online*: https://www.gospeltruth.net/booth/boothbiovol1/boothbiovol1ch24.htm.
31. Green, *The Life and Ministry of William Booth*, 128.
32. Roger Green, "William Booth's Theology of Redemption," *Christian History Institute*, 1990: https://christianhistoryinstitute.org/magazine/article/william-booths-theology-of-redemption.
33. William Booth, *In Darkest England, and the Way Out* (BiblioLife, 2008), 40.
34. Benge, *William Booth*, 146.
35. Mike Asselta, "SATERN Commerates 'Tragedy to Triumph,'" *Salvation Army*, June 2012: http://ksarrl.org/satern/SATERN_June_2012.pdf.
36. Benge, *William Booth*, 120.
37. Faye Michelson, "Do What Makes You Come Alive," Salvation Army, August 3, 2018, https://others.org.au/features/do-what-makes-you-come-alive/.
38. Green, *The Life and Ministry of William Booth*, 153.
39. Roger Green, "Catherine Booth, The Salvation Army, and the Purity Crusade of 1885," *Christians for Biblical Equality International Online*: https://www.cbeinternational.org/resources/article/priscilla-papers/catherine-booth-salvation-army-and-purity-crusade-1885.

40. Green, "Catherine Booth."

41. Benge, *William Booth*, 166.

42. Benge, *William Booth*, 166.

43. Benge, *William Booth*, 167.

44. Benge, *William Booth*, 167.

45. Green, *The Life and Ministry of William Booth*, 164.

46. Green, *The Life and Ministry of William Booth*, 165.

47. Green, *The Life and Ministry of William Booth*, 165–166.

48. Green, *The Life and Ministry of William Booth*, 165–166, 177.

49. Benge, *William Booth*, 169.

50. Roger Green, "Why Social Holiness? – Part Three," *The Salvation Army Online:* http://www1.salvationarmy.org/IHQ/www_ihq_isjc.nsf/vw -dynamic-index/3799C9D3162B0396802578AF004DA791.

51. Roger Green, "Why Social Holiness?—Part Three."

52. Green, *The Life and Ministry of William Booth*, 185.

53. Benge, *William Booth*, 173.

54. Benge, *William Booth*, 174–175.

55. Benge, *William Booth*, 189.

56. Benge, *William Booth*, 189.

57. Benge, *William Booth*, 190.

58. Norman H. Murdoch, "Sayings of William Booth," *Christianity Today Online:* https://www.christianitytoday.com/history/issues/issue-26/sayings -of-william-booth.html.

59. Benge, *William Booth*, 192.

60. Benge, *William Booth*, 193.

61. Benge, *William Booth*, 194.

62. Benge, *William Booth*, 195.

63. "Transforming Lives Since 1865," *The Salvation Army*: https://story .salvationarmy.org/.

CHAPTER 5: SERGEANT ALVIN YORK

1. Alvin York, *Sergeant York: His Own Life Story and War Diary* (New York: Racehorse, 2018), 36.

2. York, *Sergeant York*, 147.

3. York, *Sergeant York*, 168.

4. York, *Sergeant York*, 171.

5. Douglas V. Mastriano, *Alvin York: A New Biography of the Hero of the Argonne* (Lexington, KY: University Press of Kentucky, 2014), 39.

6. York, *Sergeant York*, 171.

7. York, *Sergeant York*, 174–175.

8. York, *Sergeant York*, 175.
9. York, *Sergeant York*, 194.
10. York, *Sergeant York*, 199.
11. Mastriano, *Alvin York*, 52.
12. Mastriano, *Alvin York*, 58.
13. Mastriano, *Alvin York*, 58.
14. Mastriano, *Alvin York*, 60.
15. Mastriano, *Alvin York*, 62.
16. York, *Sergeant York*, 62–63.
17. Mastriano, *Alvin York*, 65.
18. York, *Sergeant York*, 67.
19. Mastriano, *Alvin York*, 69.
20. York, *Sergeant York*, 215.
21. York, *Sergeant York*, 219–220.
22. Mastriano, *Alvin York*, 98.
23. Mastriano, *Alvin York*, 101.
24. Mastriano, *Alvin York*, 107.
25. Mastriano, *Alvin York*, 110.
26. Mastriano, *Alvin York*, 111.
27. Mastriano, *Alvin York*, 111.
28. Mastriano, *Alvin York*, 113.
29. Mastriano, *Alvin York*, 113.
30. Mastriano, *Alvin York*, 113.
31. York, *Sergeant York*, 235.
32. Mastriano, *Alvin York*, 114.
33. Mastriano, *Alvin York*, 137–139.
34. Mastriano, *Alvin York*, 137.
35. Mastriano, *Alvin York*, 140.
36. Mastriano, *Alvin York*, 141.
37. Mastriano, *Alvin York*, 147.
38. Mastriano, *Alvin York*, 147.
39. Mastriano, *Alvin York*, 156.
40. Mastriano, *Alvin York*, 181.
41. Mastriano, *Alvin York*, 187.

CHAPTER 6: ALEXANDER SOLZHENITSYN

1. Joseph Pearce, *Solzhenitsyn: A Soul in Exile* (Ada, MI: Baker, 2011), 8–9.
2. David Aikman, *Great Souls: Six Who Changed the Century* (Lanham, MA: Lexington, 2003), 132.
3. Aikman, *Great Souls*, 134.
4. Aikman, *Great Souls*, 135.

5. Aikman, *Great Souls*, 137.
6. Aikman, *Great Souls*, 138.
7. Aikman, *Great Souls*, 138.
8. Pearce, *Solzhenitsyn*, 61.
9. Pearce, *Solzhenitsyn*, 65.
10. Pearce, *Solzhenitsyn*, 68.
11. Aikman, *Great Souls*, 138.
12. Aikman, *Great Souls*, 140.
13. Aikman, *Great Souls*, 140.
14. Aleksandr I. Solzhenitsyn, *The Gulag Archipelago* (New York: Harper & Row, 1974).
15. Pearce, *Solzhenitsyn*, 89.
16. Pearce, *Solzhenitsyn*, 90.
17. Pearce, *Solzhenitsyn*, 92.
18. Pearce, *Solzhenitsyn*, 92.
19. Pearce, *Solzhenitsyn*, 95.
20. Pearce, *Solzhenitsyn*, 98.
21. Pearce, *Solzhenitsyn*, 99–100.
22. Solzhenitsyn, *The Gulag Archipelago*, 7.
23. Pearce, *Solzhenitsyn*, 103.
24. Pearce, *Solzhenitsyn*, 103–104.
25. Pearce, *Solzhenitsyn*, 105.
26. Aikman, *Great Souls*, 150.
27. Solzhenitsyn, *The Gulag Archipelago*, 612.
28. Solzhenitsyn, *The Gulag Archipelago*, 612.
29. Pearce, *Solzhenitsyn*, 154.
30. Solzhenitsyn, *The Gulag Archipelago*, 616.
31. Aikman, *Great Souls*, 153.
32. Solzhenitsyn, *The Gulag Archipelago*, 616.
33. Pearce, *Solzhenitsyn*, 124.
34. Pearce, *Solzhenitsyn*, 124.
35. Pearce, *Solzhenitsyn*, 129.
36. Pearce, *Solzhenitsyn*, 129.
37. Pearce, *Solzhenitsyn*, 129.
38. Solzhenitsyn, *The Gulag Archipelago*, 420.
39. Pearce, *Solzhenitsyn*, 136.
40. Pearce, *Solzhenitsyn*, 137.
41. Pearce, *Solzhenitsyn*, 139.
42. Pearce, *Solzhenitsyn*, 139.
43. Aikman, *Great Souls*, 156.
44. Aikman, *Great Souls*, 158.

45. Aikman, *Great Souls*, 159.
46. Aikman, *Great Souls*, 161.
47. Aikman, *Great Souls*, 162.
48. Aikman, *Great Souls*, 164.
49. Aikman, *Great Souls*, 165.
50. Aikman, *Great Souls*, 165.
51. Aikman, *Great Souls*, 167.
52. Aikman, *Great Souls*, 168.
53. Pearce, *Solzhenitsyn*, 197.
54. Aikman, *Great Souls*, 173.
55. Aikman, *Great Souls*, 175.
56. Aikman, *Great Souls*, 176.
57. Aikman, *Great Souls*, 176.
58. Aikman, *Great Souls*, 177.
59. Aikman, *Great Souls*, 178.
60. Pearce, *Solzhenitsyn*, 235.
61. Pearce, *Solzhenitsyn*, 239.
62. John Lewis Gaddis, *George F. Kennan: An American Life* (New York: Penguin Press, 2011), 622.
63. Pearce, *Solzhenitsyn*, 243–244.
64. Aleksandr I. Solzhenitsyn, "A World Split Apart: Commencement Address to Harvard University on June 8, 1978," *The Aleksandr Solzhenitsyn Center:* https://www.solzhenitsyncenter.org/a-world-split-apart.
65. Simon Reid-Henry, *Empire of Democracy: The Remaking of the West Since the Cold War* (New York: Simon & Schuster, 2019), 160.
66. Pearce, *Solzhenitsyn*, 278.
67. Vincent J. Schodolski, "Sakharov Jeered over Army Killings Charge," *Chicago Tribune*, June 3, 1989: http://www.chicagotribune.com/news/ct-xpm-1989-06-03-8902060375-story.html.
68. Felicity Barringer, "Upheaval in the East; Solzhenitsyns Brush Off Soviet Offer for a Return," *New York Times*, December 9, 1989: https://www.nytimes.com/1989/12/09/world/upheaval-in-the-east-solzhenitsyns-brush-off-soviet-offer-for-a-return.html.
69. Pearce, *Solzhenitsyn*, 281.
70. Pearce, *Solzhenitsyn*, 313.
71. Aikman, *Great Souls*, 187–188.
72. Aikman, *Great Souls*, 188.
73. Damien Francis, "Alexander Solzhenitsyn Dies Aged 89," *Guardian*, August 4, 2008: https://www.theguardian.com/books/2008/aug/04/solzhenitsyn.dies.
74. Ian Hunter, "The Last Prophet," *Touchstone Magazine*: http://www.touchstonemag.com/archives/article.php?id=16-06-017-v.

CHAPTER 7: BILLY GRAHAM

1. Billy Graham, *Just as I Am: The Autobiography of Billy Graham* (San Francisco: HarperOne, 1997), 26.

2. Graham, *Just as I Am*, 28.

3. Graham, *Just as I Am*, 30.

4. Graham, *Just as I Am*, 30.

5. Graham, *Just as I Am*, 30.

6. Graham, *Just as I Am*, 31.

7. Graham, *Just as I Am*, 46.

8. Graham, *Just as I Am*, 46.

9. Graham, *Just as I Am*, 49.

10. Graham, *Just as I Am*, 53.

11. Graham, *Just as I Am*, 64.

12. Graham, *Just as I Am*, 82.

13. *Time* magazine, November 14, 1949, quoted in Graham, *Just as I Am*, 150.

14. Graham, *Just as I Am*, 150.

15. Graham, *Just as I Am*, 157.

16. Aikman, *Great Souls*, 38.

17. Graham, *Just as I Am*, 216.

18. Graham, *Just as I Am*, 219.

19. Graham, *Just as I Am*, 225.

20. Graham, *Just as I Am*, 225.

21. Aikman, *Great Souls*, 38.

22. Graham, *Just as I Am*, 235.

23. Graham, *Just as I Am*, 236–237.

24. Graham, *Just as I Am*, 245.

25. Graham, *Just as I Am*, 246.

26. Graham, *Just as I Am*, 204.

27. Graham, *Just as I Am*, 205.

28. Graham, *Just as I Am*, 395.

29. Graham, *Just as I Am*, 531.

30. Graham, *Just as I Am*, 656.

31. "How Billy Graham and George W. Bush Connected on Faith," *Parade*, November 14, 2017: https://parade.com/618433/parade/how-billy-graham -and-george-w-bush-connected-on-faith/.

32. Graham, *Just as I Am*, 265.

33. Graham, *Just as I Am*, 428.

34. Graham, *Just as I Am*, 428.

35. Aikman, *Great Souls*, 50.

36. Graham, *Just as I Am*, 614.